WATCH OFFICER'S GUIDE

WATCH OFFICER'S GUIDE

A Handbook for All Deck Watch Officers

TENTH EDITION

NAVAL INSTITUTE PRESS
ANNAPOLIS, MARYLAND

Publisher's Preface to the Tenth Edition

This volume is the result of an endeavor to collect and put into a compact form those details appertaining to deck duty which will be found necessary or convenient to an officer carrying on a watch.—From the preface to the original *Watch Officer's Manual,* by Ensign Charles Emerson Hovey, U.S. Navy, 1911.

The book published by Ensign Hovey in January, 1911, was the first of its kind in the U.S. Navy, although there had long been predecessors in the British Navy. The objective stated by Ensign Hovey over half a century ago still governs the content of this edition. The fundamentals of watch standing, like the fundamentals of leadership, can be learned from books, but it is only with extensive experience built upon the fundamentals that an officer can stand a competent watch or become a capable leader. The pace and complexity of modern naval operations place a substantially greater demand upon the watch officer of today in comparison with that made on such an officer at the beginning of the century. While advances in technology have changed the emphasis on the nature of the watch officer's duties, the responsibility with which he is charged by Navy Regulations remains the same.

In September of 1911, Ensign Hovey was killed in action while leading a landing party against outlaw Moros in the Philippines. He was cited for conspicuous gallantry in action, and in 1919 the destroyer *Hovey* (DD208) was named in his honor. That old four-piper is gone now, sunk by the Japanese in Lingayen Gulf in 1945, but this small volume continues as a lasting memorial to a promising young officer.

The second edition of the *Manual* (1917), revised and enlarged by Lieutenant Solomon Endel, U.S. Navy, and published by the U.S. Naval Institute, was the last to carry Ensign Hovey's name. Shortly after World War I the U.S. Naval Institute acquired all rights to the book. The extensively revised third edition (1930) was produced by Commander W. S. Farber, U.S. Navy, and at that time its name was changed to *Watch Officer's Guide* to avoid confusion with various Navy Department manuals. The third edition incorporated changes in format and style which are still followed.

This edition of *Watch Officer's Guide* has been revised and updated by Captain William C. Magee, U.S. Navy (Retired), with the advice and assistance of G. D. Dunlap and Captain Henry H. Shufeldt, U.S. Naval Reserve (Retired). A comprehensive critique of the revision work, made by Commander William H. Peerenboom, U.S.N., Chairman of the Department of Seamanship and Tactics of the U.S. Naval Academy, resulted in further refinement, particularly with those sections concerning ship-handling. In addition, certain editorial changes have been made in order to bring the book into agreement with other Naval Institute publications in the matter of terminology, ship-handling, man overboard procedures, rules of the road, and heavy weather precautions. Where applicable, the latest directives of the Chief of Naval Operations concerning enlisted men—deck watches, civilian clothes, and personal appearance—have been included. The previous multiplicity of chapters describing the general and specific duties of the officer of the deck has been eliminated; all such duties are now covered in three chapters: "The Watch in General," "The Watch Underway," and "The Watch in Port." A new chapter, "Safety," has been added.

The *Watch Officer's Guide,* as it did more than fifty years ago, still tells the watch officer what he must expect and what is expected of him. With few exceptions it cannot serve as a "how to do it" text. Modern naval operations such as underway replenishment and anti-submarine warfare are too complex for detailed description and require thorough study of pertinent publications and operation orders before going on watch. The general guidelines for such operations are presented here, with reference to the appropriate official publications or other sources of information, as necessary.

The young naval officer standing deck watches in the modern navy must have a far greater range of technical and professional knowledge than was required in the past. He must work under the stress of high speed and complicated operations and he must handle many situations that challenge his imagination, resourcefulness, leadership and energy. The *Watch Officer's Guide* has been prepared to help him meet these challenges.

NAVAL INSTITUTE PRESS

CONTENTS

WATCH OFFICER'S GUIDE

Chapter 1 INTRODUCTION

The commanding officer shall establish such watches as are necessary for the safety and proper operation of the command. —*United States Navy Regulations, 1948,* Article 1002.1.

The officer of the deck is the officer on watch in charge of the ship. He shall be responsible for the safety of the ship and for the performance of the duties prescribed in these regulations and by the commanding officer. Every person on board who is subject to the orders of the commanding officer, except the executive officer, and those other officers specified in article 1009, shall be subordinate to the officer of the deck.—*Navy Regulations,* Article 1008.

Authority

The officer of the deck of a naval ship has a unique position without parallel in the other military services, or in civilian life. While on watch, he is the most important officer aboard after the commanding officer and executive officer. A large part of his importance stems from his authority to act for the commanding officer in his absence. This in itself should emphasize the importance to every newly-commissioned officer of becoming a qualified deck watch officer as soon as possible. In no other way can he so readily gain responsibility and distinguish himself in the eyes of his associates as well as his superiors. Every newly reported ensign will receive the considerate, yet critical, observation of his seniors. One of the best ways to make a good impression on them is to stand an alert watch in an intelligent manner. Being able to carry out all the duties of the officer of the deck is one of the first and most important tests that any young officer must pass; this guide is designed to help him pass that test.

Responsibility

The authority of the officer of the deck is matched by his responsibility; for nothing that occurs in the ship or nearby should escape his cognizance. He sees that the daily routine is carried out, he is responsible for the safety of the ship and her crew in port and at sea, and he must be informed and able to take action on anything which concerns his ship, whether it pertains to administration, communications, boat traffic, navigation, ship handling, supplies or personnel. It is often difficult for officers to appreciate fully this broad range of their responsibilities. Their working hours are devoted to specific and specialized duties which require most of their energy and powers of concentration. Going on watch must be accepted as a radical break from usual duties. The officer of the deck, as he relieves the deck, must, by a deliberate and planned effort, enlarge the scope of his attention.

Emphasis on Most Important Duties

There are two aspects of this question of broad responsibility that may profitably be discussed. The first is the matter of emphasis. Certainly, the officer of the deck must devote himself to the important jobs first. If the ship is in formation, he is responsible for proper station keeping and safe handling, even if that takes all his attention. The routine of the ship and other less important matters may properly be delegated to an assistant, either a junior officer or a petty officer.

In contrast there will be occasions during a quiet watch when the officer of the deck can also direct his attention to the details of administration and routine of the ship, and at the same time devote some effort to training and instruction of men in his watch.

Limitation of Activities

A second aspect of the wide scope of an officer of the deck's responsibility is that he must not unnecessarily interfere with the duties and responsibilities of other ship's officers. While the officer of the deck must be sure that everything is running according to plan, he must not try to improve or revise matters unless a crisis or emergency exists. For example, an officer of the deck may observe that men stowing a nylon towing hawser are not being careful to avoid kinks in it. While he might remind the petty officer in charge of the proper way to handle such gear, he is not expected to step in and take charge unless safety precautions are being violated or some damage to material or injury to personnel is a possibility.

Relations with Senior Officers

The officer of the deck must clearly understand the extent of his responsibility and authority because at times he may have to exert his authority over officers *senior* to him. For example, the supply officer may want to send a storekeeper ashore with urgent requisitions at a time when approaching bad weather makes it unsafe to let a boat leave the ship. If disagreement results from this situation, the matter should be referred to the executive officer. The point here is that the authority of the officer of the deck is vested by *Navy Regulations* and by custom and usage in the *office,* not the individual *person,* of the officer of the deck.

Exercise of Authority

He [an officer in charge of a watch] shall scrupulously obey all orders and regulations and shall require the same of all persons on watch under him.

At all times he shall present and conduct himself in a man-

ner befitting his office. **His orders shall be issued in the customary phraseology of the service.**—*Navy Regulations*, Article 1005.

The first part of this chapter discussed the wide scope of the authority and the responsibility of the officer of the deck. Now follows, in broad terms, discussion of the manner in which this authority should be exercised. First of all, as the quotation above indicates, the officer of the deck must conduct his watch in a strictly regulation manner, without regard to his personal views or inclinations. His one duty and obligation is to carry out the orders of higher authority, be they *Navy Regulations* or the latest memorandum from the executive officer. The following chapters will discuss the different sources of directives and information with which the officer of the deck must be familiar. It suffices here to stress the point that the officer on watch must consider himself the dispassionate instrument by which naval doctrine, policy and directive are implemented. From the clean white hats set squarely upon the heads of his signal gang to the departure of the 1600 liberty boat exactly on the bell, every event in the watch should be handled in a correct, professional, and regulation manner. The officers and men who stand a smart watch show that they are proud of their ship.

Appeal to Pride

It is this consideration, moreover, pride in the ship, that should be emphasized. There are many small ways in which an officer of the deck can indicate his concern with the reputation of the ship. Men are usually quicker to react to an appeal to their pride and self-respect than they are to the threat of disapproval or punishment, and will work much more effectively if they want to do a good job than if they are just afraid of doing a poor one. Here lies the one most obvious difference between an excellent watch and just a good or average one. For outstanding performance the men need motivation. There is nothing mysterious about how to achieve this in the men on watch under you; the important point to understand is the necessity for it if you want to do a really good job.

Other Useful Qualities

In this general discussion of how an officer of the deck exerts his authority, it is enough to point out that he exerts it through people. The manner in which he deals with people is, in a large sense, a measure of his success.

In dealing with his seniors an officer must, of course, be tactful, alert, energetic, and resourceful. *If the commanding officer has strong views on certain matters which may appear to be at some variance with doctrine or with past practices, then by all means do them his way.*

In dealing with all juniors, exert authority with scrupulous justice and fairness. There is no room for capricious, arbitrary, or oppressive application of authority. It serves no useful purpose to become unduly exasperated with men who perform badly on watch or who try to go on liberty in a dirty uniform. There is always a cause (although not an excuse) for this sort of behavior, and there is always someone responsible for the training and appearance of each man on board.

Improper behavior, deportment, or personal appearance must be dealt with in a judicious and mature manner. The person responsible for correcting such faults in a man must be made aware of his duty.

WATCH ORGANIZATION

The basic organization of a watch aboard ship should be understood by all junior officers. Charts and functional guides *for the key watch officers* are the best means to accomplish this understanding. The peacetime watch organization described herein pertains to the normal peacetime watch underway (Condition IV) and in port (Condition V). It is derived from *Shipboard Procedures, NWP 50(A)*. The material on the Command Duty Officer is included for information.

The requirements for Condition IV are:

1. No weapon batteries are manned.
2. The engineering plant is ready for speeds as ordered.
3. Material condition Yoke is modified for access during daylight.
4. Complete surface and horizon lookout coverage is provided. Air lookouts are on duty when flight operations are in progress in the vicinity.
5. CIC is sufficiently manned for routine purposes. Exterior-interior communications are sufficiently manned to cover the circuits in use.
6. Aircraft are in the condition of readiness required by the flight schedule.

Executive Officer and the OOD

The relationship of the executive officer to the OOD is prescribed in Navy Regulations, as follows:

The executive officer may direct the officer of the deck in matters concerning the general duties and safety of the ship. When the commanding officer is not on deck, the executive officer may direct the officer of the deck how to proceed in time of danger or during an emergency, or he may assume charge of the deck himself, and shall do so should it in his judgment be necessary. (Article 1009.1)

Command Duty Officer and the OOD

When the commanding officer considers that circumstances warrant, he may delegate to another officer, for a specified watch, authority similar to that prescribed in the preceding paragraph for the executive officer in relation to the officer of the deck. Such officer shall, while on watch, bear the same relation to the officer of the deck both in authority and responsibility, as that prescribed for the executive officer, but shall be subordinate to the executive officer. (Article 1009.2)

Command Duty Officer in port and the OOD

The command duty officer in port is that officer, eligible for command at sea, who has been designated for a particular watch by the commanding officer, as deputy to the executive officer for carrying out the routine of the ship in port and for supervising and directing the officer of the deck in matters concerning the safety and general duties of the ship. In the temporary absence of the executive officer, the duties of the executive officer will be carried out by the command duty officer in port.

The command duty officer in port shall:

1. Advise and, if necessary, direct the officer of the deck in matters concerning the general activities and safety of the ship.

2. Keep informed of the ship's position, mooring lines or ground tackle in use, the status of the engineering plant, and all other matters which affect the safety and security of the ship.

3. In times of danger or emergency, take command action as appropriate until an officer senior to him in the succession to command relieves him.

4. Relieve the officer of the deck only when necessary for the safety of the ship, and inform the commanding officer when such action is taken.

5. Conduct frequent inspections to insure the security of the ship. Give particular attention to the security of the ship's boats and to the safety of personnel embarked therein.

6. In the absence of the executive officer, receive the eight o'clock reports.

7. Keep advised of routine matters affecting the internal administration of the ship.

The officer of the deck in port reports directly to the commanding officer for the safety and general duties of the ship and to the command duty officer (executive officer when CDO is not assigned) in port for carrying out the ship's routine.

The Senior Watch Officer

The senior watch officer, under the direction of the executive officer, prepares the underway and in port officer watch bills subject to the approval of the commanding officer. He prepares the enlisted underway and in-port watch bills, subject to the approval of the executive officer.

Duties of the OOD Underway (Functional Guide)

In amplification of the responsibilities prescribed in Chapter 10, Section 2, *U.S. Navy Regulations,* the officer of the deck underway shall:

1. Keep himself continually informed concerning the tactical situation and geographic factors which may affect the safe navigation of the ship and take appropriate action to avoid the danger of grounding or collision in accordance with tactical doctrine, the rules of the nautical road, and the orders of the commanding officer or other proper authority.

2. Keep himself informed concerning current operation plans and orders, intentions of the OTC and the commanding officer, and such other matters as may pertain to ship or force operations.

3. Issue necessary orders to the wheel and main engine control to avoid danger; to take or keep an assigned station; or to change the course and speed of the ship in accordance with orders of proper authority.

4. Make all reports to the commanding officer that are required by Article 1020, *U.S. Navy Regulations,* and by the

commanding officer. When a command duty officer is specified for the watch, make the same reports to the command duty officer.

5. Ensure that required reports to the OOD concerning tests and inspections and the routine reports of patrols, watches and lifeboat crews are promptly originated and that the bridge watch and lookouts are properly posted and alert.

6. Supervise and direct the personnel on watch on the bridge and ensure that all required entries are properly made in the quartermaster's notebook.

7. Prepare and sign the rough deck log and ensure that all required entries are properly made.

8. Issue orders for rendering honors to passing vessels as required by regulations and custom.

9. Ensure that the executive officer, command duty officer (when assigned the watch), and department heads concerned are kept informed of changes in the tactical situation, changes in operation schedules, and other circumstances which would require a change in the ship's routine or other action on their part.

10. Keep himself informed of the status and current capabilities of the engineering plant and keep the engineering officer of the watch advised concerning boiler power requirements and the physical situation topside so that he may operate the engineering plant intelligently.

11. Carry out the routine of the ship as published in the plan of the day and other ship directives, keeping the executive officer advised of any changes.

12. Supervise and control the use of the general announcing system, the general, chemical, collision, sonar, and steering casualty alarms, and the whistle and siren, in accordance with the orders of the commanding officer, tactical doctrine, and the Rules of the Road.

13. Permit no person to go aloft on the masts or stacks or to work over the side except when wind and sea conditions will not expose them to danger, and then only when all applicable safety precautions are observed.

14. Supervise and control all transmissions and acknowledgments on the primary and secondary tactical voice radio circuits and ensure that proper phraseology and procedure arc used in all transmissions.

15. Supervise and conduct on-the-job training for the junior officer of the watch, the officer of the deck under instruction, and enlisted personnel of the bridge watch.

16. Assume such other responsibilities as may be assigned by the commanding officer.

17. Supervise the striking of the ship's bell to denote the hours and the half-hours from reveille to taps, requesting permission of the commanding officer to strike eight bells at the hours of 0800, 1200, and 2000.

Organizational Relationships

The officer of the deck reports directly to the commanding officer for the safe navigation and general operation of the ship; and to the executive officer (and command duty officer if appointed) for carrying out the ship's routine.

The following personnel report to the officer of the deck:

1. The junior officer of the watch and the officer of the deck under instruction, for the performance of their duties and on-watch training.

2. The CIC watch officer for the conduct of air and surface radar search and tracking, for supplying combat and tactical information affecting the maneuvering and safe navigation of the ship, and for conducting sonar search on ships provided with sonar equipment but not having an ASW weapon battery.

3. The engineering officer of the watch for the speed and direction of rotation of the main engines.

4. The communications watch officer for proper and expeditious transmission and receipt of visual tactical and general information signals and other communications affecting the operations or maneuvering of the ship.

5. The quartermaster of the watch for the supervision of the steersman (when senior to the boatswain's mate of the watch) for the proper maintenance of the quartermaster's notebook, and for navigational matters.

6. The damage control watch for the reporting and control of hull damage and casualties, and for the setting and maintenance of prescribed material conditions.

7. The boatswain's mate of the watch for the supervision of lifeboat and like buoy watches; for the supervision of the steersman when senior to the quartermaster of the watch; for the proper operations of the engine order telegraph, engine revolution indicator, and general announcing system; for the supervision of the 1JV phone talkers; and for the supervision of fog and other special watches when posted.

8. The bridge talkers for the relay and display of information received from ship control stations.

9. The sonar supervisor for conducting sonar search in ASW weapon system configured ships.

Duties in Port (Functional Guide)

The officer of the deck in port shall:

1. Keep continually informed of the ship's position, mooring lines or ground tackle in use, tide and weather information, the status of the engineering plant, the status of the ship's boats, and all other matters affecting the safety and security of the ship; and take appropriate action to prevent grounding, collision, dragging or other danger in accordance with the Rules of the Road and the orders of the commanding officer and other proper authority.

2. Ensure that required reports to the OOD concerning tests and inspections and the routine report of patrols, watches, and sentries are promptly originated and that the quarterdeck watch, lookouts, anchor watch, and other sentries or patrols are properly posted and alert.

3. Prepare and sign the rough deck log and ensure that all required entries are made in the quartermaster's notebook.

4. Ensure that the executive officer, command duty officer, and department heads are informed of any circumstances which would require a change in the ship's routine or other action on their part.

5. Carry out the routine of the ship as published in the plan of the day or other directive, keeping the command duty

officer advised of any changes which may be necessary.

6. Initiate and supervise action for ship's evolutions or operations as necessary.

7. Attend one of the ship's gangways and supervise those watch personnel assigned to attend other gangways.

8. Supervise and direct the operations of the ship's boats in accordance with the boat schedule published by the executive officer and with the orders of the commanding officer and other proper authority. Ensure that boats are operated in a safe manner and that all boat safety regulations are observed. Give particular attention to changes in wind or sea conditions which may affect the safety of the boats and embarked personnel, and notify the command duty officer when the suspension of boating is deemed advisable. Assure that boats are not overloaded and reduce the allowed loading capacity to a safe margin when weather conditions require caution. Recommend use of boat officers to the command duty officer when weather or other conditions make it advisable to do so. Require all boat passengers to wear life jackets when boating conditions are hazardous. Assure that all boats assigned trips are fully equipped, manned, and fueled, and that all equipment is in working order. Provide harbor charts to boat coxswains. Give boat coxswains their trip orders and their orders to shove off.

9. Supervise and control the use of the general announcing system, the general and chemical alarms, and the whistle and siren, in accordance with the orders of the commanding officer, tactical doctrine and the Rules of the Road.

10. Permit no person to go aloft on the masts or stacks or to work over the side of the ship except when wind and sea conditions will not cause them undue danger, and then only when all safety precautions are observed.

11. Display required absentee pennants, colors, and general information signals, and supervise and direct the rendering of side honors and honors to passing ships.

12. Make all reports to the commanding officer required by Article 1020, *U.S. Navy Regulations* and by the standing orders to the OOD.

13. Supervise and conduct on-the-job training for the junior

officer of the watch, the officer of the deck under instruction, and enlisted personnel of the quarterdeck watch.

14. Assume such other responsibilities as may be assigned by the commanding officer.

15. Supervise the striking of the ship's bell to denote the hours and the half-hours from reveille to taps, requesting permission of the commanding officer to strike eight bells at the hours of 0800, 1200, and 2000.

(See Chapter X for full details on standing the watch in port.)

The following personnel report to the officer of the deck in port:

1. The junior officer of the watch and the officer of the deck under instruction for the performance of their assigned duties and training on watch.

2. The department duty officers for the security and good order and discipline of their departments.

3. The communication watch officer for the proper and expeditious transmission and receipt of operational and general information messages.

4. The quartermaster of the watch for the performance of his assigned duties.

5. The boat coxswains, or boat officers when assigned, for the safe and proper operation of the ship's boats.

6. The officer or petty officer in charge of the gangway watch for the maintenance of a properly posted and alert watch on the crew's brow or accommodation ladder.

7. The boatswain's mate of the watch for the supervision and direction of the quarterdeck watch, the anchor watch, fog lookouts, brow and dock sentries when there is no Marine detachment assigned to the ship, and security watches and patrols under the control of the officer of the deck.

8. The duty master-at-arms for the maintenance of good order and discipline in the ship and the security and processing of prisoners.

9. The sergeant of the guard for the direction of the guard in the performance of their duties (in ships having a Marine Detachment assigned to duty on board).

CHARACTERISTICS OF THE OFFICER
OF THE DECK

Forehandedness

An officer of the deck exhibits on the bridge or quarter-deck all the characteristics of good leadership that, on a broader scale, mark his professional life. Leadership, as officially defined for the Navy in General Order 21, is "the sum of those qualities of intellect, of human understanding and of moral character that enable a man to inspire and to manage a group of people successfully." The officer of the deck must be intelligent and technically competent, he must understand the men under him, their need for guidance and motivation, and he must have the moral strength not only to do his own job with meticulous care but also to exact the same high standards of performance from his watch.

It is not humanly possible to be at all times letter perfect in everything that may concern an officer of the deck. The superior watch officer, however, is always ready for any situation that may arise, and for that reason, if we assume normal personal and professional qualifications, the most important faculty to be cultivated by the officer of the deck is that of *forehandedness*. If the prospects are that you may have fog in your watch, check over the fog procedure before taking the deck. If you are to take part in fleet exercises, arrange to look over the orders before going on watch. If you are to enter New York Harbor, review the Inland Rules of the Road. If your watch is to be full of ceremonies, be letter perfect in the honors required, and put a little extra snap in your own appearance. Always look ahead, a minute, an hour, or a day, and make it your pride never to be caught unprepared.

Rehearse mentally the action you would take in the event of a fire, a man overboard, a steering failure, or any other serious casualty. This habit is not difficult to acquire and is certain to pay large dividends over the course of years. *Forehandedness* is the mark of the successful man in any capacity.

Vigilance

Next to forehandedness in being thoroughly prepared for conditions and circumstances that may reasonably be expected during your watch, the most important quality for the officer of the deck is probably *vigilance*. In no position more than that of officer of the deck is "eternal vigilance the price of safety." The officer of the deck must, of course, observe intelligently all that comes within his vision, both outside and inside the ship, but his vigilance must extend beyond this range. He must cultivate the faculty of "foreseeing" situations as well as seeing them, and must maintain and develop the vigilance of all others concerned with his watch.

Judgment

A third important quality for the successful officer of the deck is that of *judgment,* which in his position is largely a sense of proportion and of the fitness of things. Watches vary all the way from hours of tenseness where your ship and shipmates are in your hands every instant, as in high-speed work at night in a darkened ship, down to the calm of a quiet Sunday afternoon at anchor, when you are just "keeping ship." It is good to adjust to the kind of watch. On the darkened destroyer, only essentials count and you must key your mind to its keenest pitch. On the Sunday afternoon, while there is no excuse for slackness, it may be that your most important immediate responsibility is to be affable to curious visitors.

Appearance and Manner

The fourth important quality is largely a question of *appearance* and *manner;* but it is more than mere smartness, it is a manifestation of *leadership*, the exemplification of which instills in subordinates confidence, pride, and a desire to emulate. Every watch officer should cultivate dignity, force, confidence, and precision in his manner of standing watch, and should exact similar qualities from his assistants. He should be careful of his personal appearance, and should strive to avoid any indication of confusion, peevishness, or noisiness. He should always act the part of what he really is—next to the captain and the executive officer, the most important person in the ship. *U.S. Navy Regulations, 1920,* said: ". . . while never permitting anyone to perform his duties in a dilatory or perfunctory manner, the officer of the deck should display a spirit of deference to superiors and kindness to inferiors."

Technical Knowledge

The officer of the deck, no matter how well endowed with forehandedness, vigilance, judgment, and a military manner, must also have complete *technical knowledge* of his job, he must know the relative importance of his many responsibilities, and he must have experience. This book cannot cover the field of technical knowledge required by the officer of the deck, nor can it furnish him with experience; it attempts, however, in the following pages to indicate:

1. The sources of technical knowledge with which a watch officer must be familiar.

2. The relative importance of the watch officer's many responsibilities.

3. The lessons of accumulated experience so far as they can be reproduced in the printed page.

4. Certain useful information which otherwise might not be readily available when wanted.

Chapter *II* THE WATCH IN GENERAL

He [the officer of the deck] shall remain in charge and at his station until regularly relieved. He shall scrupulously obey all orders and regulations and shall require the same of all persons on watch under him. He shall instruct them as may be necessary in the performance of their duties, and shall insure that they are at their stations, attentive, alert, and ready for duty. He shall endeavor to foresee situations which may arise, and shall take such timely and remedial action as may be required.

Before relieving, he shall thoroughly acquaint himself with all matters which he should know for the proper performance of his duties while on watch. He may decline to relieve his predecessor should any circumstances or situation exist which, in his opinion, justifies such action by him, until he has reported the facts to and received orders from the commanding officer, or other competent authority.—*Navy Regulations,* Article 1005.

PREPARATION

The more thorough your preparation before going on watch, the more likely you are to perform your duties efficiently. The problem really has two aspects. You need general indoctrination in all the characteristics of the ship and her crew before you can stand a proper watch; and you also require, under certain conditions, much exact local information before you relieve the deck.

Assuming that you are a newly commissioned officer reporting to your first ship, or have been ordered to one that is unfamiliar, you must know much about the ship herself: her organization, and the people who run her. Most of this information you will have to find for yourself. You will normally be provided with a copy of the *Ship's Organization and Regulations Manual,* including notices and instructions. This can be a formidable publication, especially in a large ship. You can not possibly absorb it all at once. It is better to learn the skeleton first, then concentrate on the parts that will affect you the most. Usually you will be rewarded by gaining a reasonably clear picture of who does what, where, and when.

It is difficult to overemphasize the importance of your ship's organization book. It is the key to the proper administration of the ship. It is the single most useful reference an officer has aboard ship and his best guide in learning how the ship functions.

The other major source of information about your ship, booklets of general plans and casualty control bills, may be found in damage control central or the engineer's office. They will enable you to acquire the necessary over-all knowledge of compartmentation, fittings, piping, and wiring.

Of course, you may be put on the watch list almost immediately upon reporting. This procedure is often standard, since the junior officer watch list is never long enough to suit anyone; and besides, there is much that you can learn only by doing.

There is another kind of information that an officer of the deck requires before relieving the watch: a knowledge of the immediate situation—tactical, if underway; usually administrative, if not underway. These subjects will be discussed in Chapter V.

There are a few other aspects of being prepared to stand a watch that should be mentioned. In view of the importance of the watch to you personally and, under certain circumstances, to the safety of your shipmates, it should be considered an obligation on the part of every officer to be in good physical condition before going on watch. While it often happens that you must relieve the watch—for example, the 2000–2400— when you are dog-tired after a day that began at dawn, there are other times

when you can relax for an hour or so before going on
duty. Do so.

RELIEVING THE WATCH

Don't rush the procedure. *Get up on deck early.*
Take the time to read the message board, check the log
of the last watch, visit the combat information center
(CIC) and gather all possible information that you will
need. Not later than fifteen minutes before the hour you
should step up to the officer you are relieving, salute
him, and say: "I am ready to relieve you sir." Aside from
the obvious aspects of this formality, such as setting an
example of smartness and military courtesy for the men
and observing a time-honored custom of the service,
there are very sound reasons for this procedure. The key
word is *ready*. By declaring yourself ready to relieve the
watch, you are stating that you have made all reasonable
preparations, gathered all available information, and
need but an oral turnover to assume your duties. A mum-
bled "What's the dope?" is not an acceptable substitute.
It is more than a matter of good manners, it is an obligation to the shipmate whom you are to succeed on watch,
to say: "I am ready to relieve you, sir."

As you receive information about the watch, you have
an opportunity to observe what is going on, both on
board and outside the ship. When you thoroughly understand the situation and have heard all that your predecessor has to say and have asked him any questions you
may think necessary, it is again your duty to salute him
and say: "I relieve you, sir." It must be stressed that this
is an obligation and must not be done with a sloppy
"O.K., I've got it." Taking over a watch is serious business and must be done in a clear-cut, positive, seamanlike manner.

WHEN NOT TO RELIEVE THE WATCH

It might be useful here to discuss the problem that sometimes arises when a conscientious officer feels that he must decline to relieve the deck. The extracts from *Navy Regulations* quoted at the beginning of this chapter are quite clear on this subject. There is often a feeling among junior officers, however, that they may be considered timid if they exercise their option and decline to relieve the deck. This feeling is not warranted. It is an officer's duty to decline to relieve the deck if, for example, the ship is out of position in the formation or if a busy watch in port has become somewhat confused, with boats astray or out of fuel. Of course, reasonable judgment must be exercised. A ship may be out of position for good reason and be headed back for her station. It would then be quite proper to relieve the deck. In general, however, a careful, meticulous approach to this question is recommended. An old salt has said: "Relieve in haste, repent at leisure." A reputation for being fussy in taking over a watch is not a bad thing to acquire. It will often keep your predecessor on his toes, ready to turn over his watch with no loose ends to embarrass you. Remember that after you have said: "I relieve you, sir," the full responsibility of the watch is *yours*. It will never do then to try to pass the blame back to the officer you relieved if difficulties arise.

ORGANIZING THE WATCH

It will be easier to organize the watch and run it efficiently if you know, in general, the duties of other members of the watch, from the junior officer of the watch down to the lookouts. These are laid down in the *Ship's Organization* and *Regulations Manual,* in *NWP 50 (A),* and in various Navy training manuals. Remember that you can not admonish a man for doing a job improperly unless you are able to tell him how to do it properly.

You can not expect that every man in your watch will be a seasoned, salty old-timer. Some of them will be new to the service, new to the ship, unfamiliar with their job, and not instructed in their duties and responsibilities. Along with your other duties in standing a proper watch, it will be your job to conduct on-the-job training for such men. The advantage of such a system is that when you have the men in your watch trained, they will perform their duties in the proper fashion—if you have trained them properly.

(See also Chapter V for a discussion of organizing the watch underway, and Chapter X for a similar discussion of organizing the watch in port. The topics discussed therein are of a general nature that pertain to both the underway and the in-port watches, stood by an officer of the deck.)

PERSONNEL

The opportunities which you, as an officer of the United States Navy, have to train and mold future citizens of the United States, future naval officers and enlisted men, are unlimited. Your responsibility is accordingly great. I expect every officer in the U.S. Atlantic Fleet to accept this responsibility as a trust, and to discharge it with complete devotion and energy.—Admiral L. D. McCormick, U.S.N.

Just as the officer of the deck has special responsibilities and duties concerning the ship herself and her machinery, so does he have certain special responsibilities in his dealings with the ship's company. Junior officers should understand that a feeling of mutual respect flows both ways in the chain of command. This is respect by the enlisted men for the authority and responsibility of the officers placed over them, and by officers for the responsibilities shared by the enlisted men and their loyalty and devotion in carrying out difficult tasks.

Performance

Of great importance to an officer of the deck is the performance of the men on duty with him. They must respond quickly and intelligently to his orders. Also, while on duty and on watch, as indicated in Chapter II, a moderate degree of formality should be preserved. Call your junior officer of the watch "Mr. Jones," not "Red-dog" or "Mike." Learn the names of the men on watch and use them. When giving an order or command it is proper to address a man on watch either by his last name or by his title, such as quartermaster. Using a man's name lets him know you know who he is—but when you have Jones on the wheel and another Jones as lookout, be explicit and call them "helmsman" and "lookout." Discourage idle conversation. Letting the watch swap sea stories will help pass the time in a mid-watch, but it will also interfere with proper performance of duty. Keep the noise level down, even if you have to order "knock off the chatter" to do so. This may sound unnecessarily stern, but a policy of strict attention to duty will always pay off in the long run.

The principle of reserve and decorum on the bridge and quarter-deck applies, of course, in both directions. You may know the navigator well enough to call him by his first name on the golf course, but call him "Mister" when you have the deck. A meticulous separation of social or personal affairs from the important business of watch standing is a good rule to follow.

You have an opportunity, when organizing your watch, to exercise forehandedness. While underway, for example, you can instruct your lookouts as well as CIC to be alert to sight a particular ship or point of land. Word of anticipated changes in speed can be passed down to the engine room. If your ship is in port, the signal bridge can be alerted to inform you of the approach of expected visitors. By keeping your men informed you stimulate their interest and invariably increase their efficiency. This condition is particularly true in the ideal bridge-CIC relationship.

It is a good idea to check your quartermasters not only to be sure that they are keeping the proper records, such as weather data, compass record book, and bearing book, but also to insure that they are maintaining the DR track and navigational plot. During a busy watch it is advisable to see that proper entries are being made in the quartermaster's note book. Although kept in pencil, it is an official Navy record and entries must never be erased. The OOD will need the information in that record to write the deck log at the end of the watch.

ROUTINE

The officer of the deck shall carry out promptly and precisely the established routine and any special orders for the ship, weather and other circumstances permitting, and shall report any deviation therefrom to the commanding officer or executive officer, as appropriate. He shall follow, as practicable, the motions of the senior officer present in carrying out routine evolutions.—*Navy Regulations*, Article 1012.

An intelligently conceived and accurately implemented routine is essential to good shipboard administration. It is the officer of the deck's job to take care of the second part—the implementation. If the plan of the day calls for "turn to" at 1300, be sure that, as far as you can determine, the crew does "turn to" at that time. If reveille is scheduled for 0600, then see that all hands are turned out at that time. If something does not seem right about the plan of the day, consult the executive officer, but until he changes the routine, carry it out. The plan of the day—or morning orders, as it is sometimes called—is a directive. All hands must follow it, whether or not the word is passed over the general announcing system.

Much of the detail of carrying out the daily routine will be handled by your most important enlisted assistant, the boatswain's mate of the watch. He should be made to feel responsible for the watch routine and for instruction, behavior, and appearance of the deck watch. You should supervise the boatswain's mate in carrying out the watch routine rather than by dealing directly with the men on watch. The boatswain's mate of the watch should see that all stations are manned and that the previous watch has been relieved. One of his major duties is to carry out the plan of the day. He must know what is happening on board ship and must pass the word in accordance with the prescribed routine. The standard routine is usually written into the ship's organization book and is varied only by specific instructions in the plan of the day. When it seems advisable to recommend a change in the routine because of unusual and unforeseen circumstances, the officer of the deck always checks first with the executive officer or the command duty officer, and obtains permission for such change.

PASSING THE WORD

His [the officer of the deck's] orders shall be issued in the customary phraseology of the service.—*Navy Regulations,* Article 1005.

Not only must the ship's routine be followed, but the manner in which it is accomplished, the manner in which the word is passed, is most important. It is often possible to tell how badly or how well a ship is being run by the manner in which the general announcing system is used. A noisy uproar every few minutes, passing the word for this person and that person, with each message obviously being composed on the spot by an enthusiastic boatswain's mate, is a sure indication of a sloppy ship. In contrast, the sparing use of the general announcing system, with only important words being passed—and those in a seaman-like manner, using the customary phraseology of the service—is the trademark of a smart, taut ship. The officer of the deck himself should grant permission on each occasion for passing the word. He may give the boatswain's mate blanket permission to pass all words relating to the ship's routine. He should make sure, however, that a standard, approved terminology is used. Such expressions as "chow down" or "crew of the whaleboat, man your boat and come along side" must not be tolerated. The list of commonly used "words" in Chapter IV is a good guide. If in doubt on terminology, consult a pertinent Bureau of Naval Personnel training publication, or the *Naval Terms Dictionary*.

In passing the word, other than for the ship's routine, make every effort to curtail the use of the general announcing system. Pass the word for individuals or for small groups only if there is a real emergency. Passing the word for everyone leads to abuse; no one takes the trouble to look for anyone, and inadequate supervision of the men by their officers and petty officers is abetted. Continuous chatter from the loudspeaker tends to numb the audio perception of all hands, and as a result no one listens even when important words are being passed.

An additional precaution in using the system is to be sure that only the desired circuits are cut in. Passing "sweepers" over the officers' circuit, for example, is an unnecessary annoyance to those in officers' country. In port, it is often advisable to reduce the volume of the weather-deck speakers, since there is no point in passing the word to people in other ships, on the pier, or ashore.

The use of the boatswain's pipe (properly termed a *call*) should be encouraged, as it is one of the small but important factors that comprise the ceremony and the true nautical flavor of the Navy afloat. The pipe should not be used when passing words over the officers' circuit only. When bugle calls are used, they should immediately precede the boatswain's call.

APPEARANCE OF THE WATCH

At all times he [the officer of the deck] shall present and conduct himself in a manner befitting his office.—*Navy Regulations*, Article 1005.

The officer of the deck, circumstances permitting, must see that his watch is in clean and regulation uniform, and that the bridge or quarter-deck is orderly and neat. This starts with the officer of the deck himself, who sets an example, at all times, for the whole ship. At sea, and in bad weather particularly, he should be dressed to keep warm and dry and should see that his men on watch are similarly protected. In port, with visitors coming aboard, the maximum of spit and polish is expected; uniforms in good condition, polished shoes, and clean white hats are in order. Make the boatswain's mate of the watch responsible for the appearance of the watch, and do not hesitate to have him send men below to change who are not up to your standards. Old, patched undress blues or soiled work shoes are good enough to wear about the deck when a good uniform would be unduly soiled, but are not good enough for a messenger watch on the quarter-deck.

Similarly, the appearance of the bridge or quarter-deck should be a matter of interest to the officer of the deck. He will have the boatswain's mate of the watch keep the area picked up and clean. Sweeping the deck, emptying trash buckets and ash trays and keeping empty coffee cups out of sight, are all details that an alert boat-swain's mate of the watch should attend to.

CONDUCT ON WATCH

It would be obvious and repetitious to stress here the need for decorous and seamanlike behavior on the part of all those on watch. But there is one aspect of this subject that may escape you. It is the need for a certain formality while on watch. This does not mean that you must be pompous or stuffy; on the contrary there are many occasions when a touch of humor is quite appropriate. But the men on watch must never be permitted to forget that they are on duty and that what they are doing is important. A ship is always subject to emergency or disaster; fire, man overboard, or dozens of other events can disrupt the dullest watch. Make it a practice to run a taut watch and to prevent noisy and idle chatter; use common sense and do not be arbitrary or harsh in dealing with men. The signal gang, for example, puts in long hours on the bridge and should be permitted to relax when not busy, so long as they maintain the necessary lookout.

TURNING OVER THE WATCH

As a watch draws to a close, the officer of the deck is concerned with giving his relief all available information in order to provide the maximum continuity. Both the relieved and relieving officer must make certain that this is done. It may be necessary to make notes, or to keep a check list. Remember that even while turning over the watch, you must continue to be alert and on the job. Do not let the task of turning over the watch distract your attention from maintaining a proper watch.

When the commanding officer is on the bridge underway, the officer being relieved should report: "I have been properly relieved as Officer of the Deck by Mr. ——, Sir."

CHECK-OFF LIST FOR THE OFFICER OF THE DECK

Here is a partial list of what the OOD should know about his ship. As you become thoroughly acquainted with your ship, it is advisable to prepare a more detailed check-off list, where you can fill in required data as appropriate.

1. Length, beam, draft, displacement.

2. General structural characteristics, particularly in regard to watertight integrity.

3. Height of eye at bridge; distance to horizon at this height; how to use a stadimeter.

4. Fuel-oil capacity; endurance at high, medium, low speed (or characteristics of nuclear plant).

5. Speed on different boiler combinations.

6. Time to get additional boilers on the line.

7. Acceleration and deceleration characteristics (general).

8. Speeds at which superheaters are lighted off; are secured. Advance notice required to light off and bring additional boilers on the line; maximum speed at which additional boilers can be cut in on the line or taken off.

9. Nature, capabilities, limitations of ship's armament.

10. Normal daily consumption of water; evaporator capacity.

11. Number of degrees for standard and full rudder.

12. Tactical diameter at standard and at full rudder.

13. How to turn ship in shortest time; in least space.

14. Location on bridge of all ship control gear; general characteristics of such gear.

15. Location of and facilities at other conning stations.

16. Location and use of all equipment on bridge and in pilothouse (both daylight and dark).

17. Alarms to be sounded and procedure to be followed in event of fire, rescue and assistance, man overboard, collision, general quarters.

18. Capacity and location of boats, life rafts, etc.

19. How to release life rafts.

20. How to drop an anchor, veer anchor chain, operate anchor windlass.

21. How to use a drift lead.

22. How to lower and hoist a boat.

23. Safety precautions for men fueling, handling ammunition, working over the side, aloft, in closed compartments, using power tools.

24. How to set depth charges (if carried) on safe.

25. Stations that make up special sea detail.

26. Procedure for steering casualty.

27. How to steer from other steering stations; and without power.

28. Need for blowing tubes.

29. How to detect a gyro error.

30. How to tell if anchor is dragging, and what precautions to take.

31. How to check mooring lines.

32. How to instruct boat coxswains in handling boats in bad weather.

33. Equipment carried in ship's boats.

34. How to make preparations to receive a ship alongside.

35. How to make preparations to fuel, or to receive stores or ammunition while underway.

36. Procedure for getting ship underway.

37. Procedure for fueling boats.

38. Preparations to be made when entering or leaving port.

39. What publications are kept on the bridge; in CIC.

40. Precautions in handling classified publications on the bridge.

41. General contents of the *Ship's Organization and Regulations Manual,* including all notices and instructions.

42. How to use visual recognition signals.

43. Capabilities and limitations of CIC.

44. How to use CIC, and obligation for keeping CIC informed.

45. Characteristics, limitations, and use of all electronic equipment.

46. How to use bridge radar repeater.

47. What principal radio circuits are normally manned.

48. Own ship's voice radio call and those of immediate superiors and other units in company.

49. Organization of condition watches; what armament manned.

50. Nature and use of principal interior communication circuits.

51. Damage control organization, what closures are made.

52. Safety precautions for nuclear ordnance and control of alarms.

53. Operational and administrative organization of which your ship is a part.

54. Action to be taken if required to conduct search and rescue.

55. How and when to dispose of trash and garbage.

56. When to pump bilges; when to blow tubes.

57. Characteristics of aircraft carried, how to receive helicopter.

58. Security watches in the ship; reports to be expected

on the bridge; action to be taken when the security watch reports unusual conditions.

RELATIONS WITH THE ENGINEERS

The engineering officer of the watch shall insure that all orders received from the officer of the deck are promptly and properly executed.—*Navy Regulations,* Article 1027.

A fully qualified officer of the deck should have some knowledge of his ship's engineering plant. In a steam-driven ship he should know in detail the relationship between boilers and maximum speed, and the time required to light off and cut in additional boilers. He should appreciate the special problems that the engineering department must meet in frequent and radical changes in speed, particularly in regard to superheat, and in changing the direction of rotation of the propellers. There are many other engineering problems that sometimes involve the officer of the deck, such as fuel, water, and electrical power consumption, the need for blowing tubes, and the operation of the ship's boats. In order to make reasonable decisions and to exercise correct judgment and foresight, the officer of the deck should have a considerable basic knowledge, not only of the plant itself, but also of the organization of the engineering department as well. When on watch he must not restrict himself to his regular duties of, say, electronics of communications officer; he is then responsible for the smooth functioning and efficiency of the ship as a whole.

By far the most important point for the officer of the deck to remember concerning engineering personnel is to *keep them informed* well ahead of time. Main propulsion machinery is not automatic; men have to operate, and these men must know, in general, what is planned and what is going on topside. An efficient officer of the deck keeps the engineers informed at all times and sees that any messages or orders concerning the movement of the ship, particularly radical speed changes, are passed to the engineering officer of the watch and to the engineering officer.

RELATIONS WITH STAFF

The officer of the deck of a flagship has the additional responsibilities of keeping the embarked staff informed, of handling additional boats and vehicles, and, of course, of rendering additional honors.

The staff duty officer is normally the person who should receive special reports. In general, the incidents, events, and sightings normally reported to the commanding officer should also be reported to the staff duty officer. He bears about the same relation to his admiral or squadron or division commander, as an officer of the deck does to the commanding officer.

The flag lieutenant is usually responsible to the admiral for the scheduling of honors and advises the officer of the deck what honors to expect. In return, the officer of the deck advises the flag lieutenant, as well as the staff duty officer, of unscheduled visits that may require honors.

Staff officers exercise care to preserve the unity of command of the flagship and do not give orders directly to the officer of the deck. Routine requests may be made to officers of the flagship, but in matters of any importance the chief of staff usually deals with the commanding officer of the flagship. An officer of the deck will **not be** inconvenienced by an embarked staff as long as he remembers to consider their needs, and *above all*, to keep them informed.

Chapter III THE SHIP'S DECK LOG

The deck log shall be a complete daily record, by watches, in which shall be described every circumstance and occurrence of importance or interest which concerns the crew and the operation and safety of the ship, or which may be of historical value. . . .—*Navy Regulations,* Article 1037.

GENERAL

The deck log is the only official chronological record of the ship's history during her commission. It presents a complete, accurate narrative of noteworthy incidents in the life of the ship and events affecting her officers, passengers, and crew. All significant items, whether pertaining to the ship's personnel, material, operations, or state of readiness, are entered in the deck log. It thus becomes at once the true historical account of the ship's activities and an accurate source of factual and legal data. It also provides essential aerological and hydrographic data in plain terms for the command and in more detailed synoptic code for climatological records. Watch officers responsible for the preparation of the log must understand and appreciate the importance of their undertaking. They must insure that all entries are complete, accurate, clear, concise, and expressed in standard naval phraseology. Entries must connote a true and understandable historical and legal record of the ship.

There are two parts of the deck log to be written for each watch. The first consists of tabular data which are entered in various columns. These data include the state of the weather and synoptic weather reports as well as certain logistic data and ship's position reports. Although these entries generally are made by the quartermaster of the watch, the officer of the deck is responsible for the accuracy of all entries. He must frequently review the weather observation entries to determine that they are consistent with actual changes in the weather. Unless this is done, the weather entries may remain unchanged regardless of how much the weather itself may have changed. Constant vigilance, indoctrination, and care on the part of observing personnel are required to insure that the weather elements are accurately evaluatd and correctly entered in the log. Much of the synoptic weather data is subsequently computerized for oceanographic study and used for both weather and bathythermographic predictions. Therefore, the weather data has significance both from an historical point of view and also for future operational use. The *Manual of Synoptic Weather Observations for Ship's Deck Log* (OpNavInst 3140.37) contains detailed information and guidance in taking and recording weather observations at sea and should be consulted.

The second part of the deck log consists of the remarks of the officer of the deck concerning the miscellaneous events that took place during his watch. In order to properly evaluate and enter the required remarks into the deck log, the officer of the deck and his assistants must be familiar with, and understand, the regulations and requirements for such entries. Read *Instructions for Keeping the Ship's Deck Log* (NavPers 15876), *U.S. Navy Regulations,* and the *Manual of the Judge Advocate General* (JAGInst P5800.7, Chapter XII).

The quartermaster's notebook, in a large part, forms the basis for the officer of the deck's remarks. The officer of the deck should supervise its keeping, requiring that all pertinent information and data relative to each event or occurrence throughout the watch, including exact times, be entered accurately and chronologically as they occur. Should the OOD, in reviewing the entries of his watch in the quartermaster's notebook, deem any such entries to be incorrect or that there are omissions, he shall take appropriate steps to have the correct entries recorded. In this he should be guided by Article 1036, *U.S. Navy Regulations.* It is emphasized that the quartermaster's notebook is the initial source of recorded information from which the ship's deck log is written, and it must, therefore, be a carefully and accurately maintained document.

The quartermaster's notebook should be kept in great detail. Every event should be entered in full at the time it occurs. In writing his remarks, the officer of the deck may or may not include details found in the quartermaster's notebook, depending upon the importance of the event or the outcome of a series of events. For example, the quartermaster's notebook should include each change of course and speed. The deck log remarks of the OOD for entering or leaving port or conducting an exercise may summarize this as "steering various courses at various speeds," if the exercise was accomplished without incident. Each aid to navigation sighted (including buoys) and the times when they are passed abeam and lost from sight (for the major ones), should be entered in the quartermaster's notebook. When these aids to navigation are very numerous, the officer of the deck need only list a few of the more prominent ones. Every contact, whether visual, radar, or sonar, must be logged by the quartermaster. When visual and radar contacts prove false, their inclusion in the deck log would merely clutter up the log and obscure important remarks. However, in case of a grounding, collision, or other damage, the officer of the deck should make his account in great detail. In general, the entries in the officer of the deck's remarks section should not duplicate any data listed in tabular form.

The deck log should be written while the events are still

fresh in your memory. Never leave the bridge or deck until your log is written.

The officer of the deck shall insure that the rough deck log for his watch is complete, accurate, and clear; and he shall sign it on being relieved.—*Navy Regulations,* Article 1022.

The entries in the deck log for any one day should give a complete account of the events of that day, from 0000 until 2400, without the necessity of referring back to the logs of previous days. Therefore, the remarks for the midwatch should start off with a concise yet complete summation of the situation existing at midnight. This should include the location and status of the ship, command relations, other ships and units present, and, when appropriate, the weather conditions. Succeeding watches need only have events listed as they occur.

No erasures shall be made in the deck log, quartermaster's notebook, magnetic compass record book, engineering log, or engineer's bell book. When a correction is deemed necessary, a single line shall be drawn through the original entry so that the entry remains legible. The correct entry shall then be inserted in such manner as to insure clarity and legibility. Corrections, additions, or changes shall be made only by the person required to sign the record for the watch, and shall be initialed by him on the margin of the page for each line marked out or corrected.

Should the commanding officer direct a change or addition to one of the foregoing records, the person concerned shall comply, unless he believes the proposed change or addition to be incorrect; in which event the commanding officer shall enter such remarks on the record over his signature as he deems appropriate.

No change shall be made on a log after it has been signed by the commanding officer, without his permission or direction.—*Navy Regulations,* Article 1036.

The deck log, along with the quartermaster's notebook, magnetic compass record book, the rough engineering log, and the engineer's bell book, is at times used as evidence before courts and other legal bodies. It is therefore important that, under circumstances that might conceivably lead to legal action, the remarks be particularly complete and accurate. Under such circumstances, it is advisable that they first be written in rough draft form, then checked for completeness and accuracy by all concerned, and submitted to the navigator and the captain for comment prior to entry in the log. Erasures in either the deck log, magnetic compass record book, or the quartermaster's notebook, would open to question their validity as evidence.

The log is often consulted years later in regard to claims for pensions by persons who served in the Armed Forces and those who claim injury while in the service. A complete entry, therefore, must be made in the log of each and every injury, accident or casualty, including accidents which could lead to later disclosure of injuries to the officers, crew, or passengers on board. This is necessary both to protect the government from false claims and to furnish a record for honest claimants.

The navigator has charge of the preparation of the deck log. By regulations he is required to examine the log book to see that it is prepared in accordance with instructions, and to call the attention of watch officers to any inaccuracies or omissions in their entries. The navigator is responsible to the commanding officer that the entries in the log are in proper form; but the officer of the deck is responsible for the entries during his watch.

The deck log is no longer typed in the smooth and copies are not made. All entries must be handwritten and signed with a ballpoint pen using black or blue-black ink. The remarks must be legible, and while the junior officer of the deck may write the log, it must be signed by the officer of the deck responsible for the watch.

As a matter of custom and tradition, the first watch of the year is writen in verse. Here is the midwatch log entry for 1 January 1968, by Lieutenant Commander R. E. Lane, OOD in the USS *Bennington.*

In the Tonkin Gulf we're currently steaming
On Yankee Station with nav lights agleaming.
The Senior Officer Present Afloat
Is ComCarDiv 9 in the big nuclear boat.

While we're here in the South China Sea
We're under the Yankee Team SOP
The OTC is ComASWGru One.
Embarked in none other than our Bennington.

Although we're up in the combat zone,
We have no fear, and we're sailing alone.
But if we meet up with a group of V.C.,
We've set a modified condition Three.

The word was passed, so it's a safe bet
That our DCA has condition Yoke set.
Flight ops are run by Bennington's *tower*
While, below, four boilers are giving us power.

When the year was twenty-five minutes old.
The following aircraft returned to the fold:
Three SH-3As and five S2Es
And one E1b (or a Fudd, *if you please).*

At twelve-twenty-seven right did we go
To the southerly course of two-double-oh.
Time zero-one twenty did finally arrive,
So again we came to course three-five-five.

We commenced blowing tubes at zero-one-thirty
And succeeded in getting the flight deck all dirty.
Four minutes after the hour of two,
The snipes called up and said they were through.

Now it reads zero-two-fifteen
And, because of the haze, not much can be seen.
To help solve that problem, here's what we do—
Post the low-visibility crew.

Happy New Year!

DECK LOG ENTRIES

The following sample entries are to be used as guides for recording the remarks of a watch. The list is not all inclusive, nor can the sample entries be construed as the only acceptable ones. Any entry that is complete, accurate and couched in standard naval phraseology is acceptable.

Since the deck log is handwritten, particular care must be taken when recording numbers; proper nouns shall be printed; and where signatures are required, the name shall be printed under the individual's signature. Logs received in the Bureau of Naval Personnel that are illegible (including poor penmanship) will be returned for remedial action. No lines must be skipped.

Abbreviations shall be limited to those commonly recognized in official publications and those generally accepted throughout the Navy by reason of long and continued usage. The *Dictionary of Naval Abbreviations* is a useful guide.

Air Operations
Carrier
1000   Flight quarters.
1005   Commenced launching aircraft for (carrier qualification)

(refresher operations) (group tactics), etc. Base course . . . . . , speed . . . . . .

1025   Completed launching aircraft, having launched 40 aircraft.

1030   Commenced recovering aircraft. Base course . . . . . , speed . . . . . .

1035   Commenced maneuvering on various courses (and speeds) while recovering (launching) aircraft (while conducting task group (force) flight operations).

1055   Completed recovering aircraft, having recovered 40 aircraft.

1143   F-8E, Bureau No. 12345 of VF-75, pilot LCDR Ben B. BOOMS, USN, 987654, crashed into the sea off the port bow at Latitude 30°50′ N, Longitude 150°20′ W, and sank in 500 fathoms of water.

1144   USS NOA (DD-841) and helicopter commenced search for pilot.

1146   Pilot recovered by helicopter and delivered on board USS MIDWAY (CVA-41). Injuries to pilot: (description).

1200   Search concluded. Results negative. Pilot LCDR Ben B. BOOMS, USN, 987654, presumed dead.

1215   Secured from flight quarters.

1300   A-4C, Bureau No. 67890 of VA-9, pilot ENS John P. JONES, USNR, 899880, crashed into barriers numbers 2, 4, and 6 and overturned. Pilot sustained mild abrasion to left forearm and contusions to both legs. Damage to aircraft: (major) (minor) (strike).

1315   CDR A. B. SEA, USN, Commanding Officer, VA-9, departed with 15 aircraft for Oceana, Va., TAD completed.

1330   CDR X. Y. ZEE, USN, Commanding Officer, VA-26, landed aboard with 16 aircraft from NAS, Norfolk, Va., for TAD.

NOTE.—During flight operations, log the base course and speed. Minor changes may be covered by: "Maneuvering on various courses . . . etc." All changes, however, must be entered in the quartermaster's notebook.

All Ships

2100   Maneuvering on various courses to take plane guard station No. ...... on ...... Lighting measure ...... in effect.

2110   On station. 2115 Commenced flight operations. 2210 F-4 aircraft crashed into the sea off starboard bow. Maneuvering on various courses at various speeds to recover pilot. 2214 Recovered pilot LTJG Max M. MAXWELL, USN, 800900, of VF-74. Injuries to pilot: (description).

Helicopters

1435   Flight Quarters. 1455 Launched helicopter. Pilot: LTJG Ray JOHNSON, USN. Passenger: CLEAT, A., BMC, USN. 1505 Recovered helicopter on main deck aft. 1510 Secured from flight quarters.

Loading Aircraft

0800   Commenced hoisting aircraft of VF-21 aboard.

1000   Completed hoisting 25 aircraft of VF-21 aboard.

NOTE.—If entire air wing/group aircraft are hoisted aboard at a time, log as "aircraft of CVSG-52," etc. If only a part of the wing/group aircraft are loaded at a time (i.e., during a period of a day) log as "aircraft of VF-21, VA-26, and VAH-20."

Ammunition

1400   Commenced loading (transferring) ammunition.

1600   Completed loading (transferring) ammunition, having received from (transferred to) USS NITRO (AE-23) 400 rounds 5"/38 cal. illum. projectiles, 250 5"/38 cal. smokeless and 250 5"/38 cal. flashless charges.

NOTE.—For entries regarding expenditure of ammunition, see "Exercises."

Damage

1155   USS BRISTOL (DD-857) in coming alongside to port, carried away 30 feet of the ship's port lifeline forward, with stanchions, and indented the ship's side to a depth of 4 inches over a space 10 feet long and 4 feet high in the vicinity of frames 46-51. No personnel casualties.

1401   Starboard lifeboat carried away by heavy sea. Boat and all equipment lost. No personnel casualties.

Drills and Exercises

1000   Exercised at general drills.

Abandon Ship

1005   Held abandon ship drill, provide.
1045   Secured from abandon ship drill.

Collision

1350   Held collision drill. 1354 Material condition ...... set. 1410 Secured from collision drill. Set material condition ......

Fire

1100   Held fire drill. 1110 Secured from fire drill.

Fire and Rescue

1300   Called away the fire and rescue party.
1305   Fire and rescue party embarked in starboard boat and clear of ship.
1330   Fire and rescue party returned aboard. Further assistance not required.

Gunnery

1245   Went to general quarters. Set material condition ...... 1300 Commenced ...... exercise. 1304 (Commenced firing) (Fired one ...... missile) to starboard (port). 1308 Ceased firing. 1320 Set material condition ...... 1325 Secured from general quarters. Ammunition expended: 89 rounds 5" /38 cal. high explosive projectiles with 89 rounds full service smokeless (flashless) powder cartridges with no casualties.

NOTE.—For several exercises fired in close succession, the ammunition expended for all may be grouped in one entry. Normally material condition will be set and batteries secured before securing from general quarters.

NBC Attack

1440 Set material condition . . . . . and NBC condition . . . . . .
1450 Set NBC condition . . . . . . 1500 (Simulated) nuclear (underwater) (air) burst, bearing . . . . . . distance . . . . . . yards. Maneuvering on various courses at various speeds to avoid base surge and fallout. 1530 Rejoined formation and took station . . . . . . in formation . . . . . . Axis, course, speed, etc.

Formation

0700 Maneuvering to take station . . . . . . in formation . . . . . ., axis . . . . . ., course . . . . . ., speed . . . . . . knots. Guide is USS BOSTON (CAG-1) in station . . . . . . 0800 Rotated formation axis to . . . . . . 0900 Formation changed from 49 to 52. New course and axis . . . . . ., speed . . . . . . knots. Formation guide is USS TOPEKA (CLG-8) in station . . . . . .

Officer in Tactical Command (OTC)

0900 COMCARDIV 16 embarked in USS WASP (CVS-18) assumed OTC.
1000 Commanding Officer, USS RANDOLPH (CVS-15) was designated OTC.
NOTE.—Log all shifts of tactical command. When the OTC is the Commanding Officer of your ship, use the following terminology: "OTC is Commanding Officer, USS FRANKLIN D. ROOSEVELT (CVA-42)." In every case use command title of OTC (e.g., COMCARDIV 2) and not his name and grade. State in which ship OTC is embarked.

Rendezvous

0800 USS DAHLGREN (DLG-12) made rendezvous with this ship (the formation) and took designated station (took station in the screen) (took plane guard station).
2200 Joined rendezvous with TG 70.2 and took designated station number . . . . . . in formation 4R, with guide in USS OKLAHOMA CITY (CLG-5) bearing 095, distance 2400 yards, formation course . . . . . ., formation speed . . . . . . knots, axis . . . . . . OTC is COMCRUDIV 3 in USS CANBERRA (CA-70).

Tactical Exercises

1000   Commenced division tactical exercises. Steering various courses at various speeds (in Area HOTEL) (conforming to maneuvers signalled by COMDESRON 12) (on signals from COMDESRON 12).

Zigzagging/Sinuating

1300   Commenced zigzagging in accordance with Plan # ...... base course ......, 1400 Commenced steering sinuous course, Plan #1, base course ...... 1500 Ceased zigzagging and set course ......

Fueling

Port

1000   Commenced fueling from (USS NEOSHO (AO-143)) (Naval Fuel Depot, Craney Island), draft forward ......, aft .... 1200 Fueling completed, draft forward ......, aft ......

Underway

1945   Set the special sea and replenishment detail. Commenced preparations for refueling from USS PASSUMPSIC (AO-107) 2026 Maneuvering to take waiting station astern USS PASSUMPSIC (AO-107) 2038 On station, replenishment course ......, speed .... 2042 Commenced approach, Captain (at the conn) (conning). 2053 On station alongside port side of PASSUMPSIC 2056 First line over. 2110 Received first fuel hose. 2115 Commenced receiving fuel. 2159 Fueling completed. 2206 All lines and hoses clear. Maneuvering to clear portside of PASSUMPSIC. 2210 Clear of PASSUMPSIC, 2212 Secured the replenishment detail.

Honors, Ceremonies, Official Visits

Calls

1000   The Commanding Officer left the ship to make an official call on COMCRUDESFLOT 4.

1605   RADM George DEWEY, USN, COMCRUDESFLOT 4, came aboard to return the official call of the Commanding Officer.

Manning the Rail

1000   Manned the rail as the President of the United States came aboard for an official visit. Fired 21-gun salute, broke the President's flag at the main truck.

Personal Flags

1200   RADM D. D. PORTER, USN, COMCARDIV 3, broke his flag in this ship.

1300   The Honorable (———— ————), Secretary of the Navy, came aboard; broke the flag of the Secretary of the Navy. 1500 The Secretary of the Navy departed; hauled down flag of SECNAV.

1530   COMPHIBRON 2 shifted his flag from USS ESTES (AGC-12) to USS POCONO (AGC-16).

Visits

1430   Their Hellenic Majesties, the King and Queen of Greece, made an official call on VADM D. G. FARRAGUT, USN, COMSIXTHFLT, with their official party. Rendered honors and fired a salute of 21 guns. 1530 The Royal Party departed. Rendered honors and fired a salute of 21 guns.

Inspections

Administrative, Personnel, Readiness

0930   RADM S. DECATUR, USN, COMTRAPAC, accompanied by members of his staff and inspecting party from USS ORISKANY (CVA-34) came on board and commenced surprise (administrative) (personnel) (readiness) inspection. Broke flag of COMTRAPAC.

1100   COMTRAPAC ——, members of his staff and inspecting party left the ship. Hauled down flag of COMTRAPAC.

1110   COMTRAPAC broke his flag in USS ORISKANY (CVA-34).

Lower Deck

1315   Commenced Captain's inspection of lower decks, holds and storerooms.

1400   Secured from inspection.

Personnel

0900   Mustered the crew at quarters for Captain's inspection (of personnel and upper decks).

1010   Secured from inspection.

Midwatch Entries

Port

00-04   Moored starboard side to USS AGERHOLM (DD-826) with standard mooring lines in a nest of three destroyers. USS FECHTELER (DD-870) moored outboard of AGER-HOLM to starboard. AGERHOLM moored fore and aft to buoys B-5 and B-6, San Diego, Calif. Ships present: ......, SOPA ....

00-04   Anchored in Berth B-4, U.S. Naval Base, Newport, Rhode Island, in 12 fathoms of water, sand bottom, with 75 fathoms of chain to the starboard anchor on the following anchorage bearings: Rose Island, Light 164, etc. Ship in condition of readiness THREE, material condition ...... set, and darkened except for anchor lights. Engineering department on 30 minutes notice before getting underway. Heavy weather plan in effect. Anchor detail standing by. Wind 45 knots from 070. Weather reports indicate possibility of winds up to 60 knots before 0400. Ships present ......, SOPA ....

00-04   Moored starboard side to Pier 3, Berth 35, U.S. Naval Base, Norfolk, Va., with standard mooring lines doubled. Receiving miscellaneous services from the pier. Ships present include ......, SOPA ....

00-04.   Resting on keel blocks in Drydock Number 3, U.S. Naval Shipyard, Bremerton, Wash., receiving miscellaneous services from the dock. Ships present include ......, SOPA ....

NOTE.—On succeeding watches the first entry is "Moored as before," "Anchored as before," or "Drydocked as before."

Underway

00-04   Steaming in company with Task Group 58.1, composed of CARDIV 1, CRUDESFLOT 3 and DESRON 5, plus USS HOEL (DDG-13) and USS CLAUD JONES (DE-1033) enroute from Pearl Harbor, Hawaii, to Guam, M. I. (Operating at sea off the coast of California), in accordance with CTG 58.1 serial 061. This ship in station ...... in bent-line screen .... Formation course ......, speed ...... knots. Formation axis .... SOPA is CTG 58.1 in USS SPRING-FIELD (CLG-7), OTC is COMCARDIV 1 in USS CON-STELLATION (CVA-64). SPRINGFIELD is guide, bearing ......, distance ...... yards. Condition of readiness TWO and material condition ...... set. Ship darkened (except for running lights).

NOTE.—On succeeding watches the first entry is "Underway as before."

Navigational Entries
Aids to Navigation

0102 Sighted Cape Henry Light bearing 225, distance about 20 miles. 0157 Passed Cape Henry Light abeam to starboard, distance 7.3 miles. 0300 Cape Henry Light passed from view bearing 315, distance about 20 miles.

Anchoring

1600 Anchored in Area South HOTEL, Berth 44, Hampton Roads, Va., in 4 fathoms of water, mud bottom, with 30 fathoms of chain to the port anchor on the following bearings: Fort Wood 040, Middle Ground Light 217, Sewall's Point 072. Ships present: ......, SOPA ....

NOTE.—For "Ships Present" entries, see "Ships Present" below.

Contacts

1405 Sighted merchant ship bearing 280, distance about 6 miles on approximately parallel course.

1430 Identified merchant ship as SS SEAKAY, U.S. registry, routed independently from Aruba, NWI, to New York, N.Y. 1441 Passed SS SEAKAY abeam to port, distance about 2 miles.

1621 Obtained unidentified radar contact bearing 090, distance 28,800 yards (14 miles). 1629 Unidentified contact tracked and determined to be on course 180, speed 15 knots. CPA 042, distance 4.2 miles. 1636 Contact identified as USS HAWKINS (DD-873) by USS JOSEPH P. KENNEDY, JR. (DD-850).

1715 Obtained sonar contact bearing 172, range 2,500 yds. 1717 Contact evaluated as possible submarine. Commenced attack (tracking) (investigating). 1720 Lost contact. 1721 Contact regained bearing 020. range .... Oil slick sighted on that bearing and range. Commenced re-attack. 1724 Sonar reported bearing breaking up noises. 1725 Contact lost. Steering various courses at ...... knots to regain station in formation. 1811 Regained station.

NOTE.— (1) Contacts at sea are logged when they will pass in vicinity of your ship.

(2) Under certain circumstances the above entry would not be made either because of its classification or because of entry in war diary or action report.

Course

1204 With Navassa Island Light abeam to port, distance 12 miles, changed course to 195.

1005 With New York Harbor swept channel buoy "XA" abeam to port (close aboard) (distance 500 yards) took departure for Boston, Mass., and set course 085, speed 15 knots.

1600 Completed division tactical exercises and set course 180, speed 16 knots. In column formation, OTC in USS VESOLE (DD-878). Order of ships: BARRY (DD-933) (Guide), VESOLE and POWER (DD-839). Distance 800 yards.

NOTES.—(1) Unless otherwise noted, bearings and courses are understood to read "degrees true."

(2) Where doubt may exist as to the course when passing an object abeam, as when maneuvering on various courses, log bearing when abeam.

(3) Course is "set" upon taking departure and upon completion of maneuvers.

Drydock (entering)

1420 Commercial Tug SEAGOOSE came alongside to port. Pilot C. U. FINE came aboard. 1426 U.S. Navy Tug YTB-68 came alongside port bow, U.S. Navy Tug YTB-63 came alongside port quarter. 1431 First line to dock starboard bow. 1435 First line to dock port bow. 1440 Bow passed over sill of dock. 1442 Cast off all tugs. 1450 Caisson in place. 1455 Commenced pumping water out of drydock. 1540 Resting on keel blocks. 1545 Pilot left the ship. 1550 Commenced receiving electrical power, fresh and flushing water from the dock. 1630 Inspection completed of all hull openings.

Overhaul/Conversion/Inactivation

1635 Commenced undergoing (overhaul) (conversion) (inactivation). Commenced limited log entries for duration of (overhaul) (conversion) (inactivation).

NOTE.—Above is applicable to only shipyard periods of three or more months duration. Upon termination of overhaul or conversion, deck log entries shall commence to be recorded daily by watches.

Drydock (leaving)

0850 Inspection completed of all hull openings. 0900 Flooding commenced in drydock. 0918 All services disconnected from ship. 0920 Inspection completed of all spaces for watertight integrity. 0925 Ship clear of keel blocks. 0930 Handling lines secure on ship. 0935 Pilot C. U. FINE came aboard. 0950 Commenced moving ship clear of dock. 0958 Stern passed over sill. 1005 U.S. Navy Tug YTB-63 came alongside port bow, U.S. Navy Tug YTB-68 alongside port quarter. 1009 Bow passed over sill.

Harbor (entering)

0551 Passed Ambrose Lightship abeam to port, distance 1,000 yds. 0554 Stationed special sea detail. OOD (conning) (at the conn), Captain, and Navigator on the bridge. 0600 Commenced steering various courses at various speeds conforming to Gedney Channel. 0650 Passed lighted buoy No. 12 abeam to starboard. 0701 Stopped all engines.

0705 U.S. Navy Tug No. 216 came alongside port quarter. Pilot B. A. WATCHER came aboard and took the conn. 0706 Maneuvering to go alongside the pier.

0715   Moored port side to Berth 3A, U.S. Naval Ammunition Depot, Earle, N.J., with standard mooring lines. Ships present: ......, SOPA is COMDESDIV 22 in USS GEARING (DD-710). 0720 Pilot left the ship.

NOTE.—Salient points of the ship's navigation should be logged for clarifying the ship's position. Names of tugs, stating whether Navy or commercial, and names of pilots should always be logged, giving time of arrival and time of departure. All changes in course and speed, buoys passed, and times of entering and leaving specific channels must be entered in the quartermaster's notebook.

Mooring

1006   Moored port side to Standard Oil Dock, Berth 76, Los Angeles Inner Harbor, Calif., with standard mooring lines. 1015 Commenced receiving miscellaneous services from the pier.

Sea-Weather

1130   Visibility decreased to one mile due to fog (heavy rain). Commenced sounding fog signals and stationed (extra lookouts) (lookouts in the eyes of the ship). Winds southeast 25 knots. Seas southeast 8 feet and increasing.
1212   Visibility increased to 5 miles. Ceased sounding fog signals.

NOTE.—Entry for commencement and cessation of sounding fog signals must always be made.

Speed

1700   Increased speed to 12 knots. 1710 C/s to 14 knots. 1713 Decreased speed to 8 knots to prevent damage to small boats alongside Pier 7.

Tide

0733   Commenced swinging to flood tide, stern to port. 1046 Completed swinging to flood tide, heading 347.

Time Zone Change

0001   Set clocks ahead 1 hour to conform with +3 Zone Time.

Underway

0600 Commenced preparations for getting underway. Set material condition .... 0730 Stationed the special sea detail. 0750 Completed all preparations for getting underway. Draft : forward ......, aft .... 0800 Underway for Norfolk, Va. (for sea), as a unit of Task Group 70.2 in compliance with COMCARDIV 4 serial 063 (CTG 70.2 Op Order 10-64). Maneuvering to clear the anchorage. Captain (conning) (at the conn), Navigator on the bridge. 0810 Steering various courses at various speeds standing out of Boston Harbor. 0830 OOD was given the conn. Set readiness condition THREE, anchor detail on deck. (Secured the special sea detail, set the regular steaming watch.) 0845 Entered international waters.

Personnel

Absentees, declared

0800 Mustered the crew (at quarters) (at foul weather parade) (on stations) (at quarters for Captain's inspection). Absentees: (none) (NEDOPS, John Q., 123 45 67, SA, USN, absent without authority from muster) (BADEGG, Rosco, 234 56 78, FN, USNR, UA since 0700 this date).

NOTE.—There is no legal distinction between absence over leave and absence without leave. All are logged as unauthorized absence or UA. In the case of a man's continued absence, the initial entry indicating absence or UA will suffice until the man returns, is declared a deserter, or is otherwise transferred or detached from the ship.

0900 A systematic search of the entire ship for NEDOPS, John Q., 123 45 67, SA, USN, who missed 0800 muster disclosed that (he was not on board) (he was found to be sleeping in the Bosn's Locker Comp. A-301-A).

1000 RECSTA Boston msg 031600Z reports that CULPRET, Arch, 987 65 43, BTFN, USN, UA since 0800, 15 April 1968, returned to naval custody and was being held at that station pending disposition of charges.

NOTE.—Such an entry reflects that an absentee has returned to naval jurisdiction.

Absentees, return of

2200   ROAMER, Guy, 876 54 32, PN3, USNR (returned aboard) (was delivered on board by the Armed Services Police) having been UA since 0800 this date.

2300   HAZE, "C" A., 716 26 45, SH3, USN, UA since 0700 this date, was delivered on board under guard from RECSTA, Boston, Mass., accused of drunk and disorderly conduct at that station. By order of the Commanding Officer he was restricted to the limits of the ship pending disposition of charges.

Boards

0800   The Naval Examining Board, CAPT A. B. SEA, USN, Senior Member, appointed by COMNAVAIRLANT ltr serial 1052 of 20 April 1968, met in the case of LT Xavier Y. ZEE, USN, 997900.

0900   The Naval Examining Board in the case of LT Xavier Y ZEE, USN, 997900, adjourned until 0800, 28 May 1968 (to await the action of the convening authority).

Court of Inquiry

1000   The Court of Inquiry, CAPT A. B. SEA, USN, Senior Member, appointed by COMSERVPAC ltr serial 2634 of 2 April 1968, met in the case of the late SPIRIT, Andrew J., 417 41 14, BM3, USN.

1030   The Court of Inquiry in the case of the late SPIRIT, Andrew J., 417 41 14, BM3, USN, adjourned to meet ashore at the scene of the death.

Deaths

0416   SEA, William P., 176 45 43, GM1, USN, died on board as a result of ....

Deserters

0800   ROAMER, Guy, 876 54 32, PN3, USNR, was this date declared a deserter from this ship, having been UA since 0800 1 May 1968, a period of 30 days.

Injuries

1035   During drill on the 5″ loading machine, JONAH, Ira M., 631 42 91, GMSN, USN, suffered a compound fracture of the right foot when a drill shell fell on his foot. Injury not due to his own misconduct. Treatment administered by the Medical Officer. Disposition: placed on the sick list.

Note.—In order to protect the government from false claims and to establish a record of fact for honest claimants, it is important that accurate and complete entry, including all pertinent details, be made of *each* and *every* injury, accident or casualty, however slight, among the officers, crew, visitors, passengers, longshoremen, harbor-workers, or repairmen.

Leave

1100   COMDESRON 3 hauled down his pennant and departed on 5 days leave.

1110   The Commanding Officer departed on 5 days leave.

0700   The Commanding Officer returned from 5 days leave.

(Note.—Flag Officers and unit commanders embarked, and commanding officers are the only personnel who must be logged out and in on leave.)

Special Courts-Martial

1000   The Special Court-Martial, CDR Jonathan Q. DOE, USN, Senior Member, appointed by CO, USS FORRESTAL (CVA-59) ltr serial 102 of 1 March 1968, met in the case of WEARIE, Ralph O., 876 25 93, SA USN.

1200   The Special Court-Martial which met in the case of WEARIE, Ralph O., 876 25 93, SA, USN, recessed to meet again at 1300 this date.

Note.—A court adjourns if it will not meet again that date, but if it is to meet again on the same date, it is recessed. If known, the date and time of next meeting is logged.

Summary Courts-Martial

0900   The Summary Court-Martial, LT Abel JUSTICE, USN, opened in the case of WEARIE, Ralph O., 876 25 93, SA, USN.

1100   The Summary Court-Martial in the case of WEARIE, Ralph O., 876 25 93, SA, USN, adjourned to await the action of the convening authority.

Temporary Additional Duty

1400   Pursuant to COMNAVAIRPAC ltr serial 104 of 2 February 1968, ENS Willy A. BRITE, USN, 123457, left the ship for TAD with NAS, Barber's Point, Hawaii.

1700   ENS Willy A. BRITE, USN, 123457, having completed TAD with NAS, Barber's Point, Hawaii, returned aboard and resumed his regular duties.

Passengers

1000   Mr. Delbert Z. BROWN, Civilian Technician, embarked for transportation to Guam, M.I. Authority: CNO msg 141120Z May.

NOTE.—All passengers should be logged in and out.

Patients

1306   Transferred LT Lawrence A. LEVY, USN, 808808, to U.S. Naval Hospital, Yokosuka, Japan, for treatment. Diagnosis: . . . .

NOTE.—Patients transferred with expected length of absence over 30 days or when ship is sailing outside of continental U.S. waters should be logged. Diagnosis should be included, if known.

Personal Effects

1310   Personal effects of the late SEA, William P., 176 45 43, GM1, USN, were inventoried and forwarded to . . . .

Shore Patrol

1300   Pursuant to orders of the Commanding Officer, FORCE, Marvin A., 100 92 92, BM1, USN, in charge of 17 men, left the ship to report to Senior Shore Patrol Officer, Norfolk, Va., for TAD.

0200   The Shore Patrol detail with FORCE, Marvin A., 100 92 92, BM1, USN in charge, returned to the ship having completed TAD.

Ship Movements

1100   USS RECOVERY (ARS-43) got underway and stood out of the harbor.

1130   USS KITTIWAKE (ASR-13) stood into the harbor and (anchored in Berth D-3) (moored alongside Pier 4) (moored to port of GRANT COUNTY LST-1174).

1300   USS RIGEL (AF-58) got underway from alongside this ship and anchored in Berth D-8.

1600   USS COURTNEY (DE-1021) stood in and moored alongside (to port) (outboard) of USS YOSEMITE (AD-19).

Ship's Operational Control

0705   Changed operational control to CINCUSNAVEUR, deactivated TG 85.3 and activated TG 65.4, composed of DESRON 6 and DESRON 34 enroute to Mediterranean area from Norfolk, Va.

1045   Detached by COMDESDIV 62 from TG 65.4 to proceed independently to San Remo, Italy.

1435   Detached from CTU 58.3.2, changed operational control to CTU 57.4.3.

NOTE.—For sample entries regarding commencement of operational control and changes thereto, see "Formation—Rendezvous" and "Navigational Entries—Underway."

Ships Present

Ships present: USS ENTERPRISE (CVAN-65) (COMCARDIV 4 embarked), USS COLUMBUS (CG-12), USS RECOVERY (ARS-43), and various units of the U.S. Atlantic Fleet, and service craft. SOPA is COMCARDIV 4 in ENTERPRISE (CVAN-65).

Ships present: Task Group 63.1 less DESDIV 12 plus USS ALBANY (CG-10) and various units of the British and French Navies. SOPA is COMCRUDESFLOT 2 (CTG 63.1) in ALBANY (CG-10).

Special Operations

0904   Underway for Special Operations in accordance with CINCLANT Patrol Order .... Maneuvering on various courses at various speeds conforming to ...... channel. Captain (at the conn) (conning).

1125　Secured the maneuvering watch. Commenced Special Operations.

1840　Ceased Special Operations in accordance with CIN-CLANT Patrol Order .... Commenced operating in accordance with COMSUBRON ...... Transit Order ....

Note.—Upon termination of special operations, deck log entries shall commence to be recorded daily by watches which adhere consistently to the regular schedule. For further guidance, refer to Sample Deck Log Remarks Sheet for Ships Conducting "Special Operations."

Chapter IV COMMUNICATIONS

Communications are essential to the exercise of command and extremely important to the success of any mission. The officer of the deck assumes many of the responsibilities of command which he exercises through the use of voice radio circuits. He must know enough about all such circuits, as well as other forms of communications, to discharge his duties efficiently.

INTERNAL

The first general classification for communication equipment and knowledge may be termed "internal" or "interior." Internal communications have to do with the ship itself and provide the means for informing and directing the ship's company. In their entirety they are complicated, mastered only by those specialists responsible for their maintenance. But, as far as they relate to the duties of the officer of the deck, internal communications employ a relatively limited number of circuits and types of equipment.

The officer of the deck should know in detail the internal communication facilities installed in the bridge-pilothouse area Sound-powered telephone circuits are numerous, but many of them are used only for some special purpose.

Sound powered telephone circuits aboard most ships include:

JA	Captain's battle control
JC	Ordnance control
JF	Flag officer
1JG	Aircraft control
JL	Battle lookouts
2JC	Dual-purpose battery control
1JS	Sonar control

1JV	Maneuvering, docking, catapult control
JW	Ship control, navigation
JX	Radio and signals
JZ	Damage control

The major circuits, such as the JA (captain's battle control), are most commonly used. Remember that *where* they go and *who* mans them and *when* are important details. The proper voice procedure to use on these circuits is different in some respects from voice radio procedure. Know both procedures and enforce their usage at all times. It may appear unimportant to you at first that a great variety of homemade conversation is being passed over the sound-powered telephones, but it will be evident when an emergency arises that only trained talkers, using standard phraseology, can get the correct word from station to station. The ship that permits any originality over its telephones is not only incapable of first-rate performance in an emergency, but is liable to experience confusion and mistakes during routine operations.

The intercommunication voice (MC) units, or "squawk-boxes," installed in important stations of most ships are another vital means for passing information. They are normally used by officers and should be limited to emergency business if paralleled by sound-powered telephones. Here again circuit discipline and correct procedure must be enforced by the officer of the deck. In order to avoid confusion and speed up transmissions, the standard sound-powered phone talker's procedure is used on the MC circuits.

A complete list of MC circuits follows:

Circuit	Announcing system
	One-way system
1MC	Battle and general
2MC	Engineers

3MC	Hangar deck
4MC	Damage control
5MC	Flight deck
6MC	Boat control
7MC	Submarine control
10MC	Docking control
11MC	Turret
16MC	Turret
17MC	Antiaircraft
18MC	Bridge
	Two-way system
19MC	Readyroom
20MC	Combat information
21MC	Captain's command
22MC	Radio room
23MC	Distribution control
24MC	Flag officers command
25MC	Wardroom
26MC	Machinery control
27MC	Sonar control
28MC	Squadron
29MC	Sonar information
30MC	Bomb shop
31MC	Escape trunk

Passing the Word

His [the officer of the deck's] order shall be issued in the customary phraseology of the service.—*Navy Regulations,* Article 1005.

While this subject has been discussed in an earlier chapter, it is considered important enough to justify some slight repetition. It is in the use of the general announcing system (1MC) that an officer of the deck can establish most decidedly the tone and smartness of his watch. First of all, require that each use of the general announcing system be referred to you or your junior officer of the deck for permission. If it is a routine word, such as "Pipe to dinner," you need only be sure that the standard phrase or expression is used or, in some cases, that just the boatswain's call is sounded (see list at the end of this chapter). If the word to be passed is not routine, be sure that there is good reason for using the general announcing system. Having certain individuals paged is certainly never justified unless a real emergency exists. Passing the word for a small group is similarly not advisable, yet many ships resound all day with pleas for "the five-man working party from the B Division to lay up to the quarter-deck." It is much better to have someone search out the persons concerned than to abuse the ears of all the ship's company. The general announcing system is not used between taps and reveille except for emergencies.

In passing the word the officer of the deck should be meticulous in using standard, seamanlike phraseology. The term "all hands," for example, means just that: all men and officers aboard ship. "All hands, man your battle stations" is correct. "All hands, shift into the uniform of the day" is similarly correct and should be enforced. If certain personnel are excepted, they should be listed— "All those not on watch shift into the uniform of the day," for example. The most common abuse of "all hands" is its use when "all those" is meant; for example, "All those taking typhoid shots lay down to sick bay" is correct. Be brief, as in using: "Mail call," instead of "Mail call. All division mail petty officers lay down to the post office and draw mail."

Know the difference between *secure, retreat,* and *pipe down. Secure* means to stop, as "Secure from fire drill," which means to stop fire drilling and to put away gear. *Retreat* means to leave a formation or inspection, as: "Retreat from quarters." This word is passed after *secure. Pipe down* means strike below, as: "Pipe down aired bedding."

EXAMPLES OF COMMONLY PASSED WORDS

Many ships have boatswain's mates (or men skilled with the boatswain's pipe) on watch most of the time. When passing the more common "words," these men first sound the appropriate call on the boatswain's pipe. Among such calls are "all hands," "pipe down," "mess gear," and "attention." On many ships "the word" is preceeded with "now hear this," or "now hear there." If the boatswain's call is used, there is no need for "now hear this." "All hands" is piped before any word concerning drills and emergencies, and "attention" before any miscellaneous words. The following "words" are commonly used:

Event	Word to be passed
AIR BEDDING	"All divisions air bedding."
ARRIVALS AND DEPARTURES	Title of officer, preceded by proper number of boat gongs.
BOATS	"Away, the motor whaleboat. (gig) (barge) away."
CHURCH CALL	"Divine Services are now being held (location). Maintain quiet about the decks during divine services."
COLLISION	"Collision. Collision, port side. frame twenty" (or other location).
EIGHT O'CLOCK REPORTS	"On deck all eight o'clock reports" (never the "twenty hundred reports").
EXTRA DUTY MEN	"Lay up to the quarter-deck for muster, all extra duty men" (or other special group).
FIRE	"Fire. Fire, compartment A–205–L" (or other location, including deck, frame, and side).
FLIGHT QUARTERS	"Flight quarters. Flight quarters, man all flight quarters stations to launch (recover) aircraft (helicopters)."

Event	Word to be passed
GENERAL QUARTERS	"General quarters. General quarters, all hands man battle stations."
HOIST IN BOATS	"First division stand by to hoist in (out) number——motor launch (gig)."
IDLERS	"Up all idlers" (at sea).
INSPECTION *(personnel)*	"All hands to quarters for captain's personnel inspection."
INSPECTION *(material)*	"Stand by all lower deck and topside spaces for inspection."
KNOCK OFF WORK *(before evening meal)*	"Knock off all ship's work. Shift into the uniform of the day." (First pipe "All hands.")
KNOCK OFF WORK *(before noon meal)*	"Knock off all ship's work." (First pipe "All hands.")
LATE BUNKS	"Up all late bunks."
LIBERTY	"Liberty to commence for the (first) and (third) sections at 1600; to expire on board at (hour, date, month)."
MAIL	"Mail call."
MEALS	"All hands, pipe to breakfast (noon meal or dinner; evening meal or supper)." (First pipe "Mess call.")
MESS GEAR *(call)*	"Mess gear (call). Clear the (all) mess decks." (First pipe "Mess call.")
MISTAKE OR ERROR	"Belay that last word."
MUSTER ON STATIONS	"All divisions muster on stations."
PAY	"The crew is now being paid in the mess hall."
PREPARATIONS FOR GETTING UNDERWAY	"Make all preparations for getting underway."
QUARTERS FOR MUSTER *(regular parade)*	"All hands to quarters for muster."
QUARTERS FOR MUSTER	"All hands to quarters for muster.

Event	Word to be passed
(inclement weather)	"Foul weather parade." (First pipe "All hands.")
RAIN SQUALL *(before)*	"Haul over all hatch hoods and gun covers."
READINESS FOR GETTING UNDERWAY REPORTS	"All departments, make readiness for getting underway reports to the officer of the deck on the bridge."
RELIEVING THE WATCH	"Relieve the watch. On deck the (———) section. Lifeboat crew on deck to muster. Relieve the wheel and lookouts." (First pipe "Attention.")
RESCUE AND ASSISTANCE	"Away rescue and assistance party, (———) section."
REVEILLE	"Reveille. Reveille, all hands heave **out and trice (lash) up."** Or "Reveille. Up all hands. Trice up **all bunks."** (First pipe "All hands.")
SHIFTING THE WATCH	"The officer of the deck is shifting his watch to the bridge (quarter-deck)."
SIDE BOYS	"Lay up on the quarter-deck, the side boys."
SMOKING	"The smoking lamp is lighted." (Unless the word applies to the whole ship, the location should be specified.)
SPECIAL SEA DETAIL	"Go to (man) your stations, all the special sea detail." Or "Station the special sea detail."
SWEEPERS	"Sweepers, start (man) your brooms. **Make a clean sweep** down fore and aft." (First pipe "Sweepers.")

Event	Word to be passed
TAPS	"Taps. Lights out. All hands turn in to your bunks and keep silence about the decks. Smoking lamp is out in all living spaces." (First pipe "Pipe down.")
TURN TO	"Turn to (Scrub down all weather (decks) (Scrub all canvas) (Sweep down compartments) (Dump trash)."
UNDERWAY	See *Preparations* and *Readiness*.

Use of Alarm Signals

The general alarm is a distinctive sound signal of a pulsating ringing tone which is used to call all hands to their general quarters stations—as, for example, for an actual fire or collision. Alarms should never be sounded for drill or test without first announcing the test over the general announcing system. Thus, when an alarm sounds without prior announcement, all hands will know it is an emergency.

The chemical alarm is a distinctive, 1,000-cycle steady tone used only for warning of impending gas or nuclear attack. Some new ships have a special howler, as part of the general announcing system, that is sounded when a collision is imminent. The FZ alarm is a rapid-ringing bell installed on those ships which carry nuclear weapons. This alarm unlike the others mentioned above, is triggered automatically whenever the security of a nuclear weapons space is violated or when temperatures exceed authorized limits. Antisubmarine vessels have an ASW alarm.

The ship's bell is used in conjunction with the fog gong for sounding fog signals when anchored either in Inland or International waters by being rung rapidly for five seconds at intervals of not more than one minute. When a ship more than 350 feet long is anchored in International waters, a distinctive gong shall be sounded in the after part of the ship for five seconds immediately after the bell is rung. It is standard Navy practice to follow the rapid ringing of the bell with strokes indicating the last two digits of the ship's hull number. The bell is rung rapidly for not less than five seconds, followed by the number of strokes necessary to indicate the last two digits of the ship's hull number. In international waters this is followed by sounding the fog gong for five seconds.

Another use of the bell is the traditional one of keeping time. When prescribed, the bell is sounded on the hour and the half hour, following the motion of the senior officer present, from reveille or "up all idlers" until taps.

Boat Gongs

Boat gongs are sounded in port on most ships to indicate the prospective departure of officers' boats and the arrival or departure of visiting officers, unit commanders embarked, and the commanding officer. The gongs should be sounded in time to make the departure known. (On some ships, the arrival or departure of officials is preceded by "beeps" on the chemical alarm rather than by use of gongs.) As a boat signal, the gongs are sounded *three* times, ten minutes before departure of the boat; *twice,* when there are five minutes to go: and *once,* with one minute to go before the boat leaves.

When used to indicate the arrival or departure of an officer, the gongs are sounded in pairs, the same number as the side boys the officer rates, followed by the name of the officer's command or by the word "staff." Gongs, when used this way, are not honors but merely inform those aboard ship of the arrival and departure of senior officers and the departure of crew's boats. Side boys and gongs rated by the various ranks are as follows:

Rank	Side Boys/Gongs
Fleet admiral through vice admiral	eight
Rear admiral and commodore	six
Captain and commander	four
Lieutenant commander through ensign	two

EXTERNAL

"The officer of the deck shall make no official signals except to warn others in company of immediate danger, or as otherwise authorized by the commanding officer."—*Navy Regulations,* Article 1015.

It is also important that the OOD be competent in the use of those facilities, directives, and procedures that concern communicating with other ships, units, or forces ashore. He should have a general understanding of the communication plan under which the ship is operating, know what circuits are being manner, who is on those circuits, who is net control, and what types of transmissions are authorized and know circuit designators, frequencies, calls and authenticators for all voice radio circuits. For the officer of the deck on the bridge this usually involves three circuits over which he must maintain a continuous and smart guard. There are numerous other voice circuits in CIC over which the CIC watch officer has cognizance.

The officer of the deck should be familiar with the communication facilities he has on the bridge. Of these, voice radio is a major one. Know correct voice radio procedure, such as the exact use of "over," "out," "wilco," and "acknowledge." Remember that many people are listening—some of them senior officers who will evaluate your performance. Few things mark a smart ship more firmly than a brisk, correct, and seamanlike use of voice radio, especially when underway in formation.

Visual communications, including flashing light, semaphore, and flag signals, play a large part in the daily work of an officer of the deck. Whether or not you are a proficient signalman, you must know enough of the techniques of visual communications to supervise the watch and to insure first-rate performance. This means that you should be able to tell when someone is calling you by light. It also means that you should be able to translate the heading of a message by glancing at the signalman's rough copy and noting who the originator is, to whom the message is addressed, what the precedence is, etc.

The proper use of flaghoist signals is another important aspect of bridge communications. While you will have a signalman on watch to read visual signals from the flag or other ships, you must be able to interpret them and know how to execute any orders transmitted thereby. Familiarity with the *Allied Naval Signal Book (ATPIA, Vol. II)* is a must not only for handling visual signals but more importantly for handling tactical voice signals which are transmitted in its very precise format. A similar grasp of the effective tactical publications is also a requirement of the officer of the deck. A quiet watch can suddenly become tumultuous if a visual or voice radio tactical signal addressed to your ship is not answered or executed properly. Looking up the signal, interpreting it and executing it may all have to be done in a minute or so.

Chapter V THE WATCH UNDERWAY

An officer in charge of a watch shall be responsible for the proper performance of all duties prescribed for his watch, and all persons on watch under him shall be subject to his orders. —*Navy Regulations,* Article 1005.

The officer of the deck underway has tremendous responsibility, matched by wide authority. He is required to expend much energy and to demonstrate considerable intelligence in order to perform his duties efficiently. He is rewarded, however, not only by a sense of personal satisfaction, but by the respect of his fellow officers. Short of command itself there is no finer goal for a young officer to strive for than that of being qualified as a top watchstander underway.

PREPARATION FOR ASSUMING THE WATCH

It is important to your efficiency while on watch that you make certain physical preparations. Naturally you should wear warm, comfortable clothing; draw foul weather gear, if necessary. Equip yourself with a good pair of binoculars. Ask the quartermaster for a stopwatch if you need one to time navigational lights. (All navigational lights sighted for the first time should be timed for positive identification.) At night a red flashlight is most important—*no officer should stand a watch without one.* In this connection, read the section on dark adaptation which follows in this chapter.

The following is a partial list of the information that should be obtained before relieving the deck. Experience or special circumstances will suggest additional items.

Navigational Information

1. The position of the ship on the chart, and how and when determined.

2. Course and speed of the ship.

3. Land or aids to navigation in sight or expected.

4. Changes of course and speed ordered, and by whom, and any such changes that are expected.

5. The depth of water, if on soundings.

6. Sonar conditions.

7. Navigational equipment in use, including loran, radar, sonar, Fathometer, radio, etc.

8. Weather expected (condition of the barometer and the trend of the barometer readings).

9. Current (set) experienced or expected.

10. Direction of true and relative wind.

11. Aircraft launching (recovery) course.

12. Navigational hazards to be considered, danger bearings, etc.

Tactical Information

1. Operation plans, orders, etc., under which operating.

2. The formation or disposition prescribed.

3. Own ship's assigned station, or patrol limits.

4. Identity and location of the guide and the OTC.

5. For single and multiple line formations, the prescribed order and distance.

6. For all dispositions and formations, the stations of all ships or units, formation or disposition axis, and screen axis.

7. The zigzag plan in effect.

8. Formation course (true, by gyro, and by magnetic compass).

9. Speed: signaled speed or normal speed, and the speed then being made; stationing speed.

10. Station-keeping data: amount and frequency of changes in revolutions to keep station, as well as amount of rudder (if any) being carried.

11. Radio guards assigned.

12. Recognition data.

13. Tactical circuits manned and who mans them (CIC or conn), with voice calls of OTC, own ship, and ships in formation, including screen.

14. Information of enemy, including unidentified air and surface contacts on radar screen.

15. Status of antiair warfare measures, including combat air patrol.

16. Airborne early warning information.

17. Radar guards.

18. EMCON condition in effect.

19. Flight operations scheduled or in progress.

20. Pertinent facts concerning ships in company, unusual movement, unfamiliarity with Allied procedures, radars inoperative, etc.

21. Anticipated changes in formation, tactical employment, mission or operations, such as rendezvous with replenishment group.

Ship Information

1. Condition of readiness and material condition set.

2. Status of lookouts, sea details, and the watch on deck.

3. Lifeboats ready.

4. The condition of ground tackle.

5. Status of the watch being relieved.

6. Boilers in use, and anticipated speed changes. Reserve speed available. Maximum speed requirements.

7. Important engineering machinery, electronic equipment, or gunnery equipment out of commission, and the status of repair work.

8. Important events scheduled by the plan of the day to take place during the watch.

9. Any outstanding or unexecuted orders.

10. The location of the captain and navigator (and, if a flagship, the admiral, his chief of staff, and his staff duty officer).

11. Officer who has the conn.

12. Read the current message file aboard, deck log, as far back as your last watch, and the captain's night order book.

In preparation for night watches, the captain's night order book is of major importance. It must be read carefully and initialed by the officer of the deck, junior officer of the deck, and the CIC watch officer. The standing orders that are a part of the night order book should also be read again each time before taking over a night watch. Operation orders (plans) that pertain to your watch are also highly important and should be reviewed before going on watch.

THE NIGHT ORDER BOOK

[The commanding officer of a ship] shall keep a night order book, which shall be preserved as part of the ship's official records, in which shall be entered the commanding officer's orders with respect to courses, any special precautions concerning the speed and navigation of the ship, and all other orders for the night for the officer of the deck.—*Navy Regulations*, Article 0751.

Most ships have a set of standing night orders which provide directions for night watches at *all* times; in addition, when underway, the captain will write night orders for every particular night. *Both* must be thoroughly understood and initialed by all watch officers.

The officer of the deck's major responsibility in regard to the night order book (see Appendix A for sample night orders) is to read it carefully, comprehend it, and comply with its directives. Initialing the night order book prior to relieving the watch signifies that the order book has been read and understood. A pitfall to be avoided is looking at the wrong page; ships have even made a change of course directed by an officer of the deck who was looking at the wrong night orders. If there is any reason to deviate from the captain's night orders, notify him of such deviation and the reasons therefore.

DARK ADAPTATION

Thorough knowledge of the night orders and complete understanding of all the fleet tactical and operational doctrines will not help the officer of the deck very much if he can not see where he is going at night. The safety of the ship at night depends on the ability of the officer of the deck—and the lookouts—to see in the dark. This is called dark adaptation. Cats, owls, and other nocturnal animals have acute night vision because their eyes, which are essentially color blind and see neither detail nor distant objects, are very sensitive to motion. Humans, having evolved as basically diurnal in nature, developed eyes adapted to seeing color and distant objects in daylight. You can see at night, but you can see much better if you understand the physiology of the human eye.

All vision depends on light-sensitive nerve endings in the retina of the eye, called rods and cones, which transmit to the brain an impression of the image formed on the retina by the lens of the eye. The cones, in the center, are color sensitive. The rods, in a circle around the cones, detect only variations in light intensity, but they are more sensitive to motion. So, at night when there is no color to see, the cones will tend to "make spots in front of your eyes" if you stare at a fixed point too long, but if you "look out of the corners of your eyes" the motion-sensitive rods take over; they won't tell you the color of a ship ahead, but they may enable you to see her moving in time to avoid running into her.

Daylight, in which the rods furnish color perception, is composed of all the colors in the spectrum. The cones are active only in the lower, red range of the spectrum; thus dim red lights have a minimum effect on night vision. It is possible to work in a bridge or pilothouse so lighted, then move out to the bridge wing and be able to see perfectly. The same effect is made possible by wearing red goggles for half an hour before going on watch. However, it is good practice for someone going off watch topside at night to wait until his relief knows his eyes are completely dark adapted.

Any exposure to a white light at night will greatly reduce night vision. A carelessly used flashlight, an open hatch, even the flare of a match, may reduce the conning officer's perception so he fails to see a small craft or other object in the water.

Good night vision depends on a slow, roving gaze which systematically covers the field of vision in a simple geometrical pattern. Dim objects, almost invisible if you look at them directly, will be picked up. If you sight something and then lose it, don't concentrate on where you think it should be, but move your eyes all around the spot in a circle. If you did see something, and it is moving, the rods in your eyes will find it again.

The effect of bright sunlight on the eyes lasts long after the sun goes down. Men exposed to strong sunlight during the day can see only half as well at night; they should wear dark sun glasses topside on bright days. The amount of light by which your eyes perceive motion at sea on a clear, star-lit night is only $1/150,000,000$ that of bright sunlight: give them all the help you can.

RELIEVING THE WATCH

Having completed all reasonable preparations, you are ready to get your oral turnover after informing your predecessor that you are ready to relieve him. This is a critical period, since the whole watch is usually being relieved at the same time, to say nothing of the same procedure going on in other ships in the formation. Do not divert the attention of the officer you are relieving from his duties if the watch is busy. You can always use an extra few minutes on the bridge getting oriented.

Before you say the irrevocable words: "I relieve you," be certain that you understand the situation. Check on the status of the watch standers; know what progress has been made in their relief.

After relieving, report the fact to the commanding officer if he has so instructed.

By custom the watch is always relieved fifteen minutes before the hour, unless the tactical situation is such that it is impractical because of maneuvers in process.

ORGANIZING THE WATCH

Upon taking over the watch, the first item on the agenda should be to get it organized. Begin by checking each important or key man to be sure that he knows what is expected of him. Too often an untrained or partially trained man will be jammed into the watch bill because of an oversight or of necessity, and such a man will likely not be noticed until he has made a mistake or has failed in his duties. If you do not recognize the men on watch with you as qualified and experienced, by all means check on their qualifications. On-the-spot instruction by the junior officer of the deck or an experienced petty officer might be sufficient to enable them to stand a watch. If you have any serious doubts about their qualifications, however, do not hesitate to refer the matter to the senior watch officer (in the case of officers) or to the division officer concerned. A green lookout or an unqualified helmsman can get you into serious trouble very quickly.

Remember that a normal watch, and particularly a quiet and uneventful one, offers many opportunities to train the men in their own duties and even in other jobs with which they should be familiar. By the exercise of a little ingenuity on the part of the officer of the deck, even the dullest watch can be made interesting and worthwhile. Lookouts can take a trick at the wheel, the quartermaster can teach the boatswain's mate some navigation, the boatswain's mate can drill the messenger in man overboard procedure, and use of the various general alarms.

An especially important part of indoctrination and training is that given to new men reporting aboard for duty. The officer of the deck can play a vital part in giving the new men a good first impression. Check to see that they are provided at the earliest possible moment with bunks and lockers and are assigned to a division. The executive officer usually will arrange a conducted tour of the ship for the new men. Make certain they know their way around: they will be of little use either in work or in an emergency until they do. A well-administered ship has detailed plans ready for receiving new men; the officer of the deck is responsible for starting this procedure.

Another source of potential trouble is a noisy bridge. Important voice radio messages or reports over interior communication circuits may be missed if the noise level is high. Unofficial conversation in low tones may be permitted (not for the helmsman, however), except under circumstances of tension and exceptional alertness, such as steaming darkened in formation.

It is advisable to organize your bridge personnel so

that everyone has specific duties, such as answering telephones or call bells, leaving you partially free from administrative detail. An officer or experienced enlisted man familiar with correct voice radio procedure can be detailed to answer on the bridge voice radio circuits when your ship is called.

There are many other details too numerous to mention here that should be specifically delegated. The point in all of this meticulous organization is that the officer of the deck can never justifiably tie himself down to a succession of small tasks when his major responsibilities concern the efficient operation and safety of the whole ship. The officer of the deck should normally be looking out in the direction in which the ship is moving and should not have his head buried in the pilothouse answering a phone.

THE CONN

The officer of the deck is the officer on watch in charge of the ship. He shall be responsible for the safety of the ship and for the performance of the duties prescribed in these regulations and by the commanding officer. Every person on board who is subject to the orders of the commanding officer, except the executive officer, and those other officers specified in article 1009, shall be subordinate to the officer of the deck.—*Navy Regulations*, Article 1008.

To *conn* means to control, or direct by rudder and engine order telegraph, the movements of a ship. The officer of the deck may at times have both the deck and the conn. It is customary for commanding officers of most U.S. naval vessels to take the conn at times when intricate or dangerous maneuvers are to be performed. It is also customary for officers of the deck to assist in such maneuvers by checking the performance of duty of members of the bridge watch and by keeping a watchful eye on the entire maneuver in order to inform the commanding officer of anything which might escape his notice and which consequently might endanger the safety of the ship. Likewise, when the officer of the deck has the conn during delicate maneuvers or in restricted waters, the commanding officer is customarily on the bridge watching the over-all picture to guard against mishap. In effect, then, there is a two-intellect system in which one person has the conn, giving all orders to the wheel and the engines, and another person is assisting and advising. By careful observation and prudent advice the latter endeavors to prevent an accident which might result from a momentary lapse of memory or an oversight on the part of the person conning.

Navy Regulations, Chapters 7 (Sec. 2) and 10 (Sec. 2), establishes a bridge organization which provides this safeguard, in which one human intellect supplements another, by assigning to both the commanding officer and the officer of the deck definite responsibility for the safety of the ship, regardless of which person has the conn. In fact the word *conn* does not appear in *Navy Regulations,* and no direct statement is made about the duties of the officer of the deck when another person is exercising control of the ship's movement—a matter in which he has considerable legal interest.

The following basic principles have long been accepted by experienced seagoing naval officers:

1. One and only one person can give orders to the wheel and to the engine order telegraph at any one time.

2. The identity of the person giving these orders must be known to the personnel on the bridge.

3. The officer of the deck may be relieved of the conn by another officer, but retains a considerable measure of responsibility for the ship's safety.

4. The commanding officer may take over the deck, or

he may take over the conn. In the former case, the officer of the deck has no legal responsibility for the safety of the ship, except as specifically detailed by the commanding officer. But when the commanding officer takes over the conn, the officer of the deck carries out all the duties assigned to him by *Navy Regulations,* assisting and advising the commanding officer.

5. In taking the conn from the officer of the deck, the captain should do so formally, in such a manner that all personnel of the bridge watch will be notified, unless emergency action is required. In the latter case the issuing of an order direct to the wheel or engine order telegraph will, in itself constitute assumptions of responsibility for directing the ship's movements. When taking the conn in this manner the commanding officer will then retain the conn until he formally turns it over to another person.

6. Each commanding officer establishes a procedure by which positive indication is given by him whenever he has assumed direct control of the ship and thereby relieved the conning officer of all responsibilities for such control. The procedure for delegating authority to control of the ship to a conning officer must be equally positive. It is usually done by informing all bridge personnel "This is the Captain (Mr. Jones). I have the conn (deck)." All bridge personnel, especially the helmsman and lee helmsman, will then acknowledge "Aye, Aye, Sir." It is also customary for the helmsman and the lee helmsman to respond by sounding off the course being steered and the speed and RPM indicated on the ship control console.

The officer of the deck has no problem to solve if the well-recognized principles mentioned above are observed at all times in his ship. But even the best of commanding officers is a fallible human being and may, while concentrating on the vital matters at hand, neglect to follow the recommended procedure in taking over or relinquishing the conn. Under these circumstances it is up to the officer of the deck to understand his commanding officer's actions and to clarify the situation with a polite: "Do you have the conn, sir?" or "I have the conn, sir." Then see that important bridge personnel know who has the conn.

When the officer of the deck does not have the conn he assists the conning officer in many specific ways. One of the most important is to insure that the orders from the conning officer are *understood and acted upon correctly* by the helmsman and other bridge personnel. In addition, he should make sure that the conning officer knows that his orders are being executed. Under conditions of high noise level this is sometimes difficult. In addition, the officer of the deck may take station where he can best assist the conning officer in maintaining a lookout.

COMBAT INFORMATION CENTER (CIC)

A knowledge of the purpose, capabilities, and limitations of CIC is a requisite for every qualified officer of the deck. The ideal arrangement, which is achieved on many ships, is to rotate the junior officers standing deck watches between the bridge and CIC. An understanding of both stations and how they mutually support each other is important.

CIC has as its major purpose the gathering, displaying, and evaluation of data and information in order to assist the commanding officer in handling his ship. It also disseminates information. How well it performs the first task, that of collecting data, depends somewhat on the officer of the deck. The latter must appreciate his responsibility of keeping CIC informed. It cannot be a one-way process; for CIC to do its best job, it must be furnished with visual bearings and fixes, lookout reports, visual signals and messages, decisions made by the captain or the officer of the deck, etc.

The capabilities of CIC are limited only by its equipment and the state of training of its personnel. A good CIC has the whole tactical picture and knows where all units are and what they are doing. With this knowledge and the advantages of space, good lighting, and equipment, CIC is capable of providing invaluable information and advice to the conning officer. Maneuvering problems are worked out and radar fixes are obtained which permit the CIC officer to recommend courses and speeds.

Note, however, that CIC always provides *information* and *recommendations,* not *decisions.* CIC operates as a staff officer who is always careful to *recommend* a course of action to his admiral. Decisions are made by those responsible—and the officer of the deck (or the officer who has the conn) is the one responsible.

There are exceptions to this. Control of gunfire in shore bombardment is directed from CIC. An increasing number of other operations, such as ASW and AAW, are now handled from CIC; the commanding officer stations himself there and directs the OOD who conns the ship from the bridge. The fact remains that in conning the ship, CIC's function is to recommend, the bridge's function is to conn.

AIRCRAFT CARRIER FLIGHT OPERATIONS

In an aircraft carrier the officer of the deck will meet some situations not encountered in other ships. Flight operations themselves greatly complicate the routine of the ship. The very size of a large carrier, for example, makes efficient administration difficult unless the ship is skillfully organized. Men may have long distances to travel between their duty stations and their berthing and eating spaces.

In large carriers the officer of the deck is supported by a junior (assistant) officer of the deck as well as a junior officer of the watch. The latter frequently handles routine matters underway, such as passing the word, mast reports, dumping trash, etc. The assistant officer of the deck handles tactical circuits and relays information between the commanding officer and the officer of the deck when necessary. The officer of the deck is, of course, in general charge and usually has the conn.

There is a real necessity for the nonflying line officer who stands deck watches on a carrier to become familiar with certain aspects of the problems concerning aircraft. Some of these are:

1. Aircraft turn-ups and jet blasts, with the attendant safety precautions.

2. Operation of aircraft elevators and hangar bay doors.

3. Operation of the helicopters.

4. Co-operation between the weapons department and the air department in the matter of respotting aircraft and boats.

5. Special need for smoking discipline during fueling and defueling of aircraft, tractors, helicopters, etc.

6. Plane crash procedure, the use of rescue destroyers and helicopters, and the need for keeping them informed.

7. Special restrictions on blowing tubes (never during launching and recovery, and never when soot may blow over flight deck).

8. Special wind and weather information needed before flight operations.

9. Limiting and optimum wind velocities and direction over the deck, with time needed to accelerate to desired speeds.

10. Messing of air group and air department personnel before, after, and during flight operations.

11. Need to inform air department of high winds expected so aircraft may be secured.

SUBMARINE OPERATIONS

The duties of officer of the deck of a surfaced submarine differs from those in a surface ship in several ways. First of all a submarine is extremely vulnerable should she be involved in a collision. The officer of the deck must remain fully conscious of this and accordingly he should never allow the submarine to get into any situation involving appreciable risk of collision. He must always be alert for other vessels because a submarine presents a deceiving appearance both night and day to another ship. This is especially true at night because the special lights of a submarine, which may not conform to the rules of the road, are so closely grouped as to give the appearance of a fishing boat or a very small ship. There is a tendency, then, for vessels approaching a surfaced submarine at night to be unconcerned. Similarly, a submarine tends to present a small "pip" on radar, which also leads to her classification by approaching ships as a small vessel.

The submarine OOD must be cognizant of the status of "rig for dive" at all times. When the submarine is underway at sea she should be ready to dive at any time. Once the ship has been reported "rigged for dive" permission to alter the rig for dive status or to do anything which might interfere with diving must be obtained from the commanding officer.

Because a submarine is extremely low in the water, certain safety precautions must be followed at all times at sea. Some of these are:

1. Never allow anyone on the main deck without the commanding officer's permission. Save in exceptional circumstances the commanding officer will prescribe the use of life jackets and safety lines for all personnel going to the main deck.
2. If the seas are rough the OOD, and lookouts should wear safety belts and have life lines secured to part

of the ship that would not be carried away by a boarding sea.

3. If seas are rough the OOD should shut the conning tower or upper bridge hatch to prevent flooding due to water taken over the bridge.

4. With a following sea, be alert to prevent "pooping" or taking water into the ship through the air induction system. In submarines equipped with dual induction systems the main air induction should be shut and the snorkel system used to get air into the ship.

When a submarine submerges, the OOD becomes the diving officer. The conning officer takes over the functions of the OOD.

The duties and responsibilities of the OOD of a surfaced nuclear-powered submarine are not a great deal different from those in a conventional submarine. The nuclear submarine spends so little time on the surface, however, that bridge personnel may become rusty through lack of practice. Following a prolonged period of submergence, prior to assuming the watch on the bridge, the OOD should carefully review the standing instructions and orders covering surface watch standing procedures and should brief his watch section as necessary.

HELICOPTER OPERATIONS

The use of the helicopters has become routine in ASW, underway replenishment, and rescue operations. Most naval vessels either carry and operate them or could readily be equipped to do so. An officer of the deck on almost any ship should know something of helicopter characteristics, capabilities, and limitations.

Wind is a critical factor. Know the velocities that affect helicopters, including those that govern the engagement and disengagement of rotors.

Consideration must also be given to the direction of the relative wind when maneuvering the ship to launch or receive helicopters. Cruisers, destroyers, and other ships with considerable superstructure forward of the launching area must maneuver to obtain a relative wind near the beam in order to avoid turbulence over the landing area on the fantail. For ships that land helicopters forward of the superstructure, such as a carrier, the relative wind should be forward of the beam. This can be determined by watching signal flags or the steaming colors.

Shipboard Procedure

The following general discussion of shipboard procedure for helicopter operations, applies in all important particulars to most ship types. All officers of the deck should read their ship's helicopter launching and recovery bill for a more complete discussion of the subject.

The officer of the deck (under the executive officer) coordinates the ship's movements with the helicopter launching and recovery operations. He normally orders the helicopters to be launched and recovered, keeping the executive officer and the commanding officer informed. After obtaining permission, the officer of the deck may direct the helicopter struck below or brought on deck, or may change its degree of readiness.

When the helicopter is to leave the immediate vicinity of the ship, the operations officer briefs the pilot and the officer of the deck on pertinent details, such as:

1. Time of take off and time of return.
2. Mission of the flight.
3. Position and prospective movements of own ship and of other ships as pertinent at time of take off.
4. Bearing and distance of objective at time of launching.
5. Bearing and distance of nearest land.

6. Wind and weather data as available.
7. Recognition signals and procedures.
8. Lost plane procedure.
9. Communication frequencies to be employed.
10. Magnetic variation in the operating area.

The officer of the deck should have a rescue boat manned when flight operations are in progress. He should also check on CIC to insure that it tracks the helicopter and maintains the required communication watch.

The weapons officer or the first lieutenant ordinarily meets all helicopters landing aboard that carry passengers, and insures that the passengers are directed to the people on board with whom they have business. Personnel from the captain's office meet helicopters carrying guard mail and sign for all except officer messenger mail. The officer of the deck should anticipate mail trips and have the right people on deck to receive and sign for the mail.

Readiness

Unless conditions of readiness or emergencies dictate otherwise, the helicopter must be in all respects manned and ready, with the engine warmed up and rotors spread, ten minutes prior to the scheduled launch. The sounding of flight quarters for the helicopter may be based on this time, depending on the location and status of the plane. The senior helicopter pilot should be informed of any unscheduled flight as far in advance as possible. This will enable him to plan fuel loadings and to assemble any special gear that may be required.

Safety Precautions

The main rotor blades of a helicopter are fragile control surfaces and are treated with great care. In the event of damage to one blade, the matched pair or set must be replaced, at a very high cost. An object as small as a care-lessly thrown softball can damage a blade sufficiently to require the replacement of the set. The rotor blades are flexible and will bend when exposed to strong wind. Special precautions are needed to secure the blades as well as the helicopter itself, which has a higher center of gravity than conventional planes.

The rotating blades with their high tip velocity present a missile hazard of great potentialities for damage and injury to personnel. Even when there appears to be sufficient clearance beneath the rotors for personnel on deck to pass or work safely, it must be remembered that the blades may be deflected downward. If the blades should accidentally touch a fitting or part of the ship's deck or hull while rotating, they may shatter, resulting in the loss of life or severe injury. The number of men in the vicinity of helicopter operations must be kept at a minimum. As a matter of routine, the area should always be cleared of all men not engaged in necessary activities.

Downwash from the main rotor is very strong during landing and take off. All rags, hats, and other loose gear must be kept clear of the launching and landing area.

Your ship may have to receive a helicopter, on very short notice, for in-flight transfer of men, mail, movies, or spare parts. Preparations to handle the "chopper" include changing to a course which will provide proper relative wind, clearing the deck area, and notifying necessary people.

SEARCH AND RESCUE (SAR)

The armed services and the Coast Guard maintain jointly an almost worldwide search and rescue organization, which uses existing commands, bases, and facilities to search for and rescue personnel from air, surface, and sub-surface casualties. Certain commands, such as Commander in Chief Atlantic, are designated as SAR Coordination Centers for the purpose of coordinating the activities of ships and aircraft when an accident occurs. The senior naval officer (or one designated by him) at the scene of a disaster is known as an SAR Commander. Specified radio frequencies are named upon the occurrence of an accident, and a carefully planned procedure is followed. Detailed information giving the SAR organization and procedures, with a description of facilities at each location, is usually found in fleet instructions or in an operation order. The SAR folder on the bridge and in CIC contains copies of the *National Search and Rescue Manual NWP 37(A)*, and pertinent SAR directives from current operation orders.

The officer of the deck should be generally familiar with these directives, should know the radio frequencies to be used, the rescue procedures, and special signals made by ships and aircraft.

REPLENISHMENT (UNREP)

Underway replenishment (UNREP) involves the transfer of fuel, provisions and stores, ammunition, mail, spare parts and personnel from one ship to another while both are underway. Such an operation is normally scheduled several days in advance, but an UNREP of opportunity may be ordered whenever circumstances require it. An UNREP requires special skills and techniques with which all officers must be familiar, whether or not they may be on watch during the operation. This is especially true in small ships, where it becomes an "all hands" evolution.

When an UNREP is scheduled, the OOD should:

1. Notify the heads of departments concerned of the operation as soon as practicable.

2. Order information passed over the 1MC circuit concerning time of operation and stations to be manned.

3. Supervise use of prescribed signals during approach and while alongside.

4. Assist the conning officer in relaying orders to the helmsman and operator of the engine order telegraph and revolution indicator.

5. See that smoking is controlled in accordance with ship's regulations.

Prior to an UNREP operation, review *Replenishment at Sea (NWP 38D)* for details of the entire procedure. Check *Knight's Modern Seamanship* for a description of the equipment used. Refer to Chapter VI of this text for a brief discussion of shiphandling involved, and to Chapter XI for safety precautions to be observed.

Communications equipment utilized for UNREP includes radio, flashing light, electric megaphones, sound powered telephones, flags, paddles, and wands. During the actual UNREP, the use of radio between delivery and receiving ships normally is confined to emergencies. Electric megaphones are employed during the approach until telephone lines are connected. Thereafter, they comprise the main standby method of communicating.

HEAVY WEATHER

One of the attributes of a good naval officer and seaman is weather wisdom. Know what weather is expected and plan accordingly, to meet its effects on shipboard routine and operations.

When heavy seas and winds of high intensity are anticipated, the officer of the deck shall take the following precautions:

1. Have the word passed over all circuits, "Prepare ship for heavy weather."
2. Designate divisions to rig inboard life lines on weather decks.

3. Pass, as appropriate, the word, "Close all hatches on main deck forward," "Close all topside hatches forward or aft of frame ———," "Close all topside hatches, doors and ports (on starboard or port side)." Pass the word for personnel to remain clear of the weather decks as necessary for safety.

4. Require personnel who are required to work topside in heavy weather to wear life jackets and safety lines. In this exposed work only kapok jackets shall be worn.

HURRICANES AND TYPHOONS

Cyclonic storms, known as hurricanes in the Atlantic and typhoons in the Pacific, can have devastating effects on even the largest ships. Warnings of such storms and conditions of readiness may be delineated as follows:

Condition Four

The path of the cyclone has been fairly well established and its trend indicates a possible threat of destructive winds of the force indicated within 72 hours. Take preliminary precautions.

Condition Three

The cyclone continues to advance (and approach) and destructive winds of the force indicated are possible within 48 hours. Take appropriate action to safeguard personnel and property.

Condition Two

Destructive winds of the force indicated are anticipated within 24 hours. Take additional action required to permit the setting of an appropriate state of readiness on short notice.

Condition One

Destructive winds of the force indicated are imminent. Take appropriate action to minimize injury to personnel and damage to property.

As officer of the deck, you will probably never have to face a hurricane without plenty of company on the bridge, but you should know the following procedures.

1. Determine the bearing, distance, and track of the storm from the official warnings, or from your own calculations if there are no warnings. From this information, plan how best to avoid the dangerous semicircle of the storm. Relationship to shoal water must be considered.

    a. If you are near a storm and have no warnings, determine the bearing of the storm by the direction from which swells are arriving and by adding 115° to the direction from which observed true wind is blowing.

    b. If the wind gradually hauls to the right (clockwise), the ship is in the dangerous semicircle, *i.e.*, the right side of the hurricane in relation to storm track. If it hauls to the left (counterclockwise), the ship is in the safe or navigable semicircle.

    c. If the wind remains steady in direction, increases in speed, and the barometer continues to fall, you are directly in the path of the storm.

2. Use radar.

3. Do not try to outrun or cross the "t" of a hurricane; it usually means trouble from the front-running swells of the hurricane, which build rapidly in size with the approach of the center. These can cut down ship speed by several knots, while the hurricane keeps on at its own appointed pace—or speeds up.

4. If sea surface temperature charts are available and maneuvering plans permit, avoid the areas of warmest waters. Hurricanes like these as a path if their speed is slow, say 10 knots or less. If the storms are moving fast,

16 knots or more, the warmer waters have little influence.

5. If actually caught in the hurricane circulation, even the fringes, take these steps:

a. If dead ahead of the center, bring the wind on the starboard quarter (160° relative) and make best speed on this course. This will get you away from the center most quickly, and put you in the safe semicircle.

b. If in the safe or navigable semicircle, bring the wind on the starboard quarter (130° relative) and make best speed.

c. If in the dangerous semicircle, bring the wind on the starboard bow (45° relative) and make as much headway as possible.

d. If necessary to heave to, do so head to sea.

e. Proximity to land areas, coastlines, or islands must be taken into account in maneuvering. An evasive course which brings you close to shore is dangerous, particularly if you are in the sector of the storm with onshore winds.

DAMAGE CONTROL SETTINGS

The qualified officer of the deck requires a reasonably thorough knowledge of the damage control organization of his ship. He must know how certain closures are made as a matter of routine, and must know the system in force for maintaining watertight security. The usual practice in small ships includes a watertight closure log, kept by the quartermaster of the watch, in which are recorded the openings permitted, upon request, by the officer of the deck. Both time of opening and time of closure are logged. At general quarters the log is maintained in damage control central. In large ships, damage control central is manned at all times, and the watertight log is maintained there.

While this business of opening and closing doors and hatches may appear rather dull and routine, it is a matter of great importance to the safety of the ship and the lives of the crew. A ship can go along for years and never suffer for having neglected her watertight integrity, but a sudden grounding or collision may result in disaster if the ship lacks watertight integrity. Even half a ship will stay afloat and permit the rescue of many men if the watertight integrity has been maintained. The officer of the deck must always be cognizant of the need for combatting carelessness and for making sure that the proper closure setting is maintained.

MATERIAL CASUALTIES

The officer of the deck must insure that all machinery and electronic gear is operable, within, of course, the limits of his capabilities. This means that foresight is necessary in testing equipment such as winches, radar, and voice circuits that may be used in the immediate future. In addition, the officer of the deck should follow up any material casualties that occur so that he may be certain that the cognizant officer is notified. The officer of the deck must know the effect of any casualty, and make necessary reports to the OTC, as well as intra-ship reports. An important electronic failure, for example, should be reported to the electronics officer as well as to the captain and admiral (if embarked), and information should be obtained concerning estimated length of repair time.

CLASSIFIED PUBLICATIONS

It is usually necessary to maintain on the bridge (in the pilothouse) an extensive collection of classified material. Signal books and tactical publications are often registered and must be in someone's custody at all times. Upon getting underway it is customary for the ship's custodian to bring the classified publications up to the bridge and to obtain the signature of the officer of the deck or junior officer of the watch then on duty. Whoever signs must in turn obtain the signature of his successor as the watch is relieved. It is best for the junior officer of the watch to assume this recurrent duty and to keep custody of the bridge publications. He should sight each publication before signing the list.

BINOCULARS

The officer of the deck should know how to adjust, clean, and use a pair of binoculars. He should know his own focus and interpupillary setting. He should also instruct his lookouts and other personnel in the care and use of the glasses. Careless handling, especially dropping, can soon render a pair of glasses unfit for use until repairs are made by a tender or shipyard. The men should be taught to use the neck strap and to keep the glasses in a case when not actually in use. Nothing is more lubberly, unseamanlike, and just plain wasteful of public funds than leaving binoculars adrift. The top of a chart table may seem like safe stowage until the ship takes a roll and you are faced with the embarrassment of having to lean over and pick up a pair of useless glasses. Remember that binoculars are cleaned only with lens paper.

REFUSE DISPOSAL

Except as authorized by law or by regulations issued by competent authority, no oil or refuse shall be discharged into inland and coastal navigable waters.—*Navy Regulations,* Article 1272.

It shall be unlawful for any person to discharge . . . oil . . . into or upon the coastal navigable waters of the U.S. from any vessel . . . or suffer, or permit the discharge of oil by any method, means, or manner.—*Oil Pollution Act of 1924.* (See also *"Pollution Control".*)

During wartime the scattering of boxes, cans, garbage, and other trash from ships can reveal their presence to the enemy. Special precautions are found in *Allied Naval Maneuvering Instructions,* and additional directives may be promulgated. During peacetime the dumping of trash and garbage and pumping of bilges must be controlled. Seacoast communities object to the pollution of their coasts and beaches and state and federal regulations are supporting such objections. In general, trash and garbage should not be thrown overboard underway, and bilges should not be pumped without permission of the officer of the deck. He will be guided by current directives usually found in a ship's instruction or in an operation order.

SPECIAL SEA DETAILS

The commanding officer shall insure before departure for sea that the officers and crew have been properly organized, stationed, and trained to cope effectively with any emergency that might arise in the normal course of scheduled operations. —*Navy Regulations,* Article 0746.

While the officer of the deck is not responsible for the assignment of the special sea details, he is often involved in their performance of duty—particularly if it is not up to standard. Some of them, particularly the helmsman, telephone talkers, and the engine-order telegraph operator, must be experienced and reliable men. Their mistakes or inattention to duty can result in serious trouble for the officer who is handling the ship, and could lead to collision or grounding. The OOD must be aware of the importance of the special sea details and should check their stationing throughout the ship, both topside and below decks. When a new man is assigned to special sea detail, his qualifications should be determined at once. No man, of course, is indispensable, and changes in assignments are natural. But if a proper training program is carried out in which the ood can assist, there should always be qualified men stationed as special sea details.

Specific duties of the special sea details are usually covered in the *Ship's Organization and Regulations Manual.* See Appendixes D and E for typical procedures for getting underway and entering port.

INSPECTIONS

The officer of the deck shall require frequent inspections to be made to insure the security of the ship, including watertight integrity, degree of closure, condition of the armament, condition of ground tackle or mooring lines in use, good order and discipline of the crew and all other matters which may affect the safety or operations of the ship. Such of the above inspections as are not made and reported to him by another regularly established watch shall be made by members of his watch.—*Navy Regulations,***Article 1013.**

No matter how busy or even hectic a watch may be, the officer of the deck must remember that his responsibilities include the whole ship. The security of the ship depends on frequent inspections to insure that no fire hazards exist and that watertight fittings required to be closed are actually dogged down. Gambling, smuggling of liquor, or the introduction of drugs, can not be permitted, and only an alert watch and thorough inspection will prevent all three. A well organized ship, properly inspected, will have substantially less trouble than a loosely organized, poorly disciplined ship.

Inspections normally include a watertight integrity security patrol made at regular intervals by damage control personnel. Tanks and voids are sounded during these patrols. In most ships a check-off list of all inspections and patrols is a useful device that should be maintained by the boatswain's mate or the quartermaster of the watch. This list should be inspected regularly by the OOD or

JOOD in person after first reporting to the boatswain's mate of the watch or the quartermaster.

POLLUTION CONTROL

One of the items on the check-off list for entering port (Appendix E) concerns dumping garbage and trash, and pumping bilges when conditions permit, with reference to the prohibitions of the *Oil Pollution Act of 1954*. This is not a recent innovation—the first *River and Harbor Act,* passed in 1899, prohibited the discharge of any refuse into any navigable waters. However, increasing public concern over environmental pollution, and particularly over oil spills, has resulted in many new international, national, state and local acts and laws. These concern not only the pumping of bilges, but dumping of trash and garbage, and overboard discharge of sewage in inland as well as international waters. Enforcement of such laws is strict, and penalties are becoming severe.

Pertinent portions of the *Oil Pollution Act* and the *River and Harbor Act* are usually prominently posted. Local regulations may be found in the SOPA Instructions or various port or base information folders. The officer of the deck must be cognizant of all such regulations, and religiously enforce them.

NUCLEAR WEAPONS SECURITY

Special security patrols to safeguard nuclear weapons are established by the weapons officer or the nuclear weapons officer, in accordance with instructions specifically covering such weapons. The reports of such patrols will be made to the officer of the deck.

REPORTS

The officer of the deck shall promptly report to the commanding officer all matters which affect or which may affect the safety of the ship or personnel, or ships in company. All land, shoals, rocks, lighthouses, beacons, buoys, discolored water, vessels, aircraft, or wrecks detected; any marked change in the barometer, force or direction of the wind, state of the sea, or indications or warnings of storm or bad weather; all changes of formation, course, or speed ordered by the office in tactical command, or changes of course or speed made by the ships in company or by himself; derangements to equipment which may affect the safety or operations of the ship; all serious accidents; the winding of the chronometers; the hours 0800, 1200, and 2000; and, in general, all occurrences worthy of notice of the commanding officer shall be reported to him, subject to his orders. When a flag officer is embarked, similar reports shall also be made to him, subject to his orders.—*Navy Regulations,* Article 1020.

There is one point that often confuses junior officers standing night watches. Should they comply literally with *Navy Regulations* and wake the captain for every item listed above? The answer is an unqualified affirmative. You have no choice but to obey the letter of the *Regulations.* If the reports are not desired, he may limit you in some arbitrary fashion, depending on the particular circumstances. The standing night orders or other instructions for watch standers may provide guidance on when the captain desires to be called; otherwise, be meticulous in making your reports. If there is doubt in your mind, play safe and call the captain. Do not be concerned with waking him; he is accustomed to interrupted sleep when underway at night and will gain peace of mind and reassurance by your conscientious attention to duty. Some people can acknowledge without really awaking, so be certain that important messages are actually understood. It is best to make such reports in person, rather than by messenger, when possible.

Chapter VI SHIPHANDLING

The commanding officer of a ship shall afford frequent opportunities to the executive officer, and to other officers of the ship as practicable, to improve their skill in ship handling.—*Navy Regulations*, Article 0754.*

The officer of the deck may expect to handle the ship in keeping station, in making turns in formation for changes of course, and on other occasions when no great risk is involved. If his commanding officer is so disposed, the officer of the deck may even handle the ship when making a landing alongside a wharf, pier, or other ship. In any event, the officer of the deck must prepare himself by study and observation to handle his ship. Occasions may arise, as they have in the past, in which junior officers must take their ships to sea because of an emergency owing to weather or enemy action.

This guide cannot be a definitive textbook on shiphandling. It is proposed, however, to outline in this chapter some of the important matters the officer of the deck should know. Further study in such standard reference books as Crenshaw's *Naval Shiphandling* is recommended. That book discusses the basic principles of shiphandling, and special problems in handling various types of ships.

DEFINITIONS

Pivot point: The point of rotation within the ship as she makes a turn. This point is generally about one-

* Effective 23 September 1970 the Chief of Naval Operations authorized competiton in ship-handling for all officers except commanding officers and lieutenant commanders serving as executive officers. Participation is on a voluntary basis. The foregoing competition does not include enlisted senior petty officers, but such petty officers may be assigned to ship-handling duties after proper training. (Z—gram 31.)

third the length of the ship from the bow and fairly close to the bridge (when going ahead).

Turning circle: The path described by the ship when turning. The turning circle will vary with amounts of rudder and with speeds used.

Advance: For any turn, the advance is the distance gained in the direction of the original course from the time the rudder is put over until the ship is on the new course.

Transfer: For any turn, the transfer is the distance gained in a direction perpendicular to that of the original course from the time the rudder is put over until on the new course.

Tactical diameter: For any amount of constant rudder angle, the tactical diameter is the distance made good in a direction perpendicular to that of the original course line from the time the rudder is put over until the ship is on a reverse heading. It is the transfer for a turn of 180 degrees.

Standard rudder: Standard rudder is the angle of rudder for that particular ship which under normal conditions will give standard tactical diameter.

Full rudder: Full rudder is a prescribed angle of rudder for that particular ship, usually a safe distance—five degrees—short of the stops which will give reduced tactical diameter.

Acceleration and deceleration rates: Acceleration and deceleration rates are the rates at which a ship picks up or loses headway after a change of speed.

An officer who desires to become an efficient shiphandler must first know his ship and how each of the foregoing terms applies to her.

GENERAL PRINCIPLES

An officer should also know certain general principles and their specific application to his ship, some examples of which are given below:

1. *The effect of the wind upon turning.* Most ships, particularly those with high bows, turn slowly into the wind when going ahead, but more rapidly when turning away from it. Conversely, they will turn rapidly into the wind when backing. The effect on a particular ship can be estimated by comparing the "sail area" forward of the pivot point with that abaft the pivot point. If the "sail area" is greater forward, the ship will have the above tendencies. If greater aft, her tendencies will be the opposite; this is particularly true of aircraft carriers. The "sail area" is composed of the fore-and-aft vertical surfaces of the hull and superstructure against which the wind exerts force.

2. *Effect of speed upon turning.* With constant rudder angle, for speeds any appreciable amount above steerageway, any increase in speed will result in an increased turning circle. This is a result of the inertia of the ship, which tends to keep her going in the original direction of motion. This increased turning circle will vary from ship to ship and will be most noticeable when ships of different types are operating together. Since the guide is usually a large ship and will use the same amount of rudder or standard rudder for all speeds, you must know what rudder for your ship will match the turning circle of the guide for the speed at which any turn is made.

For speeds approaching bare steerageway, a decrease in speed will result in an increased turning circle. This is owing to the decreased effect of the rudder acting against the inertia of the ship which tends to keep the ship moving in a straight line. In making a turn at low speeds, therefore, an increased amount of rudder is needed. You should always know what is the minimum speed at which you will still have steerageway.

3. *Effect of shallow water.* Reduced space between the ship's hull and the bottom in shallow water prevents the screw currents from flowing freely and from acting upon the hull and rudder in the normal manner. As a result, the ship may be sluggish or erratic in answering the rudder. In addition, there is a great waste of power, and the speed through the water will be less than that indicated by the propeller revolutions.

4. *Time lag in response to orders.* There is a noticeable lag between the time an order is given to the wheel or engines and the time that the effect of the response is felt. For example, in order to have your rudder go over at the same spot as that of the ship ahead so that you will turn in her wake, you must give your order to turn when the kick of the preceding ship's rudder is near your bridge.

5. *Backing power available.* The backing power available may be considerably less than the power for going ahead, for two reasons: a backing turbine has fewer impeller blades, so produces less power, and the propellers are less efficient when turning astern. "Back one-third" and "Back two-thirds" normally call for one-third and two-thirds, respectively, of the power available for backing. The turns for "Ahead one-third" and "Ahead two-thirds" are based upon one-third and two-thirds of standard speed. There is no "Back standard" speed. There is a probability that "Ahead one-third (two-thirds)" and "Back one-third (two-thirds)" will not have quite equal effect. As a result, in addition to twisting when one engine is backing and the other going ahead (both at one-third or two-thirds), the ship can be expected to pick up a slight amount of way in the direction of the stronger force.

6. *Factors affecting acceleration and deceleration.* The manner in which ships gain and lose headway, carry their way, and respond to changes of engine speed, varies with the size of the ship, her underwater lines, condition of bottom, wind, and state of sea. A heavy ship, a clean-bottomed ship, or a ship with fine lines, will tend to hold her way, and vice-versa. A heavy ship, a foul-bottomed ship, or a ship with full lines, will tend to pick up headway slowly in response to changes of engine speed.

7. *Factors affecting turning.* As officer of the deck you should not only know how to make a normal turn, but how to turn your ship in the shortest time and how to turn her in the shortest space.

The procedures for these two maneuvers are quite different. To turn your ship in the *shortest time,* go ahead with full power and put your rudder hard over just short of the stops. To turn your ship in the *shortest possible space,* you may have to vary your procedure, depending upon the ship herself and, sometimes, upon wind conditions. A ship with twin rudders and screws is the easiest and probably the quickest to turn, and is the least affected by the wind conditions. Simply put the rudders over full in the direction of the desired turn, and keep them there. Ring up "Ahead two-thirds" on the outboard engine and "Back two-thirds" on the inboard engine. The speed of the inboard engine can be adjusted to keep the ship from going ahead or astern as she turns on her heel.

To turn a single-rudder, twin-screw ship in the shortest space is slightly more difficult. If the screws are set well off from the centerline, and if the turn is not adversely affected to any degree by the wind, the turn can be made by going ahead on the outboard engine and backing on the inboard engine. When the wind adversely affects the turn, or when the screws are not sufficiently offset for a good, powerful couple, motion ahead and astern may be necessary to supplement the effect of the rudder. As a general rule, when the ship is going ahead with steerageway, the rudder should be put over in the direction of the desired turn; when the ship is going astern with steerageway, the rudder should be in the opposite direction; when the ship has no way on or less than steerageway, the rudder should be amidships. The amount of way on and the position of the rudder should be carefully watched. Some ships with large single rudders will show a somewhat similar tendency to a twin-rudder ship; that is, to answer to the effect of an ahead-turning screw on the rudder even when they have a small amount of sternway. The officer of the deck must know the characteristics of his own ship in this regard.

Turning a single-screw ship in the shortest space is the most complicated maneuver of all. Most ships of this type have right-handed propellers. To turn a ship of this type requires some way on. Therefore, to turn in the shortest space, alternate between headway and sternway. Whenever the engine is going ahead, throw the rudder in the direction of the desired turn. Knowing when to shift the rudder after starting the engines backing is a matter of knowing the ship. Normally, the rudder should be shifted sometime shortly after the ship loses headway. It should then be kept there until the engine is put ahead.

HANDLING IN FORMATION

Handling a ship in company with others requires a sound knowledge of the effective tactical instructions, and a thorough understanding of the relative motion of ships. Information on the first essential is found in *ATP 1,* Volumes 1 and 2. Every officer standing deck watches at sea should be so familiar with this important directive that he can find at once the proper guidance for any circumstance that may arise involving the movements of his ship. The opening chapters are particularly important, since they provide the basic concepts and definitions upon which all subsequent instructions are based.

The second essential for efficient shiphandling in formation—an understanding of relative motion—can be attained by study and practice in working maneuvering board problems. An authoritative reference is the chapter on the maneuvering board in *Dutton's Navigation and Piloting*. Many naval schools provide excellent courses in relative movement, but any officer can become proficient by a moderate amount of study and much practice. It is recommended that problems be solved both with your own ship at center and with the guide at center. The former method is almost always employed in cic; the latter is often useful on the bridge, particularly for a vessel in the screen. A sense of timing can be acquired by a thorough knowledge of the definitions and general principles cited at the beginning of this chapter.

An important result of skill in using the maneuvering board is the ability to visualize problems and to solve them mentally. For a complicated evolution, such as taking a new and distant station in a formation, your mental solution would, of course, be only approximate and would be subject to modification by cic or by a junior officer of the deck who actually works out the problem. But the mental solution permits you to make an instant change of course and speed which expedites the maneuver, demonstrates a ship's smartness and gets you "on the way." For simple problems, such as gaining 10 degrees in bearing on the guide while maintaining distance, the mental solution is sufficient since it is subject to constant confirmation by periodic bearings and ranges.

Close Station-keeping

The mental process discussed above, of visualizing simple problems in relative motion and solving them correctly, is the key to proficient station-keeping in close formation. Ships do not steam in close formation now as often as formerly although it is still an important requirement, demanded by most type commanders. Patrol and escort vessels, destroyers, cruisers, carriers, and amphibious ships still must, on occasion, be able to steam in column or in line of bearing at standard distance, or in circular formation darkened at night and at high speed.

Steaming in close column demands a keen appreciation of speed and how your ship carries her way. It is largely a matter of speed adjustment.

The stadimeter is an essential instrument when in close formation. Every watch officer should be familiar with its use and should know its capabilities and limitations. It is more accurate at closer ranges than most radars. It is particularly helpful in that it will give you quick and accurate information about whether you are opening, closing, or holding a steady distance.

Reports of distance should be given with the distance followed by the information about whether it is "closing," "opening," or "steady." The terms "increasing" or "decreasing" should not be used, as there is chance of confusion with reports concerning bearings.

Develop your sense of distance. Find some spot on the bridge where you can later stand and from which you can line up some object on your ship, such as the jackstaff, with objects on the ship ahead or to the side. When your distance to an adjacent ship has been measured, make a mental note of how the objects aligned for future reference.

There may be times on dark nights when there is not

enough light to take stadimeter readings and when you are too close for radar ranges or when radar silence is imposed. Binoculars can then be used to obtain a fair estimate of distance if during the day, when you can measure exact distance to a ship you look at it through binoculars and note the amount of the binocular field that she fills. It takes much practice to become proficient in this use of the binoculars, but it is worth it. See *Naval Shiphandling*, Chapter *IV*.

If you are the first ship in the column, or if your ship is the guide, make every effort to ensure good steering and steady speed. Watch the helmsman carefully and, at the same time, see that the proper revolutions are actually being made. The officer of the deck on the ship astern will appreciate your efforts.

When following another ship, the keeping of proper distance depends largely on your ability to detect early indications of opening or closing motion and to make proper speed adjustments to counteract that motion. In this regard you should remember that a ship following in the wake of another requires a few more revolutions than she will in still water to make good the same speed as the ship ahead because of the necessity to overcome the weak turbulence or "kick" of the preceding ship. An erratic helmsman who takes you in and out of the wake of the ship ahead will make your problem of speed adjustment a difficult one. Therefore, keep a close watch on your helmsman. Make your speed correction with care, remembering that there is a time lag before the effect of change is felt. If you do not allow for this time lag you are liable to correct twice for the same error. That will result in a need for a correction, probably larger, in the opposite direction. Once such surging starts, it is hard to stop. Study the time lag of your ship intently until you get to know it. Observe the effect of one correction carefully before applying another. Remember that excessive use of the rudder acts as a brake. Always correct the steering before increasing speed.

In general, when in column, it is safer to be inside rather than outside the prescribed distance because it is easier to drop back than to close up. Know the allowable tolerances and keep within them, because it is also easy to hit the ship ahead if she slows without your noticing it. Remember the fellow next astern, and keep your course and speed as steady as possible. The reputation of being a good ship to follow is a difficult one for a ship to earn, but it is worth trying for.

When in column, always keep in mind your number in the column and to which side you should sheer out in an emergency. This is the same side as that of your position when in column open order, and it follows the standard pattern—odd ships to starboard, even ships to port. When for any reason you find yourself getting uncomfortably close to the ship ahead, ease your bow out very slightly on the side to which you would sheer out in an emergency.

Course changes for a formation in column may be made in two ways: by individual ships turning together, and by wheeling (changing course in succession, following the ship ahead).

When change of course is made by turning together, be sure to put your rudder over the proper amount promptly on the execution of the signal. Inform the steersman of the new course, and see that he does not swing past it nor use an excessive amount of rudder in meeting the swing. Either of these errors by the steersman will cause you to end up behind bearing in the line of bearing resulting from the maneuver. Keep the nearest ship toward which you are turning under constant visual observation. Check the bearing of the guide as the turn progresses, with a view to detecting promptly any tendency to gain or lose bearing.

In practice, ships do not maintain perfect position, particularly when making frequent simultaneous turns, and the officer of the deck must know how to adjust a turn to improve his position. This ability is largely a question of experience in visualizing the situation, and in looking ahead. Of course, any such adjustments must consider adjacent ships on both sides.

In wheeling, when nearing the turning point of the ship ahead, remember that when she starts to turn her stern will swing out, and the helmsman may, if steering by keeping steady on the stern of the ship ahead, continue to steer by her stern and thus sheer out. If this happens you will start your turn *already outside* and will have to make a large turn, both in degrees turned and distance traveled, which will cause you to lose distance. In order to prevent this loss, if you are properly in station astern of the guide, order the helmsman, at the instant the signal for the turn is executed, to steady on course. Specify in your order what that course is. If you are not directly astern of the guide, take a bearing of the guide at the instant the signal is executed, and then order the helmsman to steer that as a course. This adjustment will ensure your passing through the turning point of the guide.

Assuming that the ship ahead has turned properly, you will turn in the same water. The knuckle of her wake should be slightly on the bow, in the direction of the turn. Slick water inboard of the wake is caused by the stern of the ship sliding in the turn; the inboard edge of the slick marks the path of the ship's bow, the outboard edge, that of her stern.

Conn from the wing of the bridge, where you can watch the ship ahead and the one astern, if any. Knowing exactly when to start the turn takes experience, but usually you will order the rudder put over when the knuckle is abreast the bridge. If the turn is correctly timed, the bow of your ship will follow around at the inboard edge of the slick.

If you turn too late, you will go outside the proper turning circle, and the wake of the ship ahead may tend to hold you there. If this happens, do not swing beyond the new course, but remain steadied parallel to the column on its new course. Wait until the ship next astern has completed her wheel before gradually regaining station; you will almost always have to increase speed to regain station.

If you turn too early, you will go inside the proper turning circle. A slight easing of the rudder will correct this, but it must be realized that a reduction of speed will probably be necessary to avoid coming dangerously close to the ship ahead. A common error in such a situation is to ease the rudder too much, with the result that your ship will cross the wake ahead and you will be outside after all.

The danger in turns lies in starting a large change of course when too close to the ship ahead. You will then have to choose between a larger rudder angle to stay inside the turn, while slowing, stopping, or backing, or else ease the rudder and go outside. It is safer to continue the turn inside; if you hesitate and then ease the rudder to go outside, your ship may forge ahead while her bow is still inside the stern of the ship ahead, and be in danger of collision.

If the ship ahead turns too soon or too late, don't attempt to follow her but turn correctly in the wake of the guide. If your own ship is slightly out of position when a turn is ordered, use the maneuver to correct. If you are behind station, cut the corner; if too close, don't turn too soon, but turn a bit late, with full rudder.

At night, or in fog, you may not be able to see the

knuckle. Time the signal to execute, or the whistle signal; based on your speed and distance from the guide, you can determine when you reach the point of turn.

Line of Bearing

When in line of bearing, station-keeping is somewhat more complicated, since you are then concerned with both your distance and your bearing. It is in this situation particularly that you will benefit by a thorough understanding of the relative motion of ships. While steaming in close formation, you will rarely have time to plot bearings and distances and obtain a solution if you are not in position. You have to visualize the problem, and then change course and speed properly and promptly as soon as you detect a deviation from your correct bearing and distance.

You can quickly determine whether you are ahead or behind bearing by lining up your alidade on the prescribed bearing of the guide and then sighting through it. If your line of sight falls ahead of the guide, you are ahead; if astern, you are behind.

When the line of ships is a line abreast, a speed that is greater or less than the guide's speed will cause you to advance or retard your bearing with negligible change of range. A slight change of course toward or away from the guide will cause you to close or open range with a slight loss of bearing. A small temporary increase of speed, normally only a few turns, can be used, when desirable, to counteract this small bearing change.

As we have seen, when the line of bearing is a column, the opposite of the above is true. A speed differential will cause you to close or open distance. A change of course will cause a change of bearing with a very slight opening of distance. A small temporary increase of speed can be used, when desirable, to counteract this small distance change.

For lines of bearing between these two extremes—line abreast and column—the effects of a course or speed differential are a little more complex. A combination of changing course and speed is usually required in order to maintain station.

Correct *bearing* is generally considered more important than correct *distance* (an error in bearing is more apparent on the flagship). It is generally considered better to be slightly behind bearing than ahead. It is, of course, best to be accurately on station in both bearing and distance.

When simultaneous turns are made in line of bearing, watch the ship toward which the turn is made in order to detect the first sign that she might be turning in the wrong direction.

Open Formation

Handling a ship in the main body of a circular formation is slightly easier than handling a ship in close formation, since normally the ships are not as close. However, since you keep station on a definite bearing from the guide, and at a definite distance, the problems of station-keeping are similar to those in line of bearing. The only additional problems are in determining what your range and bearing from the guide should be when moving to a new station. CIC can be of great assistance to the officer of the deck in these matters.

In order to determine his range and bearing from the guide, the officer of the deck must be familiar with the system of plotting formations, using polar co-ordinates. After plotting the formation, you can easily pick the range and bearing of the guide off the plot. A continuous plot of the formation should be kept so that ordered changes can be quickly translated into terms of new range and bearing from the guide.

Remember that the station numbers given are relative to the formation axis and must be plotted as such. A change in the direction of the formation axis will result in an equal change in the true bearing of your station from the formation center and in your true bearing from the guide.

Remember that the guide is not always at the center. And remember that immediately when any signal is executed, the guide is automatically on station, regardless of where she is. This condition may result in the formation center moving around the guide. If so, it causes your station to move a like amount in the same direction.

For any maneuver, determine from a plot your required range and bearing from the guide. Then obtain your actual range and bearing from the guide. Using these figures, determine the course and speed required for you to arrive at your proper station. If there is no change in your proper range and bearing, your problem is, of course, only one of station-keeping. A change of formation axis or change in the formation itself will be the only maneuvers that will change your range and bearing, or change either singularly, from the guide unless you are ordered to a new station.

Screening

Handling a ship in a screen is quite similar to handling a ship in the main body of a circular formation. Station-keeping problems are the same except that the distances from the guide are greater. The problem of determining range and bearing of your station from the guide is, however, more complex. The officer of the deck of a destroyer-type ship must be familiar with the maneuvering rules governing screening ships, in addition to the rules governing maneuvers of the various types of formations.

A continuous, up-to-the-minute plot of the entire formation should be kept, just as for a circular formation, so that any ordered change can be quickly translated into terms of a new range and bearing from the guide.

In order to keep the plot of the screen, you must know the location of the screen center and the direction of the screen axis. For certain types of screens, the screen center may shift. You must be able to distinguish the signals which will cause such a shift from those that do not. And you must know how to determine the amount and direction of such a shift, and how to allow for it in your maneuver, whether or not a reorientation of the screen is required.

You should keep in mind that, in addition to those shiftings of the screen center which are caused by course changes, there are also shiftings of the screen center caused by the rotation of the formation axis. When the formation guide is not at the center of the formation, a shift in the direction of the formation axis will cause the formation center to move relative to the guide. This repositioning causes the screen center and all screening stations to move a like amount and in the same direction.

The screen axis may also change. As officer of the deck you must know under what conditions it changes without a specific signal to change it, and how to determine its new direction in such cases.

Every effort should be made to start for your new station promptly. A little forehandedness will help toward this end. After each maneuver you should start anticipating the next one. You should check your plot and then determine what will be the minimum change of formation course in each direction that will cause a reorientation in which you will have to change station. And when applicable, you should determine what will be the minimum change of course that will require your initial turn to be in a direction opposite to that of the course change. With these figures firmly in mind, you can quickly translate a signal into action and can start the initial turn while the final solution is still forthcoming.

In working your solutions, be sure that you use the course and speed for the guide that he will actually be following while you are en route to your station. This policy is particularly applicable when you start for station prior to the execution of a signal which changes the guide's course or speed, or both.

There are two final points to be made about screening. The first is that exact station-keeping is not normally necessary because most screening plans require the escorts to patrol on station, changing course and speed in a random manner. At such times you can afford to devote more time to other matters, perhaps delegating, under supervision, the duty of station-keeping to the junior officer of the watch.

The second point is that when reorienting the screen or changing screening station, the officer of the deck must keep an alert watch over the whole formation, using his own eyes to a maximum extent. Others can work out maneuvering board solutions to check your quick calculations; your primary job under many conditions is that of chief safety officer.

Range to the Guide

In steaming in formation, it is always necessary to know the range to the guide. This requirement often puts such a burden on the surface-search radar operator in cic that he will keep his radar on short scale and concentrate on giving range-to-the-guide information to the officer of the deck. This situation can be very dangerous at night or in low visibility when the surface-search radar must be used for detecting and tracking ships that may pose a threat of collision.

To avoid diverting CIC from its major job of search and tracking, do not ask for ranges constantly. During daylight, use a stadimeter when possible; it can also be used at night under good visibility conditions with running lights as targets. Use the bridge radar to check on CIC and to free them of supplying continuous ranges.

MAN OVERBOARD

The first necessity in a case of a man overboard is prompt action. An alert officer of the deck will see that the men in his watch know their duties for such an emergency and will be prepared to take rapid action depending on weather and operating conditions, to carry out the following:

1. Maneuver the ship according to prescribed doctrine.
2. Have the word passed twice: "Man overboard, port (starboard) side. Section 1 (2)."
3. Sound six or more short blasts on the ship's whistle, and make appropriate visual signals as specified in Volume I of *ATP 1:* "By day hoist OSCAR and at night (in peacetime) display two pulsating red lights or fire one white rocket (Very light)."
4. Notify ships in company and the OTC.
5. Inform the commanding officer, executive officer, and flag duty officer, if appropriate.
6. Take steps to keep the man in sight if practicable.
7. Establish communications with the deck recovery detail.
8. Keep the deck recovery detail informed of the recovery side of the ship.
9. Have life raft or other life-saving equipment released as instructed by the commanding officer. Use searchlights if the situation dictates.

A helicopter offers the quickest rescue, with the advantage that it can pick up a man who is unable to help himself. If a helicopter is not available, a small boat may be used.

There are a number of man overboard recovery methods. (See diagrams and descriptions following.) The three most used are: one turn or Anderson, fastest but requires most skillful shiphandling; Williamson turn for night or low visibility; race track for fastest recovery when proceeding at high speed in clear weather; and Y-backing, for ships with large turning circles and great backing power, proceeding at slow speeds. Very large ships often use a small boat to recover a man from the water. Smaller vessels will use the boat recovery method as well when the sea is very rough and there is little chance of getting the man close alongside the ship. Swimmers with life jackets and tending lines should be ready to go into the water.

Regardless of which recovery method is used, the same basic principles and required action apply. Swing the stern away from the man with full rudder. If it is possible to stop the shaft on the side toward the man before he reaches the screws, this should be done. If it is not, which is likely, continue the recovery without attempting to stop the screw. CIC must be informed immediately, in order to provide continual ranges and bearings to the man.

Man overboard maneuvering instructions for naval vessels involved in tactical evolutions can be found in *ATP 1(A)*, Volume I, Chapter 5. Of specific importance are the instructions for column formation. In this situation, the ship that loses the man takes action to avoid him, and others do as well, with odd-numbered ships in the column clearing to starboard, and even-numbered ships clearing to port. The ship in the best position to recover the man does so, keeping the other vessels informed of her actions.

METHODS OF MAN OVERBOARD RECOVERY

METHOD AND PRIMARY USE	DIAGRAM (SHIP ON COURSE 090; NUMBERS REFER TO THE EXPLANATION)	EXPLANATION	ANALYSIS	
			ADVANTAGES	DISADVANTAGES
WILLIAMSON TURN USED IN REDUCED VISIBILITY BECAUSE IT MAKES GOOD THE ORIGINAL TRACK. USED WHEN IT IS BELIEVED THAT A MAN FELL OVERBOARD SOME TIME PREVIOUSLY AND HE IS NOT IN SIGHT.		1. PUT THE RUDDER OVER FULL IN THE DIRECTION CORRESPONDING TO THE SIDE OVER WHICH THE MAN FELL. STOP THE INBOARD ENGINE. 2. WHEN CLEAR OF THE MAN, GO AHEAD FULL ON ALL ENGINES, CONTINUE USING FULL RUDDER. 3. WHEN HEADING IS 60° BEYOND THE ORIGINAL COURSE, SHIFT THE RUDDER WITHOUT HAVING STEADIED ON A COURSE. 60° IS PROPER FOR MANY SHIPS, HOWEVER, THE EXACT AMOUNT MUST BE DETERMINED THROUGH TRIAL AND ERROR (50° FOR YP's). 4. COME TO THE RECIPROCAL OF THE ORIGINAL COURSE, USING FULL RUDDER. 5. USE THE ENGINES AND RUDDER TO ATTAIN THE PROPER FINAL POSITION (SHIP UPWIND OF THE MAN AND DEAD IN THE WATER WITH THE MAN ALONGSIDE, WELL FORWARD OF THE PROPELLERS).	SIMPLICITY MAKES GOOD THE ORIGINAL TRACK	SLOW TAKES THE SHIP A RELATIVELY GREAT DISTANCE FROM THE MAN, WHEN SIGHT MAY BE LOST.
ONE TURN USED BY DESTROYERS, SHIPS WHICH HAVE CONSIDERABLE POWER AVAILABLE AND RELATIVELY TIGHT TURNING CHARACTERISTICS.		1. PUT THE RUDDER OVER FULL IN THE DIRECTION CORRESPONDING TO THE SIDE OVER WHICH THE MAN FELL. STOP THE INBOARD ENGINE. 2. WHEN CLEAR OF THE MAN, GO AHEAD FULL ON THE OUTBOARD ENGINE ONLY. CONTINUE USING FULL RUDDER. 3. WHEN ABOUT TWO-THIRDS OF THE WAY AROUND, BACK THE INBOARD ENGINE 2/3 OR FULL. ORDER ALL ENGINES STOPPED WHEN THE MAN IS WITHIN ABOUT 15 DEGREES OF THE BOW, THEN EASE THE RUDDER AND BACK THE ENGINES AS REQUIRED TO ATTAIN THE PROPER FINAL POSITION (AS FOR THE OTHER METHODS). 4. MANY VARIATIONS OF THIS METHOD ARE USED, DIFFERING PRIMARILY IN RESPECT TO THE USE OF ONE OR BOTH ENGINES, AND THE TIME WHEN THEY ARE STOPPED AND BACKED TO RETURN TO THE MAN AND TIGHTEN THE TURN. THE VARIATION USED SHOULD REFLECT INDIVIDUAL SHIP'S CHARACTERISTICS, SEA CONDITIONS, PERSONAL PREFERENCES, ETC.	FASTEST RECOVERY METHOD.	REQUIRES A RELATIVELY HIGH DEGREE OF PROFICIENCY IN SHIPHANDLING BECAUSE OF THE LACK OF A STRAIGHT-A-WAY APPROACH TO THE MAN. OFTEN IMPOSSIBLE FOR A SINGLE PROPELLER SHIP.

METHODS OF MAN OVERBOARD RECOVERY

METHOD AND PRIMARY USE	DIAGRAM (SHIP ON COURSE 090; NUMBERS REFER TO THE EXPLANATION)	EXPLANATION	ANALYSIS	
			ADVANTAGES	DISADVANTAGES
RACETRACK TURN (TWO 180° TURNS) USED IN GOOD VISIBILITY WHEN A STRAIGHT FINAL APPROACH LEG IS DESIRED.		1. A VARIATION OF THE ONE TURN METHOD WHICH PROVIDES A DESIRABLE STRAIGHT FINAL APPROACH TO THE MAN. 2. PUT THE RUDDER OVER FULL IN THE DIRECTION CORRESPONDING TO THE SIDE OVER WHICH THE MAN FELL. STOP THE INBOARD ENGINE. 3. WHEN CLEAR OF THE MAN, GO AHEAD FULL ON ALL ENGINES, CONTINUE USING FULL RUDDER TO TURN TO THE RECIPROCAL OF THE ORIGINAL COURSE. 4. STEADY FOR A DISTANCE WHICH WILL GIVE THE DESIRED RUN FOR A FINAL STRAIGHT APPROACH. 5. USE FULL RUDDER TO TURN TO THE MAN. 6. USE THE ENGINES AND RUDDER TO ATTAIN THE PROPER FINAL POSITION (SHIP UPWIND OF THE MAN AND DEAD IN THE WATER WITH THE MAN ALONGSIDE WELL FORWARD OF THE PROPELLERS).	STRAIGHT FINAL APPROACH LEG FACILITATES A MORE CALCULABLE APPROACH. SHIP WILL RETURN TO THE MAN IF HE IS LOST FROM SIGHT. REASONABLY FAST. EFFECTIVE WHEN WIND WAS FROM ABEAM ON ORIGINAL COURSE.	SLOWER THAN ONE TURN METHOD.
DELAYED TURN USED WHEN WORD IS RECEIVED THAT A MAN FELL OVERBOARD, MAN IN SIGHT AND CLEAR ASTERN OF THE SHIP.		1. A VARIATION OF THE ONE TURN METHOD. 2. PUT THE RUDDER OVER FULL IN THE DIRECTION CORRESPONDING TO THE SIDE OVER WHICH THE MAN FELL. GO AHEAD FULL ON ALL ENGINES. 3. HEAD TOWARDS THE MAN. 4. USE THE ENGINES AND RUDDER TO ATTAIN THE PROPER FINAL POSITION (SHIP UPWIND OF THE MAN AND DEAD IN THE WATER WITH THE MAN ALONGSIDE, WELL FORWARD OF THE PROPELLERS).	FASTEST METHOD WHEN MAN IS IN SIGHT AND ALREADY CLEAR ASTERN OF THE SHIP. PROVIDES A STRAIGHT RUN IN THE CRITICAL FINAL PHASE. EFFECTIVE WHEN WIND IS FROM AHEAD OR ASTERN OF SHIP ON ORIGINAL COURSE.	DOES NOT ENSURE RETURN TO THE MAN. REQUIRES GOOD VISIBILITY. TAKES THE SHIP FARTHER FROM THE MAN THAN OTHER METHODS.

METHODS OF MAN OVERBOARD RECOVERY

METHOD AND PRIMARY USE	DIAGRAM (SHIP ON COURSE 090; NUMBERS REFER TO THE EXPLANATION)	EXPLANATION	ANALYSIS	
			ADVANTAGES	DISADVANTAGES
Y BACKING USED BY SUBMARINES BECAUSE THE SHIP (LOW HEIGHT OF EYE) REMAINS COMPARATIVELY CLOSE TO THE MAN.		1. PUT THE RUDDER OVER FULL IN THE DIRECTION CORRE-SPONDING TO THE SIDE OVER WHICH THE MAN FELL. STOP THE INBOARD ENGINE. 2. WHEN CLEAR OF THE MAN, BACK THE ENGINES WITH FULL POWER, USING OPPOSITE RUDDER. 3. GO AHEAD, USE THE ENGINES AND RUDDER TO ATTAIN THE PROPER FINAL POSITION (SHIP UPWIND OF THE MAN AND DEAD IN THE WATER WITH THE MAN ALONGSIDE, WELL FORWARD OF THE PROPELLERS).	THE SHIP REMAINS COMPARA-TIVELY CLOSE TO THE MAN.	MOST SHIPS BACK INTO THE WIND/SEA, RESULTING IN POOR CONTROL WHILE BACKING.
BOAT RECOVERY USED BY SHIPS LACKING SUF-FICIENT MANEUVERABILITY TO MAKE A GOOD APPROACH FOR A SHIP RECOVERY. USED WHEN THE SHIP IS DEAD IN THE WATER WITH THE MAN CLOSE ABOARD BUT NOT ALONGSIDE. CAN BE USED IN CONJUNC-TION WITH ANY OF THE METHODS SHOWN ABOVE.		BASIC BOAT RECOVERY METHOD: 1. PUT THE RUDDER OVER FULL IN THE DIRECTION CORRE-SPONDING TO THE SIDE OVER WHICH THE MAN FELL. STOP THE INBOARD ENGINE. 2. WHEN THE MAN IS CLEAR, BACK ALL ENGINES FULL TO NEARLY STOP THE SHIP. USE RUDDER TO THE SIDE OF THE READY LIFEBOAT TO PROVIDE A SLICK IN WHICH THE BOAT CAN BE LOWERED. STOP THE ENGINES WHILE THE SHIP STILL HAS VERY SLIGHT HEADWAY TO PERMIT BETTER CONTROL OF THE BOAT AND TO KEEP IT OUT OF THE PROPELLER WASH.	SIMPLE FOR ANY GIVEN TYPE OF SHIP, THE SHIP WILL REMAIN CLOSER TO THE MAN THAN BY ANY OTHER METHOD. DOES NOT REQUIRE THAT A PARTICULAR FINAL POSITION BE ATTAINED.	THE MAN MUST BE IN SIGHT. SEA AND WEATHER CONDI-TIONS MUST BE SATISFAC-TORY FOR SMALL BOAT OPERATIONS.

The man should be recovered in the shortest possible time. For small vessels in good weather this means the race track method. At night or in low visibility, the Williamson turn, though not the fastest recovery method, must be used to bring the ship back along her track. For any method, the desired final position is beam to the wind slightly to windward of the man, with all way off. When in this position a lee is provided for the man, and since the ship will make more leeway than will the man, she will drift toward, rather than away from him.

It is important to keep the man *forward* of the main condenser injection intakes, particularly if he may still have a parachute attached, as a parachute can clog the intakes. The intakes are ordinarily aft of the midships section, on either side; the best final position should be with the man just off the leeward bow.

REPLENISHMENT AT SEA (UNREP)

The ability of the fleet to sustain itself at sea with a high degree of mobility and flexibility has been made possible by development of the procedure for transferring stores, fuel, ammunition and personnel between ships while underway. Replenishment at sea, or *underway replenishment* (UNREP), requires top performance in ship handling, communications, and seamanship.

Standard doctrine for UNREP is provided by *Replenishment at Sea, Naval Warfare Publication NWP 38.* Fueling and transfer of light cargo or personnel often occur simultaneously, while the handling of heavy stores and ammunition are usually separate operations. Although the rigging and stations differ for fueling, transferring heavy stores and ammunition, and for light cargo and passenger transfer, the key personnel involved and communications employed are practically the same.

The delivery ship maintains course and speed while

the receiving ship makes the approach, takes station alongside, and clears the delivery ship on completion of replenishment. The delivery ship is thus the control ship. Weather conditions permitting, the normal speed of the control ship is between 10 and 15 knots. Speeds less than 8 knots are inadvisable because of reduced rudder effect. When speeds exceed 15 knots, venturi effect (the pressure differential created around the hull of a moving ship resulting in a decreased pressure or suction amidships) dictate the need for a greater lateral separation. Read Chapter 10 of *Naval Shiphandling* for a detailed description of how to bring a ship alongside a delivery ship.

When the delivery ship is steady on course and speed, she indicates preparations in progress to receive a ship alongside by flying ROMEO at the dip on her rigged side. The receiving ship replies that she is ready to come alongside by flying ROMEO at the dip on the side rigged. When the delivery ship is ready for the approach, she hoists ROMEO close up. The receiving ship hoists ROMEO close up and increases speed 3 to 10 knots, depending on ship type, over signaled UNREP speed. She slows down so as to be moving at replenishment speed when in position. When the ships are in proper relative position, transfer rigs are passed and hooked up; as the first line is secured, both ships haul down ROMEO. Both ships fly BRAVO if transferring fuel or ammunition.

Fifteen minutes before the receiving ship expects to complete replenishment, the officer of the deck orders PREP hoisted at the dip to so notify the next ship scheduled to replenish. On completion of the UNREP, all nets, slings, lines, and hoses are returned to the delivery ship. Messengers are passed back last.

Just prior to disengaging, the receiving ship hoists PREP close up. When the last line is clear, she hauls it down. When clearing the side, the conning officer increases speed moderately from 3 to 10 knots depending on ship type, and clears ahead, changing course outboard in small increments. Propeller wash caused by radical changes in speed and course can adversely affect steering of the delivery ship and a dangerous situation may develop if a ship is on her other side.

PILOTS

A pilot is merely an advisor to the commanding officer. His presence on board shall not relieve the commanding officer or any of his subordinates from their responsibility for the proper performance of the duties with which they may be charged concerning the navigation and handling of the ship.—*Navy Regulations*, Article 0752.

There are certain exceptions to the principle stated above, notably in the use of pilots in the Panama Canal and when entering a dry dock. By and large, a pilot must be considered as an advisor, even though he takes the conn upon invitation of the commanding officer. Pilots are often unfamiliar with the type of ship they are handling, and may use nonstandard commands to the annunciator or to the helsman. The OOD should assist the pilot and co-operate with him fully but must not relax his vigilance for the safety of the ship. In addition, he can profitably observe the pilot and thus learn much about ship handling and about local conditions of tide and current. The OOD assisting a pilot should ensure that actions of tugs conform to the pilot's orders. See Chapter IX for standard whistle and hand signals to be used with tugs.

Among preparations that can be made for a pilot's arrival are: an interpreter (if needed), tug radio frequencies available on bridge (if needed), a ladder rigged over the side, and the junior officer of the deck on hand to meet him as he comes aboard.

Chapter *VII* RULES OF THE NAUTICAL ROAD

He [the officer of the deck] shall thoroughly familiarize himself with the laws to prevent collision and shall strictly comply with them.—*Navy Regulations,* Article 1010.

This chapter is a guide and ready reference for the officer of the deck in regard to the rules to prevent collisions—rules which are required to be followed while navigating or piloting upon the high seas and the adjacent inland waters of the United States. It will be noted that vessels and seaplanes navigating the high seas are required to follow the International Rules, while vessels navigating inshore of the boundary lines dividing the high seas from inland waters are required to follow the Inland Rules and the Pilot Rules established pursuant thereto. These statutory and regulatory Rules are to be found in *CG 169,* entitled *Rules of the Road, International—Inland,* and in *Farwell's Rules of the Nautical Road.* The latter publication is of special value to the officer of the deck in that it contains a thorough, up-to-date treatment of the practical and legal aspects of the subject, as well as the material published by the Commandant, U.S. Coast Guard, in *CG 169.*

The officer of the deck must be familiar with all aspects of the *International* and *Inland* rules. Other rules, not discussed here, are *Rules of the Road, Great Lakes* (**CG 172**), and *Rules of the Road, Western Rivers* (**CG 184**), which should be studied if a ship is to operate in those waters. The following discussion is based on the *International Rules of the Road* which went into effect 1 September 1965, and the *Inland Rules,* effective 1 January 1969.

DEFINITIONS

Vessel: This term includes every description of watercraft, other than a seaplane on the water, used or capable of being used as a means of transportation on water.

Seaplane: An aircraft designed to maneuver on the water.

Power-driven Vessel: Defined in the International Rules as any vessel propelled by machinery—including one partially propelled by sail.

Steam Vessel: Defined in the Inland Rules as any vessel propelled by machinery, including one partially propelled by sail; i.e., a power-driven vessel as defined by the International Rules.

Privileged Vessel: A vessel which is required to *hold course and speed.*

Burdened Vessel: A vessel which is required to *keep clear* of a privileged vessel.

Underway: Said of a vessel or seaplane on the water which is not at anchor, made fast to the shore, or aground.

Cross Signals: An illegal response of one blast on the whistle or siren to a signal of two blasts, or vice versa, by a steam vessel in inland waters.

Moderate Speed: Ordinarily, bare steerageway or such speed as will enable a vessel proceeding in fog or other similarly restricted visibility to stop in one half the distance of visibility; in extremely close visibility, the requirement to moor, come to anchor, or not to get underway.

In Extremis: A crossing, meeting, or overtaking situation which has developed to such a dangerous degree that both vessels must take prompt and effective steps to avoid collision.

IMPORTANT ASPECTS OF THE RULES

In obeying and construing the rules of the road, any action taken should be positive, in ample time, and with due regard to the observance of good seamanship.

Boundary Lines

Specific boundary lines of inland waters have been established in most of the areas subject to the Inland Rules. These may be obtained by reference to *CG 169* or to *Farwell's Rules of the Nautical Road*. In areas where no specific boundary lines have been established, boundary lines of inland waters are determined by:

1. The shore line.

2. At buoyed entrances, a line approximately parallel with the general trend of the shore, drawn through the outermost buoy or other aid to navigation.

As officer of the deck, it is important that you know where the boundary lines dividing the high seas from inland waters are. The Inland Rules and the Pilot Rules for Inland Waters apply *inshore* of these lines. On the other hand, the International Rules apply *outside* these lines. If you do not know where they are, the actions, lights, and sound signals of vessels approaching your vessel from the other side of a boundary line may mislead you. Always enter in the log the exact time at which the vessel enters *international* or *inland* waters.

Passing Signals

There is a fundamental difference in the meaning and the method of prescribing the conventional one and two short-blast passing signals under International and Inland Rules. Under the International Rules, the signals are purely rudder signals, to be given when, and only when, a change in course is executed. Accordingly, a general rule is stated in these Rules which provides for a signal in every situation when the course is changed. Under the Inland and Pilot Rules, on the other hand, the one and two short-blast signals are not for the purpose of announcing a change in course, but to indicate the side on which an approaching vessel will pass. In these Rules, it is, therefore, necessary to specify the use of a signal in a particular situation. The appropriate signal is not covered by a general rule, but is prescribed in the rule referring to a specific situation, and is required to be given and answered, whether a change of course is involved or not.

Navigational Lights (see chart, page 129)

The importance of proper running and riding lights can hardly be over-emphasized. It is the function of these lights to give a vessel such timely and effective notice of the proximity of another that all doubt about her character and intentions will be settled before there is any serious risk of collision. More than half the Rules relate to them, and in collision cases, the courts construe strongly against vessels which disregard their requirements. You should make a special study of the differences in lights required under the International Rules, the Inland Rules, and the Pilot Rules for Inland Waters. Whether at sea or in the inland waters of the United States, the Rules concerning lights in that area must be obeyed literally in all weathers from sunset to sunrise (*not from darkness to daylight*). Moreover, during such times, no other lights which may be mistaken for the prescribed lights or which impair their visibility or distinctive character, or interfere with the keeping of a proper lookout, may be exhibited. It is true that naval and Coast Guard vessels of *special construction* are allowed to vary the number, position, range or arc of visibility of the lights

LIGHTS FOR POWER VESSELS UNDER WAY

LIGHTS			SHAPES	
LIGHT	INTERNATIONAL RULES	U.S. INLAND WATERS	INT'NAT'L. RULES	U.S. INL. WATERS
MASTHEAD	1 W/20 ——————————→		POWER VESSEL PROCEEDING UNDER SAIL ▼ BLACK CONE	NONE
RANGE	1 W/20	1 W/32		
SIDE	1 R,G/10 ——————————→			
STERN	1 W/12 ——————→(WHEN REQUIRED)			

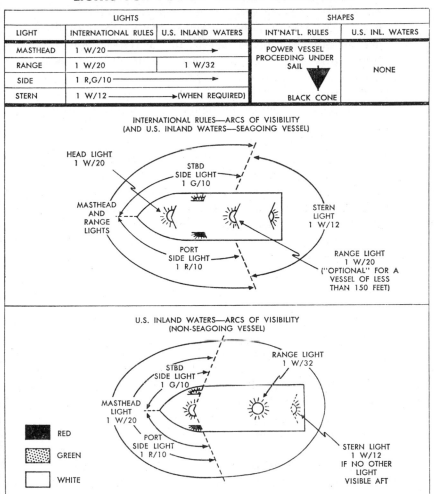

INTERNATIONAL RULES—ARCS OF VISIBILITY
(AND U.S. INLAND WATERS—SEAGOING VESSEL)

HEAD LIGHT
1 W/20

STBD
SIDE LIGHT
1 G/10

MASTHEAD
AND
RANGE
LIGHTS

STERN
LIGHT
1 W/12

PORT
SIDE LIGHT
1 R/10

RANGE LIGHT
1 W/20
("OPTIONAL" FOR A
VESSEL OF LESS
THAN 150 FEET)

U.S. INLAND WATERS—ARCS OF VISIBILITY
(NON-SEAGOING VESSEL)

RANGE LIGHT
1 W/32

STBD
SIDE LIGHT
1 G/10

MASTHEAD
LIGHT
1 W/20

PORT
SIDE LIGHT
1 R/10

RED

GREEN

WHITE

STERN LIGHT
1 W/12
IF NO OTHER
LIGHT
VISIBLE AFT

required by the Rules, *provided they maintain the closest possible compliance with the pertinent Rules,* but this is not a matter within the discretion of the officer of the deck or other shipboard officers. In this respect, your responsibility is limited to knowing which vessels have been found to be of special construction by the proper authorities, and what lights are carried by them. (Two recent opinions concerning lights expressed by the Admiralty Division of the Judge Advocate General will be of interest to all officers of the deck:

1. Anchor lights are not required to be shown by a vessel in drydock unless the vessel is in an open-end dock with part of the vessel projecting out over the sill.

2. A vessel dragging an anchor on the ground at short stay to assist in shiphandling should continue to display underway lights, not anchor lights.)

The required characteristics of navigational lights are stated in detail in the rules themselves, to which reference should be made if exact information is desired. A practical familiarity with lights necessitates knowledge of the following characteristics:

1. Name

2. Occasions when carried

3. Number, color, and arc of visibility. These can be expressed as "2 W/20," meaning two white lights, showing an unbroken light over an arc of the horizon of 20 points.

4. General location on the ship and location in respect to other lights.

5. Distance of visibility.

The navigational lights, *running* (under way) and *riding* (not under way), which are prescribed by the rules *must* be exhibited in all weathers from sunset to sunrise. They may also be used during the hours of daylight in restricted visibility and in all other circumstances when it is deemed necessary. During the times when lights are required by the rules, no other lights may be exhibited, "except such lights as cannot be mistaken for the prescribed lights or impair their visibility or distinctive character, or interfere with the keeping of a proper lookout." All of the various lights which are visible on a ship, regardless of their purpose, must meet these criteria. Within the limits of the foregoing, naval vessels use the signal searchlight, carrier deck lights, and speed lights (steady or flashing, white for ahead speeds, red for stopped and backing speeds). All vessels, regardless of size, must have some kind of navigational lights. (See examples of navigational lights in *"Light Displays"* pages 151-166.)

Speed

The Rules require every vessel *in* or *near* fog, mist, falling snow, heavy rainstorms, or any other condition similarly restricting visibility to:

1. *Go at a moderate speed,* having careful regard to the existing circumstances and conditions.

2. *Stop her engines,* and *then navigate with caution* until danger of collision is over, upon hearing, apparently forward of her beam, the fog signal of a vessel the position of which is not ascertained.

Both these requirements are strictly enforced by the courts, and departure from them is permitted only to avoid immediate danger. Therefore, you must always proceed at moderate speed in fog; stop the engines upon hearing a fog signal forward or apparently forward of the beam; and from then on maintain bare steerageway as long as danger of collision exists. Courts have ruled that "stop engines" as used here means "stop ship." There is no general rule in either the International or Inland Rules which limits the speed of vessels in good visibility. However, every vessel is liable for damage caused by her swells, whether that damage is to property along the shore or to passing vessels and their tows. Consequently, there will be times when speed will have to be reduced in good visibility, as well as in fog.

Radar

Court decisions have held vessels equipped with radar at fault in collisions in reduced visibility, not only for failure to use radar, but also for failure to employ it intelligently. The possession of radar does not give any vessel the right to use greater than moderate speed in restricted visibility *or* excuse her failure to have adequate and proper lookouts, to stop her engines when a fog signal is heard apparently forward of the beam, or to take all the precautions required by the practice of good seamanship. Radar is merely an additional and useful aid to navigation. Properly used, radar enables a ship to proceed on a mission which might be otherwise impossible to carry out, and makes it possible to conn a ship in reduced conditions of visibility with greater confidence than otherwise could be expected.

STEERING AND SAILING RULES

When two vessels approach in such a manner as to involve risk of collision, at least one vessel is required to keep out of the way of the other. In a general sense this "burden" is placed on the more maneuverable of the two vessels, according to the following classification, in which the relative right of way of vessels is established in order of decreasing burden:

> Power vessel under way (not engaged in fishing)
> Sailing vessel under way (not engaged in fishing)
> Vessel engaged in fishing under way
> Vessel not under command engaged in special operations (International Rules only)
> Vessel not under way

The actions of two vessels of the same classification is governed by whether they are in a meeting, overtaking, or crossing situation. With vessels of different classifications, the one in the higher classification is required to keep clear of the other.

Seaplanes on the water are, in turn, required to conform to the Rules governing the actions of power-driven vessels in these three situations, while sailing vessels are given the right of way over power-driven vessels, except when overtaking them.

This Rule shall not give to a sailing vessel the right to hamper, in a narrow channel, the safe passage of a power-driven vessel which can navigate only inside such channel.

It is nesessary that you have a clear mental picture of the meeting, crossing, and overtaking situations, and understand the conditions of privilege and burden in each, in order to be a competent officer of the deck. Study the following discussion and accompanying diagrams thoroughly.

The following provisions of the Rules must be understood:

Meeting Situation (see diagram, page 134)

Both vessels are burdened.

Two power-driven vessels are held to be meeting if their courses are substantially opposite or within a point or two of being opposite, or if, as in the case of a winding river, they will become opposite at the point where they meet, even though they may first sight each other at right angles. In open water, this will be when you can see the masts of the vessel ahead in a line, or nearly in a line, with the masts on your vessel by day, and both sidelights of the vessel ahead by night. Neither vessel is privileged in this situation. On the contrary, the two meeting vessels are required to pass port to port, unless they are already

STEERING AND SAILING RULES

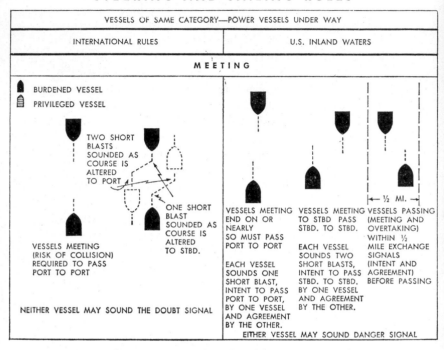

so far to the starboard of each other that they will clear on that side at a safe distance without changing course. In order that they may pass safely port to port, a sufficient change of course to the right is required of both vessels, not in the jaws of collision, but at such a safe distance apart and of a sufficient number of degrees that they will avoid even getting in dangerous proximity to each other.

Overtaking Situation (see diagram, page 135)

The overtaking vessel is burdened and the overtaken vessel is privileged; no subsequent alteration of bearing

STEERING AND SAILING RULES

VESSELS OF SAME CATEGORY—POWER VESSELS UNDER WAY	
INTERNATIONAL RULES	U.S. INLAND WATERS

OVERTAKING

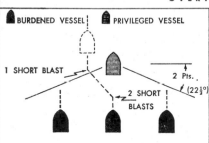

BURDENED VESSEL   PRIVILEGED VESSEL

1 SHORT BLAST

2 Pts. (22½°)

2 SHORT BLASTS

OVERTAKING VESSEL SOUNDS STEERING SIGNALS ONLY AS IT CHANGES COURSE.

OVERTAKEN VESSEL (PRIVILEGED) MAY SOUND THE DOUBT SIGNAL.

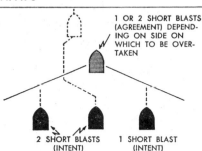

1 OR 2 SHORT BLASTS (AGREEMENT) DEPENDING ON SIDE ON WHICH TO BE OVERTAKEN

2 SHORT BLASTS (INTENT)   1 SHORT BLAST (INTENT)

SIGNALS OF INTENT AND AGREEMENT MUST BE EXCHANGED BEFORE THE OVERTAKING VESSEL PASSES THE OTHER. SIGNALS ARE 1 OR 2 SHORT BLASTS ACCORDING TO THE SIDE ON WHICH THE OVERTAKEN VESSEL IS TO BE PASSED.

EITHER VESSEL MAY SOUND DANGER SIGNAL.

CROSSING

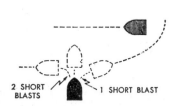

2 SHORT BLASTS   1 SHORT BLAST

BURDENED VESSEL SHOULD NOT CROSS BOW OF PRIVILEGED VESSEL IF CIRCUMSTANCES PERMIT. BURDENED VESSEL MAY TURN IN ANY DIRECTION AND/OR SLOW TO AVOID THE PRIVILEGED VESSEL. STEERING SIGNALS SOUNDED EVERY TIME COURSE IS CHANGED.

PRIVILEGED VESSEL MAY SOUND DOUBT SIGNAL.

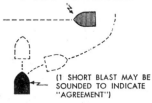

(1 SHORT BLAST FOR INTENT)

(1 SHORT BLAST MAY BE SOUNDED TO INDICATE "AGREEMENT")

BURDENED VESSEL SHOULD NOT CROSS BOW OF THE PRIVILEGED VESSEL. BURDENED VESSEL MAY TURN <u>RIGHT</u> AND/OR SLOW TO AVOID THE PRIVILEGED VESSEL.

EITHER VESSEL MAY SOUND DANGER SIGNAL.

between the two can make the overtaking vessel a crossing vessel within the meaning of the rule, or relieve the overtaking vessel of her duty to keep clear of the overtaken vessel until she is finally pas tand clear.

An overtaking vessel is one going in the same direction, or within six points of the same direction, as a slower vessel ahead; that is, an overtaking vessel is one which is approaching a vessel ahead from two points or more abaft her beam. In this situation the leading vessel is recognized as having been there first, and the overtaking vessel is required to take positive action to keep clear of her as long as risk of collision remains. Thus, the situation is clearly one of privilege and burden; and the overtaken vessel, being privileged, must keep her course and speed, while the overtaking vessel, being burdened, must take all the positive action necessary to keep clear of the overtaken vessel.

Crossing Situation (see diagram, page 135)

The power vessel having the other to starboard is burdened and the vessel to starboard is privileged. The privileged vessel must maintain course and speed until the situation is in extremis.

Two power-driven vessels are held to be crossing when one approaches the other on either side in the arc between meeting and overtaking; that is, from a point or two on the bow to two points abaft the beam. Here, too, the situation is one of privilege and burden. The privileged crossing vessel—that is, the one having the other on her port hand—is required to keep course and speed, unless definite remedial action should become necessary; while the burdened vessel is required to keep clear, to avoid crossing ahead, and, if necessary, to slacken speed, stop, or reverse. It is only when the two crossing vessels have arrived in dangerous proximity that the privileged vessel in the crossing situation is allowed to take positive action to avert collision—and then, she *must* do so.

Thereupon, always remember that you must take bearings of vessels approaching or appearing to approach your vessel on either side in the arc from right ahead to two points abaft the beam. If the bearing draws forward appreciably, the other vessel will pass ahead. If it draws aft appreciably, the other vessel will pass astern. On the other hand, if the bearing remains the same, or nearly so, or changes very slowly, there is a definite risk of collision, and proper and effective action to prevent collision must be taken at once. Remember that, except for vessels on opening or divergent courses, a steady bearing means that collision is imminent, unless corrective action is taken. The taking of prompt and effective action will normally avoid situations where your vessel is privileged and therefore bound to hold course and speed, while you have to "sweat out" the possibility of the burdened vessel taking action to keep clear at the last minute. This is especially true in instances where merchant vessels attempt to seize the right of way or maneuver to gain the right of way. In such instances their failure to observe the Rules does not relieve them of the responsibility they otherwise would have; but you, on the other hand, cannot maintain your course and speed into collision, either. In cases of doubt, as well as when routine meeting, crossing, and overtaking situations develop, the commanding officer should be notified about what the situation is and what action has been or is being taken.

Inland Rules Traffic Situations

Ships leaving or entering U.S. ports will be operating under Inland Rules. The accompanying diagrams show

Here the two colored lights visible to each will indicate their direction approach "head and head" toward each other. In this situation it is a standing rule that both shall direct their courses to starboard and pass on the port side of each other, each having previously given one blast of the whistle.

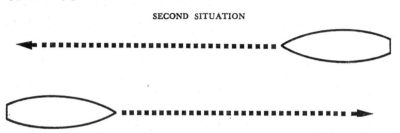

In this situation the red light only will be visible to each, the screens preventing the green light being seen. Both vessels are evidently passing to port of each other, which is rulable in this situation, each pilot having previously signified his intention by one blast of the whistle.

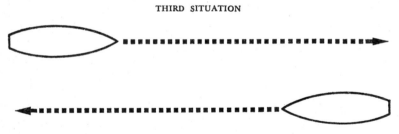

In this situation the green light only will be visible to each, the screens preventing the red light from being seen. They are therefore passing to starboard of each other, which is rulable in this situation, each pilot having previously signified his intention by two blasts of the whistle.

In this situation one steam vessel is overtaking another steam vessel from some point within the angle of two points abaft the beam of the overtaken steam-vessel. The overtaking steam vessel may pass on the starboard or port side of the steam vessel ahead after the necessary signals for passing have been given with assent of the overtaken steam vessel,

FIFTH SITUATION

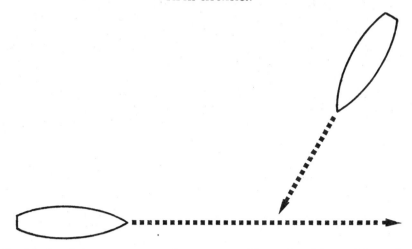

In this situation two steam vessels are approaching each other at right angles or obliquely in such manner as to involve risk of collision, other than where one steam vessel is overtaking another. The steam vessel which has the other on her own port side shall hold course and speed, and the other shall keep clear by crossing astern of the steam vessel that is holding course and speed, or, if necessary to do so, shall slacken her speed, stop, or reverse.

the five basic traffic situations, as described in Pilot Rules for Inland Waters.

Steering Signals (see chart, page 140)

Steering signals are essentially a system of "short blasts" (of one second duration) on a sound-making device used by *power* vessels which are approaching or are being approached by other vessels, used in a fashion prescribed by the steering and sailing rules.

The rules are silent as to the distance at which vessels are to sound steering signals, but require that they be sounded in the prescribed fashion when the vessels are in sight. In waters governed by the International Rules, one or two (as appropriate) short-blast signals should be sounded whenever course is changed while in sight of

STEERING SIGNAL SUMMARY

SHORT BLAST SIGNALS			
INTERNATIONAL RULES (RUDDER SIGNALS)		U.S. INLAND WATERS (SIGNALS OF INTENT-AGREEMENT)	
		MEETING	
1 SHORT	I AM ALTERING MY COURSE TO STARBOARD	1 SHORT	I INTEND/AGREE—PORT TO PORT PASSING
2 SHORTS	I AM ALTERING MY COURSE TO PORT	2 SHORTS	I INTEND/AGREE—STARBOARD TO STARBOARD PASSING
3 SHORTS	MY ENGINES ARE BACKING OR I HAVE STERNWAY ON	**OVERTAKING**	
5 OR MORE SHORTS	I DOUBT THAT THE BURDENED VESSEL IS TAKING SUFFICIENT ACTION TO AVERT COLLISION	1 SHORT	I INTEND/AGREE—BURDENED VESSEL OVERTAKE ON THE STARBOARD SIDE OF THE PRIVILEGED VESSEL
	"INTERNATIONAL SIGNAL OF DOUBT" SOUNDED BY PRIVILEGED VESSEL ONLY	2 SHORTS	I INTEND/AGREE—BURDENED VESSEL OVERTAKE ON THE PORT SIDE OF THE PRIVILEGED VESSEL
		CROSSING	OPTIONAL SIGNALS
		1 SHORT	PRIVILEGED VESSEL: I INTEND TO MAINTAIN COURSE AND SPEED
NOTE			BURDENED VESSEL: I UNDERSTAND YOUR INTENTIONS; I WILL KEEP CLEAR OF YOU
4 SHORTS	SPECIAL FOG SIGNAL, FOR USE BY POWER PILOT VESSELS ENGAGED ON PILOTAGE DUTY	3 SHORTS	MY ENGINES ARE BACKING OR I HAVE STERNWAY ON
		4 OR MORE SHORTS	"U.S. INLAND DANGER SIGNAL": DANGER EXISTS, I DO NOT UNDERSTAND YOUR INTENTIONS, I OBJECT (MAY BE SOUNDED BY EITHER A PRIVILEGED OR BURDENED VESSEL)

another vessel. The sense of the one- and two-short-blast steering signals is the same under the International Rules and those applicable in U. S. inland waters.

Special Circumstances

The International and Inland Rules both recognize that situations may arise where specific Rules will not work. Where departure from these Rules is necessary to avoid immediate danger, such action is accordingly authorized by the General Prudential Rule. (**Rule 27. In obeying and construing these Rules due regard shall be had to all dangers of navigation and collision, and to any special circumstances, including the limitations of the craft involved, which may render a departure from the above Rules necessary in order to avoid immediate danger.**) Such departure, however, is authorized *for this purpose only*—and then only to the extent necessary.

Danger Signals

Under the Inland Rules, the danger signal is a mandatory, all-purpose, all-weather alarm signal of four or more short and rapid blasts, which is required to be given by every steam (i.e., power-driven) vessel in doubt about an approaching vessel's course or intention. Under the International Rules, on the other hand, the danger signal is an optional signal of five or more short and rapid blasts, which may be given only by the privileged vessel in the overtaking and crossing situations at sea, and then only when she is in sight of another vessel and in doubt that the other vessel is taking sufficient action to avert collision. Its sole purpose is to give a power-driven vessel that is required to hold her course and speed the opportunity of calling the attention of the burdened vessel to her obligations under the International Rules to keep clear. This differentiation between the two danger signals is important, and must be understood, for each of these signals must be used in its proper manner and in its proper jurisdiction. There might be occasions when it would be highly desirable to use the Inland danger signal at sea, but you cannot legally do so. Under such circumstances you must use a signal authorized by the International Rules to attract attention, or else turn to the International Code of Signals. There are two especially useful one-letter warning signals in the latter:

1. The letter *U,* which signifies "You are standing into danger."

2. The letter *D,* which signifies "Keep clear of me, I am manuevering with difficulty."

Either one of these signals can be transmitted visually, by means of Morse code using flashing light, or by whistle or siren.

Risk of Collision

"Risk of collision begins the very moment when the two vessels have approached so near each other and upon such courses that by departure from the rules of navigation, whether from want of good seamanship, accident, mistake, misapprehension of signals, or otherwise, a collision might be brought about. . . . Risk of collision may be said to begin the moment the two vessels have approached each other so near that a collision might be brought about by any such departure and continues up to the moment when they have so far progressed that no such result can ensue." The *Milwaukee* (1871) Fed. Case. No. 9,626.

When two vessels approach each other, "risk of collision" begins when the relative bearing does not change appreciably, but continues steady until some action (change of heading or speed) is taken by one or both the vessels to eliminate the danger. Under such circumstances, small changes of heading or speed should be avoided; any change should be considerable.

Bearings of approaching vessels should be observed frequently and the approximate drift—left, right, or steady—determined. Bearings, combined with either opening or closing range, will indicate the existence and approximate degree of risk of collision. Remember that in every case of collision, the risk of collision must have existed for some time prior to the collision. A steady bearing, whether visual or radar, is an indication of existing risk.

At night, the white masthead and range lights are usually the first indication of aan approaching vessel. Observation of such lights will show whether action has to be taken to prevent risk of collision. In a crossing situation, that vessel which is showing another her red side light is privileged and has the right of way; the ship showing another her green side light is burdened and must maneuver to keep clear.

In a meeting head-on situation, each vessel will see both the red and green side lights of the other, and normal procedure is to turn to starboard and pass port to port.

In an overtaking situation where the overtaking vessel is more than two points abaft the beam of the overtaken vessel, the latter may see either the green or red or both side lights of the overtaking vessel and is the privileged vessel. The overtaking vessel will not be able to see either of the side lights of the overtaken vessel, only her stern light, and is the burdened vessel. (Refer to *Farwell's Rules of the Nautical Road* for full discussion of this subject.)

ANNEX TO THE INTERNATIONAL RULES

Recommendations on the Use of Radar Information as an Aid to Avoiding Collisions at Sea

(1) Assumptions made on scanty information may be dangerous and should be avoided.

(2) A vessel navigating with the aid of radar in restricted visibility must, in compliance with Rule 16(a), go at a moderate speed. Information obtained from the use of radar is one of the circumstances to be taken into ac-

count when determining moderate speed. In this regard it must be recognized that small vessels, small icebergs and similar floating objects may not be detected by radar. Radar indications of one or more vessels in the vicinity may mean that "moderate speed" should be slower than a mariner without radar might consider moderate in the circumstances.

(3) When navigating in restricted visibility the radar range and bearing alone do not constitute ascertainment of the position of the other vessel under Rule 16(b) sufficiently to relieve a vessel of the duty to stop her engines and navigate with caution when a fog signal is heard forward of the beam.

(4) When action has been taken under Rule 16(c) to avoid a close quarters situation, it is essential to make sure that such action is having the desired effect. Alterations of course or speed or both are matters as to which the mariner must be guided by the circumstances of the case.

(5) Alteration of course alone may be the most effective action to avoid close quarters provided that:—

(a) There is sufficient sea room.

(b) It is made in good time.

(c) It is substantial. A succession of small alterations of course should be avoided.

(d) It does not result in a close quarters situation with other vessels.

(6) The direction of a alteration of course is a matter in which the mariner must be guided by the circumstances of the case. An alteration to starboard, particularly when vessels are approaching apparently on opposite or nearly opposite courses, is generally preferable to an alteration to port.

(7) An alteration of speed, either alone or in conjunction with an alteration of course, should be substantial.

A number of small alterations of speed should be avoided.

(8) If a close quarters situation is imminent, the most prudent action may be to take all way off the vessel.

Bend Signals

Under the Inland Rules, the bend signal is a single long blast of eight to ten seconds' duration, which is required to be given by:

1. A steam (i.e., power-driven) vessel approaching within half a mile of a blind bend or curve in a channel where a vessel approaching from the opposite direction cannot be seen for a distance of half a mile. In such instances, should the signal be answered, as is required, by a vessel around the bend, signals for meeting and passing should be given and answered *immediately upon sighting each other*.

2. A steam (i.e., power-driven) vessel emerging from a slip, dock, or berth. Here the signal is not answerable, and until such time as the emerging vessel is clear and steadied on a course and speed, neither she nor an approaching vessel has a right of way. Thereupon, however, the Rules for meeting, crossing, and overtaking vessels apply.

Under Internationl Rules, on the other hand, the bend signal is a single purpose signal consisting of a prolonged blast of four to six seconds' duration, which is required to be given by a power-driven (i.e., steam) vessel within one-half mile of a blind bend or curve in a channel where a vessel approaching from the other direction cannot be seen for any distance. It must be answered by a power-driven vessel within hearing distance around the bend, but subsequent signals are given only if either vessel has to change course.

In a narrow channel a power-driven vessel of less than 65

feet in length shall not hamper the safe passage of a vessel which can navigate only inside such channel.

FOG SIGNALS

Fog signals function as a warning of a vessel's presence and give indication of its nature and maneuverability. They must be sounded under any conditions of restricted visibility, whether by day or night. This applies to all vessels within approximately 2 miles of such restricted visibility areas even though the vessel itself may not be experiencing restricted visibility.

The *maximum* interval between fog signals is *one* minute, with the exception of a power vessel under way in the International Rules (two minutes). There are occasions when fog signals should be sounded more frequently. A stop watch is best used by the man assigned the duty of sounding the fog signals. He should be directed to change the interval between signals frequently in case another vessel's signals were synchronized with his own, and therefore not heard. The disadvantages of sounding fog signals too frequently (intervals considerably shorter than the maximum) are that the period of time available for the purpose of listening for the signals of other vessels is thereby reduced, and also that the acuteness of hearing (so essential in restricted visibility) of lookouts and deck watch officers is deadened by their own vessel's signals.

Not Under Command Signals (see chart, page 147)

Not under command refers to a vessel whose ship-control equipment is involuntarily inoperative to the extent that her movements can not be controlled; as commonly expressed, she is "broken down," and must apprise approaching vessels of her plight. Outside inland waters, this condition is indicated by the use of two black

VESSELS NOT UNDER COMMAND/ ENGAGED IN SPECIAL OPERATIONS

INTERNATIONAL RULES			U.S. INLAND WATERS	
LIGHTS		SHAPES	LIGHTS	SHAPES
NOT UNDER COMMAND SIDE WHEN { 1 R, G/10 WAY ON STERN { 1 W/12 SPECIAL 2 R/32			(UNDER WAY LIGHTS)	(NONE)
SPECIAL OPERATIONS UNDER WAY (LESS MINESWEEPING) SIDE WHEN { 1 R, G/10 WAY ON STERN { 1 W/12 SPECIAL 1 R-W-R/32			VARIOUS LIGHTS & SHAPES WHICH ARE CONTAINED IN THE PILOT RULES FOR U.S. INLAND WATERS	
SPECIAL OPERATIONS AT ANCHOR* SPECIAL 1 R-W-R/32 ANCHOR LIGHTS * NOT INCLUDING VESSELS ENGAGED IN REPLEN. AT SEA, LAUNCH. /RECOV. ACFT., AND MINESWEEPING				
SPECIAL OPERATIONS (MINESWEEPING) MASTHEAD 1 W/20 RANGE 1 W/20 (OPTIONAL FOR VESSEL LESS THAN 150 FT. IN LENGTH) SIDE WHEN { 1 R, G/10 WAY ON STERN { 1 W/12 SPECIAL 2, 3 G/32		DANGER EXISTS on BOTH SIDES OR DANGER EXISTS ON SIDE INDICATED	(UNDER WAY LIGHTS)	(NONE)

■ BLACK	□ WHITE	▨ RED

balls or shapes by day, two all-around red lights at night, and whistle signals of one prolonged and two short blasts when underway in restricted visibility. In inland waters, where these signals have other meanings, inability to comply with the meeting and passing rules is indicated by a timely use of the Inland danger signal.

Special Operations include laying or picking up submarine cables or navigation marks, surveying or underwater operations, replenishment at sea, and recovery of aircraft. All vessels engaged in special operations show distinctive lights and shapes, as indicated in the accompanying chart.

Aircraft Carriers

An aircraft carrier, while launching and recovering aircraft, is considered "unable to maneuver" and has the right of way over all other *naval* vessels, regardless of their size, type or descriptions except for ships engaged in un derway replenishment. She will show the shapes and lights for vessels engaged in special operations. Other naval vessels must stay clear, and, if it is necessary to pass her during flight operations the following rules apply:

1. If the carrier is headed into the wind, pass on her starboard side.

2. If the carrier is headed off the wind, pass on her lee side.

Minesweepers

A minesweeper engaged in sweeping is conducting a special operation with distinct possibility of danger to other vessels. Vessels engaged in minesweeping operations carry lights and shapes indicating that it is dangerous to approach closer than 3000 yards astern or 1500 yards on the side or sides on which danger exists.

Small Vessels

A small vessel should not hamper the movements of a larger vessel, especially in restricted waters.

Vessels Not in Station

Vessels which are not in station should not hamper those in station. On the other hand, vessels in station should not stubbornly maintain their course and speed if danger of collision exists.

Distress Signals

When a vessel in distress requires assistance, any sound or visual equipment is used to attract attention. The Inland and International Rules specify firing a gun, sounding the fog signal apparatus, etc. In addition to signals to attract attention of other nearby vessels, the International Rules include the use of SOS transmitted by CW radio or MAYDAY spoken over voice radio.

Vessels Not Under Way (see chart, page 150)

This includes vessels not engaged in any special operation which would necessitate special lights or shapes, and also applies to vessels aground.

The anchor lights and ball for vessels at anchor should also be used when moored to a buoy, or at a pier if they project into the stream.

In addition to the lights shown in the accompanying diagram, the FAA requires all vessels not under way to show 2 red aircraft warning lights at the top of all masts.

Formation v. Single Vessel

Normally, a vessel proceeding independently should maneuver to stay clear of a formation. Merchant vessels,

VESSELS NOT UNDER WAY

	LIGHTS	SHAPES
AT ANCHOR		
VESSELS 150 FT. OR MORE IN LENGTH		
	1 W/32 FORWARD, HIGH 1 W/32 AFT, LOW	
VESSELS LESS THAN 150 FT. IN LENGTH		"ANCHOR BALL"
	1 W/32 FORWARD	
AGROUND		
INTERNATIONAL RULES		
	SPECIAL 2 R/32 ANCHOR LIGHTS 1, 2 W/32	
U.S. INLAND WATERS		
	(ANCHOR LIGHTS)	

however, will often maintain their right of way and run directly into a formation. Under favorable circumstances, in good visibility when no other naval vessels are involved, the commander of a small formation will probably maneuver his unit to clear the "stranger." But the officer of the deck of a vessel in formation cannot, and should not, count on the unit being maneuvered clear. This is a difficult, if not impossible, maneuver under many conditions. Under all circumstances, the officer of the deck is responsible for handling his own vessel in accordance with the applicable rules of the road in regard to the "stranger," and in accordance with standard naval instructions in regard to naval vessels in formation.

Timely and Positive Action

In obeying and construing the Rules of the Road, any action taken should be positive, in ample time, and with due regard to the observance of good seamanship.

LIGHT DISPLAYS

Both the International and the Inland Rules require that lights to prevent collision be displayed from sunset to sunrise, and during such time no other lights which may be mistaken for the prescribed lights shall be exhibited.

Notation is made in the legend accompanying each illustration of the rules that apply—International, Inland, or Pilot.

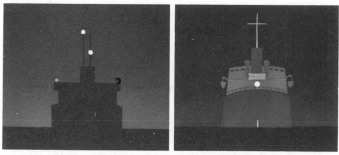

Bow and stern views of power-driven vessel under way, over 150 feet in length.　　　INTERNATIONAL RULE 2.

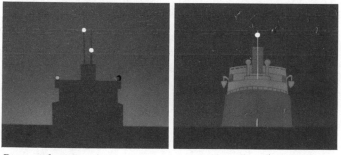

Bow and stern views of power-driven vessel under way, over 65 feet in length.　　　INLAND RULE 2.

Sailing vessels under way, or vessel in tow. A sailing vessel may also carry red-over-green, 20-point lights on the mast.

INTERNATIONAL RULE 5, INLAND RULES, ARTICLE 5.

Power-driven (or power and sail) vessel, under 150 feet in length, under way.

INTERNATIONAL RULE 2, INLAND RULES, ARTICLE 2.

Class 2 or Class 3 power-driven (or power and sail) vessel, under way. MOTORBOAT ACT, OF APRIL 25, 1940.

Small vessel uses flare-up when being approached by another vessel. INTERNATIONAL RULE 7 (f); INLAND RULES, 7.

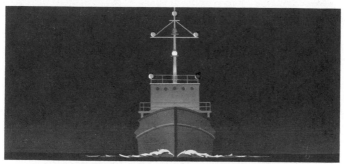

Vessel under 150 feet, engaged in minesweeping operations. INTERNATIONAL RULE 4 (d).

Vessel whose occupation limits her maneuverability. Side and stern lights are shown when making way.

INTERNATIONAL RULE 4 (c).

Ferryboat with special identifying light 15 feet above range lights. PILOT RULES, SECTION 80.15.

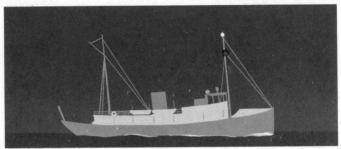

Power-driven pilot vessel under way. When on station, flare-up light is shown. INTERNATIONAL RULE 8 (a); INLAND RULES, 8.

Sailing pilot vessel under way. Flare-up light is shown when on station. INTERNATIONAL RULE 8 (b); INLAND RULES, 8.

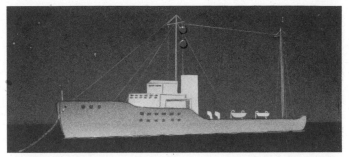

Vessel not under command. INTERNATIONAL RULE 4 (a).
Coast and geodetic survey vessel at anchor, working in a fairway. PILOT RULES, SECTION 80.33.

Vessel at anchor, over 150 feet in length.
INTERNATIONAL RULE 11 (b); INLAND RULES, 11 (b).

Vessel at anchor, under 150 feet in length.
INTERNATIONAL RULE 11 (a); INLAND RULES, 11 (a).

Vessel moored over a wreck.   PILOT RULES, SECTION 80.19 (a).

Tug with barges, length of tow not over 600 feet, without optional after range light, high seas (port-side view).
INTERNATIONAL RULE 3 (a).

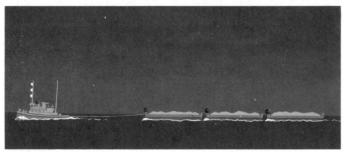

Tug with barges, length of tow over 600 feet, without optional after range light, high seas (port-side view).
INTERNATIONAL RULE 3 (a).

Tug with tow astern, showing optional arrangements.
INLAND RULES, 3 (a).

Tug with a submerged tow.   PILOT RULES, SECTION 80.18 (a).

Tug with barge, canal boat, or scow alongside.
INLAND RULES, 3; PILOT RULES, SECTION 80.16a (c).

Seaplane being towed.   INTERNATIONAL RULE 5 (a).

Special quick-flashing (90 per minute) amber light for sub-marines.   INTERNATIONAL RULE 13 (a); INLAND RULE 13.

Vessel engaged in trawling.   INTERNATIONAL RULE 9 (c).

Vessel fishing, other than trawling, with nets extending less than 500 feet.   INTERNATIONAL RULE 9.

Vessel fishing, other than trawling, with nets extending over 500 feet.   INTERNATIONAL RULE 9.

Fishing vessel less than 10 tons, showing bi-colored lantern when being approached by another vessel.

INLAND RULES, 9 (a).

Stationary dredge.   PILOT RULES, SECTION 80.20 (a).

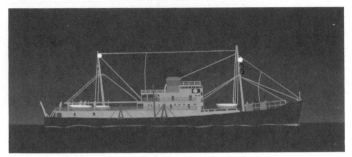

Self-propelling suction dredge, under way.
          PILOT RULES, SECTION 80.21 (a).

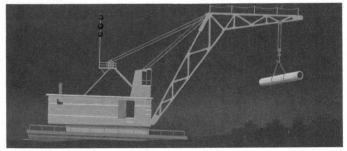

Vessel engaged in submarine construction, or similar activities.
          PILOT RULES, SECTION 80.22 (a).

DAYMARKS

Daymarks are displayed from sunrise to sunset where they best can be seen. International and Inland Rules require that daymarks must be at least two feet in diameter. When more than one mark is displayed, they must be at least six feet apart.

Vessel using both sail and power.   INTERNATIONAL RULE 14.

Vessel aground.   INTERNATIONAL RULE 11 (e).

Minesweeper. Left, sweeping port and starboard; right, sweeping starboard only. INTERNATIONAL RULE 4 (d) (1).

Vessel engaged in fishing. PILOT RULES, SECTION 80.32a.

Vessel engaged in fishing. INTERNATIONAL RULE 9 (h).

Vessel at anchor.
INTERNATIONAL RULE 11 (c); PILOT RULES, SECTION 80.25.

Vessel not under command.   INTERNATIONAL RULE 4 (a).

Vessel moored over a wreck.   PILOT RULES, SECTION 80.19 (b).

Hydrographic surveying vessel under way.
PILOT RULES, SECTION 80.33 (a).

Cable ship at work on cable. INTERNATIONAL RULE 4 (c).

Tug with a submerged tow. PILOT RULES, SECTION 80.18.

Stationary dredge. PILOT RULES, SECTION 80.20.

Self-propelling suction dredge, under way.
PILOT RULES, SECTION 80.21.

Vessel engaged in submarine construction, or similar activities.
PILOT RULES, SECTION 80.22.

Daytime distress signal, International code flags NC.
INTERNATIONAL RULE 31 (a) (vi).

Vessel or seaplane in distress showing flames (burning oil barrel, etc.).   INTERNATIONAL RULE 31 (a) (viii); INLAND RULES, 31.

Vessel or seaplane in distress, firing red rocket stars.
INTERNATIONAL RULE 31 (a) (iii).

SUMMARY OF SOUND SIGNALS

Symbol	Meaning
•	a short blast (about one second duration)
—	a blast of unspecified duration
‾‾‾	a prolonged blast (four to six seconds duration)
———	a long blast (duration at least 8 seconds, usually 8–10)
*****	ringing a bell for five seconds
o	three strokes of a bell
♯	gong, five seconds

INSTRUMENTS	International	Inland
Power Driven/Steam	Whistle, Fog Horn, and Bell	Whistle or Siren, Fog Horn and Bell
Sailing	Fog Horn and Bell	Fog Horn
Vessel Towed	Whistle, or Fog Horn	Fog Horn

VESSELS IN SIGHT OF EACH OTHER   INTERNATIONAL

	Signal
I am altering my course to starboard	•
I am altering my course to port	• •
My engines are going astern or I have sternway on	• • •
I doubt whether the burdened vessel is taking sufficient action	• • • • • or more

INLAND   Meeting

Port to port passing	•
Starboard to starboard passing	• •

Overtaking Vessel

I desire to pass on your starboard hand	•
I desire to pass on your port hand	• •

Overtaken Vessel

I assent to your passing on my starboard hand	•
I assent to your passing on my port hand	• •
It is not safe to attempt to pass	• • • • or more

Crossing Situation

Privileged Vessel—I intend to hold course and speed	•
Burdened Vessel—I intend to leave you on my port hand	•

Backing Signal

My engines are backing or I have sternway on	• • •

Danger Signal

Danger exists, I do not understand your actions, or I object	• • • • or more

VESSELS NOT IN SIGHT OF EACH OTHER

International	—½ mile from bend in channel	‾‾‾
Inland	—½ mile from bend in channel or leaving slip	‾‾‾
Inland	—Danger exists	• • • • or more

FOG SIGNALS

Type of Vessel	International		Inland	
	Signal	Maximum Interval	Signal	Maximum Interval
Power vessel under way with way on	‾‾‾	2 Min.	‾‾‾	1 Min.
Power vessel under way with no way on	‾‾‾ ‾‾‾	2 Min.	‾‾‾	1 Min.
Towing				
Power vessel	‾‾‾ • •	1 Min.	‾‾‾ • •	1 Min.
Sailing vessel	‾‾‾ • •	1 Min.		
Vessel laying submarine cable or navigation marks	‾‾‾ • •	1 Min.	‾‾‾	1 Min.
Vessel not under command	‾‾‾ • •	1 Min.	‾‾‾	1 Min.
Vessel towed	‾‾‾ • • •	1 Min.	‾‾‾ • •	1 Min.
Vessel at anchor	*****♯	1 Min.	*****	1 Min.
Vessel aground	o*****o♯	1 Min.		
Sailing vessel				
on starboard tack	—	1 Min.	—	1 Min.
on port tack	— —	1 Min.	— —	1 Min.
wind abaft beam	— — —	1 Min.	— — —	1 Min.
Vessels fishing	‾‾‾ • •	1 Min.		

NOTES: Sounding of gong aft applies only to vessels over 350 feet in length at anchor or aground in International Waters.

Vessels at anchor in International Waters may sound a three blast signal, 1 short, 1 prolonged, and 1 short to give warning of their position.

Chapter VIII SAFE NAVIGATION

The commanding officer is responsible for the safe navigation of his ship or aircraft, except as prescribed otherwise in these regulations for ships at a naval shipyard or station, in drydock, or in the Panama Canal. In time of war, or during exercises simulating war, the provisions of this article pertaining to the use of lights and electronic devices may be modified by competent authority.

The commanding officer of a ship and, as appropriate, of an aircraft, shall:

(d) Keep himself informed of the error of all compasses and other devices available as aids to navigation.

(i) Insure that efficient devices for fixing the ship's position and for ascertaining the depth of water are employed when underway on soundings, entering or leaving port, or upon approaching an anchorage, shoal, or rock, whether or not a pilot is on board. If circumstances warrant, he shall reduce speed to the extent necessary to permit these devices to be operated efficiently and accurately.

(j) Observe every precaution prescribed by law to prevent collisions and other accidents on the high seas, inland waters, or in the air.

(k) When underway in restricted waters or close inshore, and unless unusual circumstances prevent, steam at a speed which will not endanger other ships or craft, or property close to the shore.

(l) Take special care that the lights required by law to prevent collisions at sea, in port, or in the air are kept in order and burning in all weathers from sunset to sunrise, and require that means for promptly relighting or replacing such lights are available.—*Navy Regulations,* Article 0751.

When at sea, and especially when approaching land or shoal waters, the officer of the deck shall keep himself informed of the position of the ship and of all other particulars which may be of use in keeping the ship out of danger. He shall employ such means and devices as may be available for detecting and avoiding danger from grounding or collision. When there is danger of grounding or collision, he shall take immediate action to minimize and localize any damage which might occur. He shall thoroughly familiarize himself with the laws to prevent collision and shall strictly comply with them. He shall see that the ship is skillfully steered and kept on her course and that when steaming in formation, the assigned station is maintained. He shall see that nothing is done to impair the accuracy of the compasses, and that their errors are frequently verified. During low visibility or when in congested areas he shall station additional lookouts as the circumstances require. He shall see that the lights required by law for preventing collisions are kept burning from sunset till sunrise, except when not in use by orders of competent authority, and that they are inspected half hourly.—*Navy Regulations,* Article 1010.

Except as prescribed in these regulations or as authorized by the commanding officer, the officer of the deck shall not change the prescribed course or speed of the ship unless necessary to avoid collision or imminent danger.—*Navy Regulations, Article* 1011.

Young officers are inclined to look upon disasters at sea as something remote from their experience and as events that are as infrequent and as inescapable as being struck by lightning. On the contrary, collisions and groundings are altogether too common and are almost always avoidable. It is true that perfect safety records cannot reasonably be expected of any force or fleet; the business of going to sea even in peacetime is inherently dangerous. But the most important point is that collisions and groundings can be avoided for the most part by the intelligent application of the fundamental principles of good seamanship combined with the exercise of good judgment and common sense. While unusual material casualties that cannot immediately be coped with do occasionally happen, in most cases some human error has set in motion or abetted the process that leads to an accident.

COLLISIONS

Analysis of collision cases reveals that one or more of the following factors are frequently involved:

1. Failure to establish in time the fact that risk of collision exists.

2. Failure to take timely avoiding action.

3. Failure to turn on running lights in the emergency while ships were darkened.

4. Failure to notify the commanding officer of a potentially dangerous situation.

5. Failure to check for steady bearing in a closing situation until too late.

6. Excessive reliance on CIC to the exclusion of a common sense evaluation of the situation on the bridge.

7. Poor judgment in evaluating the effects of wind and tide.

8. Failure to understand the tactical characteristics of the ship.

9. Injudicious use of the power available in the ship.

10. Bridge and CIC radars both on long scale, thereby making the detection of close-in targets difficult, *or*
    Bridge and CIC radars both on short scale resulting in a failure to detect distant targets on a collision course until very close in.

11. Failure of bridge personnel to keep sharp visual lookout.

12. Failure of CIC and bridge to insure the receipt of tactical signals by the conning officer.

13. A radical course change made by one or more ships without informing ships in the vicinity.

14. Whistle signals not used.

15. The required checks between gyro and magnetic compasses not made.

16. Other ships in the formation observing the merging of pips without broadcasting a warning by voice radio.

17. Maneuvering board solutions provided by CIC not checked by the bridge, and vice versa.

18. Deck watch officers not familiar with the rules of the road, and were vague as to accepted collision prevention procedure.

19. Failure to execute tactical signals properly.

Most of these errors seem elementary and not likely to be made by able, intelligent officers. Yet, it is just these simple mistakes that are made with discouraging frequency. It does not require genius to stand a sound, proficient deck watch; but it does take vigilance, alertness, a highly developed sense of responsibility, and the exercise of good judgment.

Most of the points listed above will be discussed under separate headings farther along in the book; the others need little elaboration. The timely use of navigational lights in uncertain or dangerous maneuvering situations is proper, whether under simulated or actual battle conditions, and in any case, it should be evident in these days of radar that such action could only yield incidental information to a possible nearby enemy. Running-light panels should be kept set up, and bridge personnel should be drilled in switching them on quickly.

Frequent compass checks of the bearings of all closing ships is an absolute essential. This is the best and single most important means of preventing collision at sea. In reduced visibility, check bearings by radar. Unless your ship and another are on parallel (or exactly opposite) opening courses, a steady bearing means collision is imminent. Even a slowly changing bearing is warning of a dangerous situation. *Take action.* This means notifying the captain if time permits, changing course, or stopping and backing.

GROUNDINGS

A second major category of emergencies is grounding. Like collisions, groundings are largely attributable to human error. Here are some common examples. Most of them involve jobs which are the responsibility of the navigator, but of which the OOD should be cognizant.

1. Laying down the ship's DR plot too close to known shoal water, or over water too shallow for the ship's draft.

2. Lack of foresight in not laying down danger and turning bearings ahead of time.

3. Excessive reliance on radar navigation alone.

4. Failure of the officer of the deck to notify the captain and the navigator immediately when doubt of safe position first arises.

5. Improper application of known gyro error.

6. Failure to use visible navigational aids.

7. Failure to have latest *Notice to Mariners* concerning temporary dislocation of navigational aids.

8. Failure to use effectively a dead-reckoning plot.

9. Failure to fix position by distance run between successive bearings when only one landmark was identified.

10. Failure to take emergency action when doubt of safe position exists.

11. Failure to use Fathometer and line of soundings.

12. Failure to account for set and drift and apply the proper correction.

13. Improper identification of lights and other fixed navigational aids.

14. Failure to adjust course as necessary to remain on the DR track.

15. Failure to take fixes frequently enough.

16. Failure to stop and assess the situation or take emergency action when the plot goes awry or when doubt arises as to the ship's position.

17. Improper reliance on non-fixed aids, such as buoys, for navigational purposes.

Again, most of the errors that result in groundings are violations of the most rudimentary and basic principles of navigation, and as in collisions, the inescapable conclusion is that disaster results from carelessness and lack of exercise of good judgment rather than from a lack of knowledge. The temptation to take a chance, to slop through the watch instead of expending energy in doing the job correctly, is too often not resisted. It does not take a master mariner to slow, stop, change course, or notify the captain and the navigator that the ship's position is in doubt. Yet, every year groundings occur that would have been just that easy to avoid.

Checking the gyro should be a matter of concern for the officer of the deck. A range can often be used, or a sun azimuth or a bearing of Polaris can be taken. The old reliable check against the magnetic compass is required by *Navy Regulations*, and should not be done in a perfunctory manner. Gyro compasses can suddenly develop large errors which can be disastrous; the only way to detect these quickly is to note the relationship, at all times, between the gyro and the magnetic compasses. The quartermaster of the watch logs the readings of both in his compass record book. He should be impressed with the importance of this routine chore. After you have detected and measured a gyro error, the next important thing to do is to apply it *in the right direction.* If you do not trust your memory, refer to *Dutton's Navigation and Piloting,* which is available in every charthouse.

RADAR NAVIGATION

The commanding officer of a ship shall require that available electronic and other devices appropriate as aids to safe navigation be employed during periods of low visibility and at other times when needed.—*Navy Regulations*, Article 0751.

The increasing efficiency of electronic aids to navigation resents a definite problem. There is a tendency to rely on them too completely—even to the exclusion of using such old-fashioned but useful devices as binoculars. Radar and other electronic aids should be looked upon only as important *aids* to conning a ship in low visibility. They sometimes fail or slip out of calibration or suffer directional casualities to their gyro indicators. On those occasions of reduced visibility when the ship must be conned by electronic means, make certain that the CIC plotting team is alert, that the information and recommendations they are giving you are correct (check the various radar repeaters against each other) that all applicable equipment is in use such as sonar, Fathometer, loran, DRT, etc., in addition to the radar, and, very importantly, that an alert visual watch is maintained.

When practicable, while piloting in good visibility, use radar for training. Ask CIC for advice based on radar information, and then check against visual observations. Become familiar in good weather with typical PPI pictures; this familiarity results in confidence when you must use radar information only.

For an authoritative discussion of proper use of radar, refer to Chapter VII, *Farwell's Rules of the Nautical Road,* for the Annex to the International Rules titled "Recommendations on the Use of Radar Information As An Aid to Avoiding Collision at Sea."

DEAD RECKONING (DR) PLOT

In the days before electronics, when good fixes were rare, hard to get, and highly valued, the DR plot was one of a navigator's most important aids. it was always run up and projected ahead. It is still just as important as it ever was. When a ship's actual position is in doubt, a DR position (modified in some cases by known factors, such as current, to give an estimated position) is the best estimate of that position. A good navigator will have one or the other instantly available at all times. The mechanics of navigating—the accumulation of fixes showing where you have been—is only secondary. A navigator's primary duty in assuring himself of the safe navigation of his ship is to know *where the ship is going,* not where it has been. For this purpose a DR plot is invaluable and must always be maintained on the bridge chart in use. A mechanical means of keeping but not of advancing this plot, the dead reckoning tracer (DRT), is a sometimes neglected instrument. It should always be set up and operating when on soundings, and its setting made to conform at frequent intervals with actual fixes.

EMERGENCY ACTION

It is an absolute, immediate necessity for the officer of the deck to take action when the position of his ship is in doubt. It is difficult to imagine an officer of the deck so busy trying to get a cut that will put him where he thinks he is that he forgets that his ship is steaming on to disaster. But all too often this has happened. Sometimes the captain and the navigator are not informed; often the ship needed only a slight change of course toward deep water to insure its safety. A senior naval officer has stated, "The direct and final cause of most groundings is the failure of the conning officer to take the immediate emergency action of slowing, stopping, or turning to safe water when the possibility of grounding first develops. In restricted waters such possibility automatically develops with the first doubt as to the ship's position. There is no question of the advisability of taking a calculated risk in this respect during peacetime. Any risk is unacceptable under such circumstances. The realization of this one fact by commanding officers, navigators, and officers of the deck would have prevented most of the groundings in this force."

THE NAVIGATOR AND THE OFFICER OF THE DECK

The navigating officer shall advise the officer of the deck of a safe course to be steered and the officer of the deck shall regard such advice as sufficient authority to change the course, but he shall at once report the change to the commanding officer. In addition, the commanding officer may authorize the navigating officer, when on the bridge at sea, provided no other officer so authorized is present, to relieve the officer of the deck in an emergency when, in the opinion of the navigating officer such action is necessary for the safety of the ship.

The commanding officer shall be promptly informed whenever the officer of the deck is relieved in accordance with this article.—*Navy Regulations*, Articles 1009-3 and 1009-4.

Note the language of the article concerning navigation quoted from *Navy Regulations* at the beginning of this chapter: "The officer of the deck shall keep himself informed." If the navigator is on the bridge and maintaining the ship's track, it is an easy matter for the officer of the deck to check on the ship's position. If, however, during prolonged periods of steaming within sight of land, for example, the navigator leaves the bridge, then the officer of the deck should take a more active interest in the navigation plot and must insure accurate fixes and the projection of the ship's course into safe waters. If an experienced assistant navigator is maintaining the plot then all may be well. It often happens, however, that the navigator must depend on the officer of the deck or his assistant to obtain visual or radar fixes and to maintain the ship's navigational plot, particularly when well off shore but still within radar range of mountain peaks, etc. This time-honored and logical arrangement does not reduce the responsibilities of either the navigator or the officer of the deck.

Navy Regulations stipulates that, except as prescribed in those regulations or as authorized by the commanding officer, the officer of the deck shall not change the prescribed course or speed of the ship unless necessary to avoid collision or imminent danger. They also state that the navigating officer shall advise the officer of the deck of a safe course to be steered, and that the officer of the deck shall regard such advice as sufficient authority to change the course, but that he shall at once report any such change to the commanding officer. These regulations further require that, when in formation, the officer of the deck shall ensure that the assigned station is maintained. The officer of the deck, therefore, must make such changes of course and speed as are necessary to carry out properly the tactical orders received from higher authority, and to maintain the ship's station. When the captain is on the bridge, the officer of the deck should inform him of the tactical order and the maneuver(s) contemplated. When the captain is not on the bridge, the officer of the deck should immediately notify him. Except for changes of very minor effect, such as changing station when in mid-ocean, the navigator should also be notified of any change in course or speed. This requirement to maintain assigned station gives the officer of the deck the authority to make the small adjustments to course and speed necessary for accurate station-keeping. These adjustments are not considered changes in the prescribed course and speed.

FOG AND LOW VISIBILITY

Operating at night and in low visibility often complicates the duties of an officer of the deck. Radar has made possible the most complicated maneuvering and piloting under all conditions of visibility. Thus, despite the assistance of radar, the duties and responsibilities of a conning officer are in no way simplified. The fault of many inexperienced officers is that, with the advent of radar, they have neglected older and more reliable means of safeguarding the ship. Radar is an *aid* against disaster, not a *guarantee.*

There is a deplorable tendency among many officers to spend their watch with their noses glued to the radar scope. While this invaluable device must often be used, it must not be to the exclusion of visual observation and the intelligent use of well-trained lookouts.

An officer of the deck must have a reasonably detailed understanding of the capabilities and limitations of his radars. He should know exactly how to operate all the remote control gear, such as the bridge repeater. He should know who is responsible for the maintenance of the ship's radars, and how to reach them in a hurry. He should have the radars warmed up and checked before dark or upon the onset of fog, rain, or snow.

It is important that surface search radar equipment be used in reduced visibility. At night or during reduced visibility, radar repeaters on the bridge, or on the bridge and in CIC, should be at different scales. The surface search radars should be kept continually energized when underway (but not necessarily emitting when operating under an EMCON condition), and they should be properly checked and calibrated at intervals. Keeping all radar repeaters in both CIC and on the bridge on the same scale is dangerous, since it could lead to undue concentration on either the immediate area at the expense of detecting more distant contacts, or vice versa. The courts have held that failure on the part of a government vessel to make use of radar while under way in low visibility was directly contributory to a collision in which the vessel was involved. Rule 29 of the *Rules of the Nautical Road,* quoted herewith, was considered applicable: "Nothing in these rules shall exonerate any vessel . . . from the consequence of any neglect to carry lights or signals, or of any neglect to keep a proper lookout, or of the neglect of any precaution which may be required by the ordinary practice of seamen, or by the special circumstance of the case."

LOOKOUTS

The commanding officer of a ship shall insure that lookouts are proficient in their duties, and are stationed as necessary in accordance with the best practice of seamen, having in mind any special conditions, the results to be accomplished, and the physical limitations of personnel. When under way during low visibility, or when approaching or traversing congested traffic lanes or areas, at least one lookout shall be stationed in the bow as far forward and as near the water as is feasible.—*Navy Regulations,* Article 0751.

Nothing in these Rules shall exonerate any vessel, or the owner, master or crew thereof, from the consequences of any neglect to carry lights or signals, or of any neglect to *keep a proper look-out,* or of the neglect of any precautions which may be required in the ordinary practice of seamen, or by the special circumstances of the case."—*International Rules,* Rule of Good Seamanship, Rule 29.

An important, and sometimes much neglected, aid to safe ship operation is the lookout. The trained human eye is still superior in many respects to the most elaborate machine. Be alert to "station additional lookouts as the circumstances require." This may be in clear weather if your ship is in much traveled sea areas. See that they have some means of rapid communication with the bridge; they should not, however, wear phones. Be sure that they are instructed in accordance with the currently effective lookout manual. This is important to provide uniformity in reporting. See that your lookouts are well clothed, are rotated frequently, and are provided with an opportunity to obtain hot food and drink if low temperatures warrant it. Men cannot perform efficiently if cold, wet, or hungry; they also have a limited span of attention and cannot be expected to remain alert for long periods without a break.

Above all, let the lookout know that you are counting on his reports and consider his an important job. Be meticulous in acknowledging his reports, even if radar has already made contact. A word of praise or interest will go a long way in increasing his efficiency. Lookouts should be encouraged to qualify as "Expert Lookouts," as set forth in Article C–7411, *BuPers Manual*. Note that *Navy Regulations* requires a half-hourly report on the navigational lights. "Starboard sidelight, masthead light, bright lights, sir" and "Port sidelight, range light, bright lights, sir" are the traditional reports required.

PSYCHOLOGICAL FACTORS

There are certain psychological factors which have fully as much to do with safety at sea as any of the more strictly technical ones. A large proportion of the disasters in tactics and maneuvers comes from concentrating too much on one objective or urgency, at the cost of not being sufficiently alert for others. Thus, absorption with enemy craft already under fire has led to being torpedoed by others not looked for or not given attention; while preoccupation with navigation, with carrying out the particular job in hand, or with avoiding some particular vessel or hazard, has resulted in collision with ships to whose presence we were temporarily oblivious. There is no rule that can cover this except the ancient one that eternal vigilance is the price of safety, no matter what the immediate distractions.

No officer, whatever his rank and experience, should flatter himself that he is immune to the inexplicable lapses in judgment, calculation, and memory, or to the slips of the tongue in giving orders, which throughout seagoing history have so often brought disaster to men of the highest reputation and ability. Where a mistake in maneuvering or navigating can spell calamity, an officer shows rashness and conceit, rather than admirable self-confidence, in not checking his plan with someone else before starting it, *if time permits.* This is not yielding to another's judgment; it is merely making sure that one's own has not "blown a fuse" somewhere, as the best mental and mechanical equipment in the world has sometimes done.—(From a letter to the Pacific Fleet, by Fleet Admiral Chester W. Nimitz, U.S. Navy)

Chapter IX STANDARD COMMANDS

His [the officer of the deck's] orders shall be issued in the customary phraseology of the service.—*Navy Regulations*, Article 1005.

Nowhere in the Navy is exact phraseology as important as it is to the conning officer in giving commands to the helmsman or engine-order telegraph watch. Because misunderstanding or ambiguity can be so quickly disastrous, there must be no possibility of a mistaken meaning. There need be no confusion if only the exact and official terminology is used. Short cuts or individual variations are to be discouraged; it is important that all the enlisted men who man the ship-control instruments become accustomed to receiving their commands in the same form.

MANNER OF GIVING COMMANDS

The manner in which you give commands is important. Speak clearly, loud enough to be heard, and with a positive, incisive tone. The word helm should not be used in any command relating to the operation of the rudder.

Commands to the helmsman are given in a logical sequence. The first word, "right" or "left," indicates direction and enables the helmsman to start putting the wheel over at once. The second word indicates amount, as: "Right *standard* rudder." The purpose of giving the command in this manner is to insure the quick and accurate compliance of the helmsman, who starts turning his wheel instantly upon hearing "right" or "left," and by the time the amount of the rudder has been specified he can bring the rudder-angle indicator to rest on the exact number of degrees.

Similarly, in giving commands to the engine-order telegraph (annunciator) the first term, "port (starboard) engine" or "all engines" alerts the operator and indicates which handles or knobs he must prepare to move. The next part, "ahead" or "back," gives the direction of movement of the handles or knobs. The last part, "one-third," "full," etc., gives the amount of the speed change and tells the engine-order telegraph operator where to stop his instrument.

Following are standard commands to the engine-order telegraph:

1. "All engines, ahead one-third (two-thirds, standard, full, flank)," or "All engines back one-third (two-thirds, full)."

2. "Starboard (port) engine, ahead one-third (two-thirds, standard, full)"; "Port (starboard) engine, back one-third (two-thirds, full)."

In ships where flank speed is not otherwise provided for on the engine-order telegraph, the operator should ring up full speed twice.

In an emergency, when it is desired to abandon the normal acceleration and deceleration tables and to go ahead or back with all available power as quickly as possible, the proper command is, "All engines, ahead (back) emergency." The operator should then ring up "flank ahead" (or full astern) three or more times in rapid succession.

The exact number of turns to be made on each engine should be indicated to the engine room over the revolution indicator. If you desire turns other than the exact number for the speed ordered, you should specify the number of turns desired: *"Indicate* (ring up) one one seven revolutions." The word revolutions should always be included in this order to prevent any possible confusion with orders concerning course or bearings. When increasing or decreasing turns by small numbers, you should also state the exact number of turns desired; for instance, "Indicate one one seven revolutions," rather than order, "Up two," or "Take off three."

When specifying turns, you should, if practicable, state the *number of turns* desired, rather than ordering turns for the *speed desired*. This may not always be practical as, for instance, when you are on the wing of the bridge, cannot see or remember the turns required, and feel that you should not leave the wing of the bridge. You should then order: *"Indicate turns for _____ knots,"* and require a report of the turns rung up, as well as a repetition of the command. Memorize the turns-per-knot table as soon as possible.

One-third speed and two-thirds speed are one-third and two-thirds of the prescribed standard speed. The turns for these speeds are the number of revolutions required to make those fractions of standard speed. Full speed and flank speed are greater speeds than standard speed. They may be based on fractions of standard speed or on specified increments. The turns for these speeds are also the number of turns actually required to make them. When small adjustments in the speed are desired, the only command usually necessary is the one ordering the change in revolutions. However, when ordering a number of revolutions which will give a speed closer to another increment than the one already indicated, you should also ring up that nearest increment on the engine-order telegraph.

It is important that all commands be repeated back loudly and clearly by the helmsman or engine-order telegraph operator just as they are given by the officer at the conn. This practice serves as a check on the officer who originates the command and neutralizes any slip of the tongue, such as "left" when the opposite, "right," is meant.

In addition, and just as important, the man at the wheel

or engine-order telegraph must be required to report when he has complied with the command.

For example, the proper sequence would be:

(*Command*) "Right full rudder."

(*Repeat*) "Right full rudder, sir."

(*When carried out*) "Rudder is right full, sir."

(*Conning officer*) "Very well."

(*Command*) "All engines ahead standard."

(*Repeat*) "All engines ahead standard, sir."

(*When acknowledged by engine rooms*) "All engines indicate (answer) ahead standard, sir."

(*Conning officer*) "Very well."

It is a common practice on most ships, when maneuvering or when special sea details are manned, to have the engine-order telegraph operator wear the jv phones. By transmitting over his phones when repeating back his commands to the conning officer, the operator parallels to the engine room all orders he is given. The phones also provide standby communication with the engine room if the annunciator or RPM indicator fails.

If a command is given to change the speed of only one engine, then the operator, when making his final report (such as "Port engine answers ahead one-third, sir"), should also inform the conning officer of the position of the other handle (such as "Starboard engine is backing full, sir"). This assists the conning officer in keeping his commands to the engines in mind.

All commands to the helmsman which specify a course or heading must refer to the compass by which he is steering at the time. Each course or heading is stated in three digits. For example, the order to steer 005 degrees is, "Come right (left) to course zero zero five." If the gyro compass which the helmsman is using is in error, then the actual compass course for the helmsman to use should be given. You cannot expect the helmsman to perform mental arithmetic. Similarly, when steering by magnetic compass, the officer of the deck should apply the needed corrections and give the helmsman the course to maintain.

COMMANDS TO THE HELMSMAN

Command	Meaning
"RIGHT (LEFT) RUDDER":	A command to apply right (left) rudder instantly, an indeterminate amount. Must be followed instantly by the amount of rudder desired.
"RIGHT (LEFT) STANDARD RUDDER":	Put the rudder over to the right (left) the specified number of degrees necessary for the ship to make her standard tactical diameter.
"RIGHT (LEFT) FULL RUDDER":	Put the rudder over to the right (left) the specified number of degrees necessary for the ship to make her reduced tactical diameter.
"RIGHT (LEFT) FIVE (TEN, etc.) DEGREES RUDDER":	Turn the wheel to right (left) until the rudder is placed at the number of degrees ordered. This command is used in making changes of course. The helmsman would then be ordered to steer the new course (by such command as, "Steady on course _____," in time to permit the helmsman to "meet her" on the new course. The complete command would be, for example, "Right five degrees rudder. Steady on course two seven five."
"RIGHT (LEFT) HANDSOMELY":	Turn the rudder a small amount. The command is given when a very slight change of course is desired.

Command	Meaning
"INCREASE YOUR RUDDER TO _____ DEGREES":	Increase the rudder angle. This command is given when, with the rudder already over, it is desired to make her turn more rapidly. The command must be followed by the exact number of degrees of rudder desired.
"EASE YOUR RUDDER TO _____ DEGREES":	Decrease the rudder angle. This command is given when the ship, turning with right (left) rudder, is turning toward or is nearing the heading desired. The command can be given, for example: "Ease to fifteen (five), etc."
"MEET HER":	Use rudder as may be necessary to check her swing. This command may be given when the ship is nearing the desired course.
"STEADY," or "STEADY AS YOU GO":	Steer the course on which the ship is heading when the command is received. This command is given when, in changing course, the new course is reached or the ship is heading as desired. The helmsman responds, "Steady as you go. Course _____, sir."
"RUDDER AMIDSHIPS":	Rudder angle zero. This command is given when the ship is turning, and it is desired to make her swing less rapidly.
"SHIFT YOUR RUDDER":	Change from right to left rudder (or vice-versa) an equal amount. This command is given, for example, when the ship loses headway

Command	Meaning
	and gathers sternway, to keep her turning in the same direction.
"MIND YOUR RUDDER":	A warning that the ship is swinging off the course because of bad steering. It is also a command to steer exactly, using less rudder.
"NOTHING TO THE LEFT (RIGHT) OF _____":	A warning to the helmsman that you do not desire the ship to be steered to the left (right) of the course ordered.
"HOW IS YOUR RUDDER?":	A question to the helmsman. He should reply, "Five (ten, fifteen, etc.) degrees right (left), or full (standard) right (left) rudder, sir."
"HOW DOES SHE HEAD?" OR "MARK YOUR HEAD":	A question to the helmsman. He should give the ship's head at the time, for example, "Two seven five, sir."
"KEEP HER SO":	A command to the helmsman when he reports the ship's heading and it is desired to steady her on that heading.
"VERY WELL":	Given to the helmsman, after a report by him, to let him know that you understand the situation. (Never say, "All right," which is very bad sea language, and in addition may be confused with a command to the wheel.)
"COME RIGHT (LEFT) TO _____":	Put over the rudder right (left) and steady on new course.

In conning the ship, an officer should use common sense and knowledge of the helmsman's capabilities.

There is usually no need for all the detailed commands that are implicit in a change of course unless the helmsman is under instruction or the maneuver must be executed with extreme precision. With a moderately experienced helmsman, when making a change of course, it is sufficient to say, "Right standard rudder, Come to course _____." The helmsman repeats the command and reports when steady on the new course.

The conning officer can err in the other direction by not giving the helmsman enough information. For example, the officer of the deck gives the command, "Right standard rudder. Steady on course two seven zero." As the ship swings, the officer of the deck desires to speed up the process, and says, "Increase to right full." *He must then repeat,* "Steady on two seven zero," since each order to the helmsman cancels the preceding course order.

A final word about the helmsman: have him report properly the fact that he has been relieved and what orders he turned over to his relief. A proper report would be, "I have been relieved, sir. Steering course zero nine two, checking zero nine three."

COMMANDS TO LINE HANDLERS

Many a good approach to a landing is offset by improper use of mooring lines. Learn how to use them properly when getting underway as well as when mooring. This requires knowledge of standard commands to the line handlers.

The following examples and definitions are in common use in the fleet and can form the basis for all orders to lines. The orders should state number of line when appropriate. Mooring lines are numbered from forward aft in the order from which they are run out from the ship, but their names describe their location, use, and direction they tend as they leave the ship. 1, bow line; 2, after bow spring; 3, forward bow spring; 4, after quarter spring; 5, forward quarter spring; 6, stern line. The wait or breast line amidships is not numbered.

Command	Meaning
"STAND BY YOUR LINES":	Man the lines, ready to cast off or let go.
"LET GO" or "LET GO ALL LINES":	Slack off smartly to permit those tending lines on pier or another ship to cast off.
"SEND THE LINES OVER":	Pass the lines to the pier, place the eye over the appropriate bollard, but take no strain.
"TAKE A STRAIN ON SLACK":	Put line under tension. Take all tension off of line and let it hang slack.
"EASE":	Let line out until it is under less tension, but not slacked.
"TAKE—TO THE CAPSTAN":	Lead the end of line to the capstan, take the slack out of the line, but *take no strain*.
"HEAVE AROUND ON—":	Apply tension on line with the capstan.
"AVAST HEAVING":	Stop the capstan.
"HOLD WHAT YOU'VE GOT":	Hold the line as it is.
"HOLD":	Do not allow any more line to go out. (Caution—this risks parting the line).
"CHECK":	Hold heavy tension on line but render it (let it slip) as necessary to prevent parting the line.
"SURGE":	Hold moderate tension line, but render it enough to permit movement of the ship (used when mov-

Command	Meaning
	ing along the pier to adjust position).
"DOUBLE UP":	Pass an additional bight on all mooring lines so that there are three parts of each line to the pier.
"SINGLE UP":	Take in all bights and extra lines so there remains only a single part of each of the normal mooring lines.
"TAKE IN ALL LINES":	Used when secured with your *own* lines. Have the ends of all lines cast off from the pier and brought on board.
"CAST OFF ALL LINES":	Used when secured with *another* ship's lines in a nest. Cast off the ends of the lines and allow the other ship to retrieve her lines.
"SHIFT":	Used when moving a line along a pier. Followed by designating what line and where it is to go: "Shift number 3 from the bollard to the cleat."

Yelling at line handlers is unseamanlike and detracts from a smart operation; use telephone talkers for getting your commands out.

If it is desired to use the ship's auxiliary deck machinery to haul in on a line, the command is given, "Take one (number one) to the winch (capstan)." This may be followed by, "Heave around on one (number one)" and then, "Avast heaving on one (number one)."

It may be noted that the proper naval term for the line handling drum on the anchor windlass is *warping head*. Usage, however, has given authority to the synonyms *winch* or *capstan,* with winch the more common.

COMMANDS TO TUGBOAT

Tugs are handled more and more by two-way radio. However, these whistle and hand signals are still in use.

Hand Whistle

FROM STOP TO HALF SPEED AHEAD.	1 blast
FROM HALF SPEED AHEAD TO STOP.	1 blast
FROM HALF SPEED AHEAD TO FULL SPEED AHEAD.	4 short blasts
FROM FULL SPEED AHEAD TO HALF SPEED AHEAD.	1 blast
FROM STOP TO HALF SPEED ASTERN.	2 blasts
FROM HALF SPEED ASTERN TO FULL SPEED ASTERN.	4 short blasts
FROM HALF OR FULL SPEED ASTERN TO STOP.	1 blast
CAST OFF, STAND CLEAR.	1 prolonged, 2 short

Notes:

1. A blast is 2 to 3 seconds duration. A prolonged blast is 4 to 5 seconds duration. A short blast is about one second duration.

2. In using whistle signals to direct more than one tug, care must be exercised to ensure that the signal is directed to and received by the desired tug. Whistles of a different, distinct tone have been used successfully to handle more than one tug.

3. These signals may be transmitted to the tug by flashing light. Light signals should be used only when hand whistle or hand signals cannot be used.

4. Normally, whistle signals will be augmented by hand signals.

Hand Signals

HALF SPEED (ahead or astern)		Arm pointed in direction desired.
FULL SPEED (ahead or astern)		Fist describing arc (as in "bouncing" an engine telegraph).

Hand Signals

DEAD SLOW
(ahead or astern)

Undulating movement of open hand (palm down).

STOP

Open palm held aloft facing tug.

CAST OFF, STAND
CLEAR

Closed fist with thumb extended, swung up and down.

TUG TO USE RIGHT
RUDDER

Hand describing circle as if turning wheel to the right (clockwise), facing in the same direction as tug.

TUG TO USE LEFT
RUDDER

Hand describing circle as if turning wheel to the left (counterclockwise), facing in same direction as tug.

TUG TO USE RUDDER
AMIDSHIP

Arm at side of body with hand extended, swung back and forth.

Note:

Tug shall acknowledge all of the above signals with one short toot (one second or less) from her whistle, with the exception of the backing signal, which shall be acknowledged with two short toots, and the cast-off signal, which shall be acknowledged by one prolonged and two short toots.

Chapter X THE WATCH IN PORT

The officer of the deck shall carry out promptly and precisely the established routine and any special orders for the ship, weather and other circumstances permitting, and shall report any deviation therefrom to the commanding officer or executive officer, as appropriate. He shall follow, as practicable, the motions of the senior officer present in carrying out routine evolutions.—*Navy Regulations,* Article 1012.

While the ship in anchored or moored, the officer of the deck is spared the need for making quick decisions concerning shiphandling, tactical signals, and formation maneuvers. Nevertheless, the in-port routine, involving boats, vehicles, supplies, ship's work, personnel, visitors, honors and ceremonies, make a watch in port equally as demanding asone underway. The scope of responsibility is broad; the officer of the deck must feel responsible for all that happens on board, or is related to, his ship.

PETTY OFFICERS AS OOD

The performance of duties described in this chapter is not necessarily limited to commissioned officers, as Z-gram 44 issued by the Chief of Naval Operations on 13 October 1970 encourages the assignment of senior petty officers to officer of the deck (quarter-deck) watches in port.

There should be no confusion about the official status of petty officers so assigned; they are officers of the deck, subject only in the performance of duty to the orders of the commanding officer, executive officer, and command duty officer. The assignment of petty officers as officers of the deck should be made in writing by the commanding officer, the senior watch officer's watch list, or in the plan of the day.

RELIEVING THE WATCH

Detailed preparation is necessary before taking over the watch in port. In addition to becoming familiar with any pertinent operation plans or orders, there are usually senior officers present afloat (SOPA) instructions and port or harbor information booklets which contain important information on local services and facilities available, special hazards to boating, weather to be expected, etc. All this information is usually kept in an OOD folder.

Following are some of the most important items the officers of the deck must consider in port. Experience or special circumstances will suggest others:

1. How anchored or moored.
2. Position of ship on the chart.
3. When anchored, the anchorage bearings and nature of holding ground.
4. When anchored (or moored to a span), the anchor(s) in use, scope of chain, etc.
5. When moored to a buoy or buoys, the amount of chain or wire used.
6. When moored to a pier or alongside another ship, what lines are over, and what camels, fenders, and brows are in use.
7. When alongside, what services are being received.
8. Tide, depth of water, amount of rise and fall of the tide, state of tide, time and direction of last swing, time of next change of tide.
9. Status of engineering department: boilers in use, amount of steaming notice, if any; cold iron watch, if any.
10. Anchor(s) ready for letting go.
11. Status of gyro compass (running or secured).
12. State of the weather, and any anticipated changes.

13. Other ships present, and their locations.

14. SOPA and other commanders present, and their flagships.

15. Flags and pennants flying.

16. Guardships (military, medical, etc.), radio circuits manned, visual signal guards.

17. Status of all boats—in the water, in the skids, out of commission, at the ship, away on trips, trips scheduled, etc. Status of fuel in boats.

18. Status of vehicles—location, drivers, trips planned, fuel, etc.

19. Status of aircraft.

20. Location of captain, executive officer, and any flag officer or unit commander embarked, as well as his chief of staff and staff duty officer.

21. Time of return on board of captain or executive officer.

22. In the absence of a flag officer or unit commander embarked, the senior officer of his staff on board.

23. The officers with command duty and staff duty.

24. Work and drills in progress and scheduled.

25. Special security measures, such as fire watches and special weapons patrols, in force.

26. Visitors and workmen on board.

27. Important visitors expected.

28. Liberty—the commencement and time and location of expiration; number of men on liberty.

29. All unexecuted orders; status of prisoners, restricted men.

30. Telephone communications with the shore, including important telephone numbers (shore patrol, commanding officer's home, etc.).

31. Radio circuits with ships in harbor and beach guard; calls.

ORGANIZING THE WATCH

The watch should be organized and instructed as discussed in Chapter V, "The Watch Underway." Each key man should be checked to insure that he knows his duties and then supervised enough to insure that he performs them. Much of such supervision, as well as many administrative details, can be delegated to the junior officer of the deck or the petty officer of the watch. It is especially important that all personnel on watch, particularly those stationed on the quarter-deck, execute their duties smartly and be impeccable in their manner of wearing the uniform and in grooming.

Petty Officer of the Watch

Specifically when designated the *petty officer of the watch* (POOW) is the assistant to the officer of the deck and able to perform the duties assigned by the OOD. He inspects all packages carried aboard ship, reporting any irregularities to the officer of the deck and permits no unauthorized persons to come aboard, requiring positive identification from every individual. He prevents bumboats from coming alongside or having communication with or making sales to men on board ship, except as specifically authorized by the executive officer. He allows no enlisted men to leave the ship without authorization. He keeps a close watch on mooring lines and notifies the officer of the deck should it become necessary to adjust the lines. The POOW usually maintains a log of all occurrences during his watch, called the quartermaster's notebook (see Chapter III). See Chapter II for full discussion of duties of the boatswain's mate of the watch.

Master-at-Arms

In ships . . . there shall be assigned under the executive officer a chief master-at-arms, and such other masters-at-arms as may be required as his assistants, for the maintenance of good order and discipline.—*Navy Regulations,* Article 0806.

The chief master-at-arms, or in his absence, the duty master-at-arms, is a valuable assistant to the officer of the deck. He should be notified when changes in the day's routine are under consideration. He should also be used in making inspections. Above all, he is a major factor in maintaining order throughout the ship. See the *Ship's Organization and Regulations Manual* for detailed duties of the master-at-arms.

Messenger of the Watch

Commonly called OOD messenger, this man must be familiar with the names and locations of the various parts of the ship, with the department offices, and with the names and duties of the various officers and petty officers and where to find them.

Sounding and Security Patrol

In addition to the *"Cold Iron Watch"* (discussed later in this chapter under "Internal Security"), the in-port watch will include a petty officer who tours unmanned spaces, voids, and storerooms, reporting the results of inspections hourly to the POOW.

EXTERNAL SECURITY

At sea the officer of the deck has as his most important consideration the safety of his ship. In port, his major responsibility is security of the ship which can be threatened by many things: wind, waves, flooding, fire, sabotage from within the ship, saboteurs, sneak attack, civil disorder or riots.

Numerous threats to security may originate outside the ship. Strangers who approach the ship should be regarded with suspicion, even though they appear to be ordinary visitors, salesmen, agents, newsboys, or delivery men.

Control of Visitors

Attention is invited to the following pertinent extracts from *Navy Regulations,* Article 0733 and 0734.

The commanding officer shall not permit foreigners or representatives of foreign activities to make inspections on board naval vessels or aircraft or at naval activities, or to inspect work being done or material assembled or stored for the Naval Establishment at private manufacturing establishments, shipyards, or other places without specific permission of the Chief of Naval Operations. When such permission has been given, he shall detail an officer to accompany the visitor, and following the inspection shall advise the Chief of Naval Operations by letter as to the details of what was shown and what was refused.

Commanding officers are responsible for the control of visitors to activities of the Department of the Navy and shall comply with the relevant provisions of the Department of the Navy Security Manual for Classified Information and other pertinent directives. Commanding officers shall take such measures and impose any restrictions on visitors as necessary to safeguard the classified material under their jurisdiction. Arrangements for visiting shall always be based on the assumption that foreign agents will be among the visitors.

In general, dealers or tradesmen or their agents shall not be admitted within a command, except as authorized by the commanding officer for the following purposes:

1. To conduct public business.

2. To transact specific private business with individuals at the request of the latter.

3. To furnish services and supplies which are necessary and which are not otherwise, or are insufficiently, available to the personnel of the command.

Current fleet and force regulations restricting general and casual visiting and the approach of bumboats should be followed with great care. Persons with a legitimate reason to come on board must be received politely. But the uniform alone is not always a guarantee of trustworthiness. If circumstances warrant (and directives may so require), every person coming on board, whether in uniform or professing official government or business connections, should present proper identification. The more difficult the circumstances may be for the officer of the deck to screen visitors, the more important it is that all precautions be observed. Enemy agents may be expected to take advantage of such occasions as Armed Forces Day or the arrival of a ship at a shipyard.

Inspections

In addition to identifying all individuals coming on board, the officer of the deck should investigate all packages, parcels, brief cases, tool boxes, etc., that are introduced into the ship. The chances are that your biggest haul will be drugs or liquor, but there is always the possibility that materials for sabotage may be intercepted.

Sentries and Guards

When sentries and armed guards are required, the officer of the deck will normally have only to implement existing directives covering the use of *forecastle, fantail,* and *pier sentries.* All sentries posted for security purposes will be guided by written instructions, and must know how to challenge boats in order to identify occupants before they come alongside. The pier sentry will control flow of personnel and traffic on the pier. Forecastle and fantail sentries must check mooring lines and make periodic reports to the officer of the deck. All sentries may be armed when the situation demands. The use of armed guards should be of direct concern to the officer of the deck; he must be certain that the men assigned as sentries or guards are reasonably proficient in the use of their weapons. If doubt exists, send for a gunner's mate with the duty, and have the men properly instructed. An armed man who does not know his weapon is useless at his post, and a danger to his ship and shipmates.

In foreign ports an external security watch is usually set in accordance with a special bill in the ship's organization. This may include setting a picket-boat watch around the ship. The organization and equipment of such a boat patrol is covered in *NWP 50(A)*.

Sneak Attack and Sabotage

Particularly during hours of darkness, ships at anchor or moored are vulnerable to various forms of sneak attack or sabotage, conducted by swimmers from shore, small boats, a midget submarine, or a submarine. Limpet mines may be attached to the hull of the ship, explosive charges may be placed on the bottom below the ship, or mobile limpets may be used. Suicide swimmers and boats have been used in the past. The use of boarders posing as bumboat crews is possible. Saboteurs may mingle with the returning liberty party or pose as visitors. Surreptitious entry from the shore is possible when ships are moored to a pier. Attack may consist of contamination of food and water supplies or destruction of vital equipment by explosives or other means. Where such dangers of attack exist, normal security measures must be increased. The operations officer will organize, supervise, and coordinate all phases of maintaining security against sneak attack.

The officer of the deck will maintain gangway security by identifying all approaching boats, and consider all boats, persons, and packages suspect until positively identified and inspected.

All unnecessary lines, fenders and sea ladders should be taken in. Boats not in use should be hoisted in, and booms rigged out of reach of swimmers or boats. Guards should be posted at all topside openings and a party held in readiness to repel boarders. Automatic weapons should be manned, and all personnel armed. Unnecessary noise should be avoided. Swimmers and EOD personnel may be assigned to inspect the ship's bottom after all sentries and boats have been warned that own personnel are in the water, ensuring that no explosive charges will be dropped, and securing the sonar.

If an attack has started, the highest degree of material readiness should be set, the rail manned with armed personnel, and SOPA and all ships present notified.

Detailed instructions governing other measures will be found in the *Ship's Organization and Regulations Manual*. These include the establishment of armed boat patrols, maintainence of watertight integrity, steaming watches, darkening ship, and lighting of adjacent areas.

ANCHORAGE AND MOORINGS

The officer of the deck has his greatest responsibilities in relation to the weather when his ship is anchored, moored, or secured to a pier or wharf. At sea the commanding officer is on the bridge and makes the big decisions; in port the officer of the deck must often take action before the commanding officer can be aroused.

Meteorological forecasts are in general excellent but are not always available, nor can they be 100 per cent accurate. They may even lull inexperienced officers into a false sense of security. The *actual* weather at your position is the important factor, not the weather that is *forecast* for your position. It is advisable for the officer of the deck to know what sort of weather can be expected in a certain area at a certain time of year. Pilot charts are one source of this information. There may be very little possibility of winds over 40 knots in San Diego Bay, at any time: but at Adak in the Aleutians, the wind can whip up to 60 knots almost any afternoon. The local topography sometimes make a great difference in the incidence of high winds that could endanger an anchored ship.

Scope of Chain

It is a common practice to use a length of anchor chain equal to six times the depth of water. The following table is a more accurate guide:

DEPTH OF WATER	RECOMMENDED SCOPE
Up to 10 fathoms	Depth multiplied by 7
10 to 15 fathoms	Depth multiplied by 6
15 to 20 fathoms	Depth multiplied by 5
20 to 30 fathoms	Depth multiplied by 4
Over 30 fathoms	Depth multiplied by 3

The guide applies only when moderately severe winds, perhaps up to force 7 are expected. In extremely high winds longer scope is necessary to take advantage of the maximum holding power of the ground tackle. See *Knight's Modern Seamanship* for a table giving maximum effective scope, and an excellent discussion of ground tackle and its use in anchoring.

Dragging

When at anchor, the officer of the deck shall take proper precautions to detect and prevent dragging.—*Navy Regulations,* Article 1014.

The most certain indication of dragging is a change in your anchorage bearings, particularly those bearings near the beam. These should be checked at regular intervals even in good weather. Ships have been known to part their chain upon dropping the anchor, and will then, of course, drag at the slightest provocation, since only the anchor cable which is lying in the bottom is holding. Another sign of dragging anchor can be discovered by watching the chain or by feeling it on deck. Chain secured to a dragging anchor usually reveals by its pulsation that the anchor is not holding. Anchor chains pulsate or jump when the anchor is dragging because the flukes are alternately taking hold and then being pulled loose.

Drift Lead

A drift lead should be put over the side when there is any possibility of dragging, either owing to wind, poor holding ground, or strong currents. It can either be dropped straight down, with slack in the line, or dropped aft, with a taut line leading forward. In either case a change in the slackness or tautness of the line will indicate dragging, providing the ship is not yawing. As long as a ship is fairly steady, a drift lead will usually give notice in case of dragging, but if she sheers about considerably, it cannot be relied upon.

If the ship is discovered to be dragging, the officer of the deck should take immediate action—alert the engine room and anchor detail—then call the commanding officer. In a crowded anchorage or when near a lee shore, the general alarm should also be sounded.

Collision and Grounding

The major safeguards to prevent collision or grounding caused by dragging are (1) having an anchor ready for letting go, and (2) having steam at the throttle with the steering gear ready for use and the engine room ready to answer all bells. The latter, of course, is expensive in man hours and fuel and should not be directed without good cause. However, an officer of the deck should not hesitate to call the commanding officer and inform him of the possibility of dragging. The commanding officer will then decide what precautionary measures, in addition to the normal one of having a second anchor ready, shall be taken.

A ship secured to a mooring buoy by her anchor chain is rarely in danger except in exceedingly high winds, providing the mooring itself is well anchored. There are times, however, in very severe weather when destroyers and smaller vessels have been known to carry away from a mooring. This generally has happened when too little scope of chain to the buoy was used. The chop raised in the harbor by the strong winds was sufficient to cause the bow of the ship to rise and fall. Without a long enough scope of chain whose catenary provides a spring, the sudden strain as the bow of the ship pitches is sufficient to part the chain or the chain stopper on deck. To counter the yaw resulting from a longer scope to the buoy, an anchor dropped under foot is often useful.

Heavy Weather

Alongside a pier or wharf, with the standard mooring lines doubled up, there is little danger from high winds, except in extreme cases. When heavy seas and high winds are anticipated, the officer of the deck shall:

1. Request permission to hoist in all boats in the water, and to trice up gangways. Boat pool boats shall be returned to their base or secured astern on long painters, and a special boat watch established.

2. Call away the anchor detail and be prepared to get underway or veer chains as may be directed.

3. Have second gyro compass started and ship's posi-

tion checked continuously by bearings; shift watch to bridge.

4. Put over drift lead.

The officer of the deck usually will not have to make major decisions under these circumstances, since most of his seniors will be aboard.

Extreme Temperatures

In addition to wind there may be the hazard or extreme discomfort of very low or very high temperatures. The former can cause material damage, such as ruptured fire-main risers in exposed locations, and can also greatly diminish the ship's capacity to use her armament or equipment. It is not practicable to enumerate here the many precautions and special measures to be taken when operating in extreme cold. That information is found in *Cold Weather Operating Procedures NWP 35, Naval Arctic Operations ATP 17,* and the *Manual of Ice Seamanship HO 551.* It is merely desired to make the officer of the deck aware that special problems do exist.

Very high temperatures and humidity may affect electronics, magazines, rocket and torpedo stowage in addition to having an important influence on the health, comfort, and performance of the crew. Most modern naval ships are air-conditioned but occasionally it may be necessary to cool some spaces by rigging auxiliary blowers or by wetting the exposed deck area with a fire hose.

HURRICANES AND TYPHOONS

When there has been warning of a hurricane or typhoon moving into your area, it must be decided whether to put to sea to avoid the storm, or remain in port and ride it out. If the former, the general procedures described in Chapter VI, under "Hurricanes and Typhoons", should be followed. If the ship remains in port, it may move to a sheltered anchorage, or remain at its berth in which case all preparations for getting underway should be made, in addition to carrying out the precautions listed for heavy weather. Preliminary preparations for riding out a storm are normally prescribed in the SOPA instructions, and include the following:

Mooring lines should be doubled up, and continually inspected.

Personnel must be recalled to ship, and engineering plant and sea detail placed on stand-by.

Radio and signal watch must be maintained, radar manned, and plot of storm kept in CIC.

Dock area must be policed, topside gear secured, heavy weather gear and flashlights broken out, and rescue-assistance lockers inventoried.

Crew should be briefed on movements of storm.

If the ship is to remain in port, at anchor, the same procedure should be followed. The anchorage should allow room to swing with the longest scope of chain available. Main engines should be used to offset the wind, with RPM equivalent to from three to five knots.

Keep close watch for dragging by use of bearings on shore, radar, drift lead, and continuous echo soundings. The chain should be watched continuously for signs of dragging anchor.

For complete details on procedures to be followed in hurricane or typhoon conditions, underway or in port, read *Heavy Weather Guide*. (See Bibliography.)

INTERNAL SECURITY

The safety of the ship may also be threatened by persons or forces within the ship. Sabotage by a member of the crew is possible, particularly in times of great international tension. Abrasives in lubricating oil and nails driven into multiple conductor cables can cause great damage. A more common problem is the danger of fire or flooding owing to factors that can be anticipated and controlled. The ship's organization specifies a security patrol and a sounding patrol. Sometimes these patrols are combined. The officer of the deck should insure that these patrols are being carried out and the reports are made to him in person and on time. In addition, the quartermaster must log the reports in his notebook. The personnel involved should be instructed and supervised as necessary. In addition to routine checks for watertight closures and security, the patrols should be alert to fire hazards, such as the accumulation of trash, and the presence of combustibles, such as paint that has not been properly stowed in the paint locker.

Cold Iron Watch

In addition to routine security and sounding patrols, a ship whose main machinery is inactive or which has no auxiliary watch on duty below stations a "cold iron watch." This watch consists of men of the engineer force who at regular intervals inspect all machinery spaces for violations of watertight integrity and for fire hazards. The results of these inspections should be logged in the quartermaster's notebook.

Shipyard Security

Except in matters coming within the police regulations of the ship, the commanding officer shall exercise no control over the officers or employees of a naval shipyard or station where his ship is moored, unless with the permission of the commander of the naval shipyard or station.

The officer of the deck shall take necessary measures to prevent the introduction in or removal from the ship of unauthorized articles.—*Navy Regulations,* Articles 0766 and 1019.

A ship under repair and overhaul in a shipyard has security problems of a particularly acute nature. *All work-*

men coming on board must be identified. Their tools may be stowed in racks on deck and should be safeguarded by ship's sentries. Like all other respectable working men, most shipyard workers are honest. But a small percentage will not be able to resist a souvenir or two, particularly tools that are left adrift. It must be the unpleasant duty of the watch on deck to see that theft is kept to a minimum, both by ship and shipyard personnel.

Compartments containing classified matter must be secured, either by locking or by sentries. There are sometimes occasions when yard workmen must enter these spaces, and the officer of the deck can anticipate matters if he keeps himself reasonably well informed of the nature and location of the work being done aboard ship. *Fire watches are normally assigned each welder and burner who comes on board.* Another special precaution to be taken during shipyard work is to *inspect spaces after each shift for rubbish and other material that may be a fire hazard.*

Other Inspections

In addition to the material inspections discussed above, the officer of the deck should direct his assistants, the junior officer of the deck, the petty officer of the watch, or the master-at-arms, to make inspections throughout the ship, day and night. Particular vigilance must be exercised to prevent gambling, smuggling of liquor or the introduction of drugs, and only an alert watch and thorough inspection will prevent such practices. A well-organized ship, properly inspected, will have substantially less trouble than a loosely organized, poorly disciplined ship. All such inspections are made at irregular intervals and should be as comprehensive as practicable. Their objective is the preservation of good order and discipline and the enforcement of such items of the daily routine as reveille, tattoo, and taps. By this means the officer of the deck keeps informed of what is going on and sees that the daily routine is carried out.

Custody of Keys

A matter of minor importance that can prove difficult to the officer of the deck, is the custody of ship's keys. Heads of departments are normally responsible for the keys to locked spaces under their cognizance, except that the keys to magazines are kept by the commanding officer and those to lockers containing alcohol and drugs are usually in the custody of the executive officer or medical officer. Narcotics are kept in a safe with an officer custodian having the combination. If keys are kept in their specified places and are not carried on the person of some petty officer, then all those with proper authorization can obtain ready entry to locked spaces. More important, in the event of an emergency such as fire, access can readily be obtained to locked compartments or storerooms.

THE SIGNAL BRIDGE

An officer of the deck in port relies on his signal force on watch to keep him informed of ship and boat movements, particularly the approach of important officers, such as the captain, or of important visitors. This, of course, is but one of their duties; they are usually engaged in sending or receiving visual messages. An alert signal force is one of the marks of a smart ship, and the officer of the deck should do all in his power to gain that distinction for his ship. He should demand a sharp lookout and prompt reports. In some large ships, such as aircraft carriers, the officer of the deck is not stationed where he can maintain a proper lookout himself.

When stationed, bridge and signal watches perform, in addition to regular duties, the following functions with regard to security:

1. Notify the officer of the deck of changes in weather.

2. Maintain surveillance of the harbor and report boats approaching the ship to the officer of the deck.

3. Report any unusual disturbances or signs of distress within the harbor.

4. Report movements of other ships within the harbor.

SMART APPEARANCE

In port, particularly, the smart appearance of the ship, her boats, and her crew, is a major responsibility of the officer of the deck. The officer of the deck must first of all know the proper standards of cleanliness and smartness, and he must then enforce these standards. It takes only time and a little practice to note such things as irish pennants, slack halyards and sloppy execution of colors. But it takes energy, initiative, and patience both to observe deficiencies and to take action to correct them. Junior officers vary widely in their powers of observation and in their attitude about taking action. *The sooner an officer acquires a reputation for standing a taut watch and for being intolerant of anything that downgrades his ship, the more readily will the crew respond.* Such an officer will not be likely to have men come on watch on the quarter-deck in frayed or soiled uniforms. Men do not try to go ashore on liberty during his watch without adequate grooming. He will, in short, find his high standards easier to maintain. On the other hand, an officer who is slovenly and who has not the moral responsibility nor the pride to stand a proper watch, will find himself in continual hot water. His superiors will be constantly calling him on the appearance of the ship, and the crew will become less responsive to him. Early in your career, resolve to run a taut and efficient watch, with the ship and her personnel looking shipshape and smart at all times. Men will respect an officer who knows his job and performs his duties fairly and pleasantly but in accordancc with all directives and the traditionally high standards of the Navy.

Training

Another aspect of watch standing that should be considered is training. An important indoctrination that men receive in the Navy is on-the-job training—learning while they are doing. A normal watch, and particularly a quiet and uneventful one, offers many opportunities to train the men in their own duties and even in other jobs with which they should be familiar. By the exercise of a little ingenuity on the part of the officer of the deck, even the dullest watch can be made interesting and worthwhile. Lookouts can take a trick at the wheel, the quartermaster can teach the boatswain's mate some navigation, the boatswain's mate can drill the messenger in man overboard procedure, and use of the various general alarms.

An especially important part of indoctrination and training is that given to new men reporting aboard for duty. The officer of the deck can play a vital part in giving the new men a good first impression. Check to see that they are provided with bunks and lockers and are assigned to a division. The Executive Officer usually will arrange a conducted tour of the ship for the new men. Make certain they know their way around: they will be of little use either in work or in an emergency until they do. A well-administered ship has detailed plans ready for receiving new men; the officer of the deck is responsible for starting this procedure.

STORES, FUEL, AND PROVISIONS

When loading stores, the officer of the deck makes certain that the right people have been notified and are in charge. The deck force is responsible for operating the gear and tackle needed, and the officer of the deck should check to see that a competent boatswain's mate is on the job. The supply officer or his representative should check the stores aboard and direct their stowage.

Since the commanding officer of the ship is responsible for both the quantity and quality of fuel oil received, it is advisable for the officer of the deck to take an interest in the fuel barge that comes alongside in port. The engineer officer (or the one with the day's duty) and the "oil king" (the petty officer in charge of fuel records) should be notified. The amount of oil received aboard is also logged, as well as the ship's draft before and after fueling.

LIBERTY

Liberty is normally granted to the men by sections. Sections are the basic units of the ship's company. Each man is assigned to a section for liberty, watch standing, condition watches, messing, and berthing. Each complete section is adequate to maneuver and fight the ship within the limits of the personnel available. Each section, therefore, includes adequate ratings, numbers, and qualifications to man all required stations in emergencies, including getting underway and proceeding to sea, surprise hostile action, rescue and assistance, disaster ashore, etc. This is why it is important for liberty to be strictly controlled, so that the ship's capability to respond to emergencies can be maintained.

Inspection of Liberty Parties

The officer of the deck in port is responsible for getting men off on liberty on time and after a thorough inspection. This inspection should not be perfunctory. *Men going on liberty must be in clean, regulation uniforms, or other authorized clothing.* Men must have their hair properly cut, beards neatly shaved, and shoes shined.*

---

* Third class petty officers and above may wear civilian clothing to and from the ship on liberty, as authorized by the Chief of Naval Operations in Z-gram 05 of 30 July 1970 and Z-gram 68 of 23 December 1970.

Men who have slight deficiencies should be warned; those who definitely fail to pass inspection should be directed to correct their shortcomings. Be firm but fair; a moderately worn uniform, if clean and pressed should pass, while a new pair of shoes, dull and dusty, should not. When sending a liberty party ashore, remind the younger, less experienced men that the reputation of the Navy and the ship depends on their appearance and conduct ashore.

The return of liberty parties may be a routine matter or, under different circumstances, may be quite a lively occasion. Under normal conditions the officer of the deck has only to identify the men. If the ship has just made port after a long voyage, or is sailing the next day for an extended absence, there may be a few tipsy or noisy celebrants. Have a master-at-arms or corporal of the guard get them off the quarter-deck and persuade them in turn in below quietly. The officer of the deck must remain apart from any confusion that may arise and should let his experienced assistants handle matters. Persistent rowdies or troublemakers may require your special attention, and direct orders may be needed to control them. Avoid physical contact; let the enlisted men in the watch handle those men who will not go below peacefully. The men who are most in need of your attention are those who are brought aboard apparently drunk. Have these men taken to sick bay and examined; they may have head injuries or be drugged instead of, or in addition to, being drunk. If necessary, arouse the medical officer and have him make the examinations. Matters of this sort must be recorded fully in the log, together with the written report of the medical examination.

Loading Liberty Boats

While juniors in the Navy normally embark in boats and vehicles before their seniors, there is a time when the usual procedure may very well be reversed. When embarking liberty parties into boats or busses, allow the chief petty officers to go first, followed by the other petty officers in descending order of rank. This practice will enhance the prestige of the petty officers and provide a convenience which they well deserve. Also, in large ships with many officers waiting to go ashore, it may be necessary to limit the number of junior officers embarking in order to insure room for the senior officers.

EIGHT O'CLOCK REPORTS

Eight o'clock reports are an important part of the ship's routine. They serve two functions: to insure that the necessary security and damage control inspections and checks have been made, and to furnish the executive officer with the information he needs to make his report on the condition of the ship at 2000 to the commanding officer. (In accordance with time-honored custom of the service, the reports made to the executive officer or command duty officer by the heads of departments at 2000 are known as the *eight o'clock reports,* not the *twenty hundred reports.*)

WORKING PARTIES

The ship's schedule may often require large working parties to complete, without rest, an important evolution such as provisioning ship. These matters are normally accepted by the men with reasonable understanding. Many times, when only small groups are involved, the officer of the deck can contribute to the well-being of the crew by exercising forehandedness, good judgment, and consideration for the men's comfort. Leisure time and meal hours should be respected as much as possible. Men who are working hard through meal times should not be required to shift into another uniform just for the meal and should have complete and hot meals saved for them if they miss the regular one. Working parties leaving the ship should be provided with such comforts as rain gear, drinking water, etc., when circumstances warrant. When men are required to do work that results in loss of sleep or prevents having regular meals, it is incumbent upon the responsible officer, when the work is completed, to see that they are given rest, meals, or compensatory release from regular duties.

SHORE PATROL

When liberty is granted to any considerable number of persons, except in a city large enough to care properly for them without danger of disturbance or disorder, the senior officer present shall cause to be established a sufficient patrol of officers, petty officers, and noncommissioned officers, in charge of an officer, to maintain order and suppress any unseemly conduct on the part of any member of the liberty party. The senior patrol officer shall communicate with the chief of police or other local officials and make such arrangements as may be practicable to aid the patrol in properly carrying out its duties.

A patrol shall not be landed in any foreign port without first obtaining the consent of the proper local officials. Tact must be used in requesting this permission, and unless it is willingly and cordially given, the patrol shall not be landed. If consent cannot be obtained, the size of the liberty parties shall be held to such limits as may be necessary to render disturbances unlikely.

Officers and men on patrol duty in a foreign country shall be unarmed; when in a United States port, officers and men shall be armed as prescribed by the senior officer present.

No officer or man who is a member of the shore patrol shall, while on watch, on post, or at other times prescribed by the senior officer, partake of or indulge in any form of intoxicating liquor or other form of intoxicant or narcotic. The senior patrol officer shall see that the provisions of this paragraph are strictly observed, and shall promptly report to the senior officer present, in writing, all violations of it that may come to his notice. All officers and men of the patrol shall report to the senior patrol officer all violations of the provisions of this paragraph on the part of those under them.—*Navy Regulations,* Article 0625.

Shore patrol is established and operated in accordance with needs of the naval service for the maintenance of order, the enforcement of naval and local regulations, and the protection and assistance of naval personnel ashore.

The jurisdiction of the shore patrol extends over all persons subject to the Uniform Code of Military Justice, both male and female.

Shore patrol is vested with authority to discharge fully its duties and functions by the command establishing the shore patrol, and it is a principal agency through which the command enforces compliance with naval law and maintains naval discipline ashore. Officers, petty officers, and non-commissioned officers shall, by their conduct, command the respect of all members of the armed services, and reflect credit on the naval services. Members of the shore patrol are forbidden to partake of any intoxicating liquor, including beer and wine, at any time when on patrol duty or when subject to call for duty. Members of the shore patrol found to be violating the trust, or wrongfully using the authority vested in them, or found to be under the influence of intoxicating liquor or consuming intoxicating liquor while on duty will be tried by courts-martial.—*Bureau of Naval Personnel Manual,* Articles C–7902, C–7903, and C–7904.

The material quoted above, together with the *United States Navy Shore Patrol Manual,* provides the basic directive for shore patrol activity. The officer of the deck in port is certain to have dealings with shore patrol personnel, if only to see that the men and officers detailed from the ship are sent ashore. It is desirable that the officer of the deck know in general how the shore patrol is organized, what its purpose is, and how it operates. Normally, ship's personnel detailed for shore patrol duty will already have been instructed in their duties and responsibilities. It is a function of the executive officer to insure that a division officer or experienced petty officer does the instructing. But on occasion an officer of the deck may have to detail men who have not been instructed. It is his responsibility, then, to break out the manual and see that the men are informed.

Requirements for shore patrol are generally included in SOPA instructions.

APPREHENSION AND RESTRAINT

An officer of the deck must know the difference between *apprehension* and the three degrees of *restraint: confinement, arrest, and restriction in lieu of arrest.*

The officer of the deck will have occasion to receive custody of men charged with misconduct. The men may be delivered by the shore patrol or by an officer or petty officer aboard ship. They may even deliver themselves for minor offenses, such as being out of uniform. It is important that the officer of the deck know the legal meanings of the terms involved, and also know what action to take.

All officers, petty officers, and noncommissioned officers of any service have authority to apprehend offenders subject to the *Uniform Code of Military Justice.* Other enlisted men may do so when assigned shore patrol, military police, and similar duties. *Apprehension* is accomplished by clearly informing the person that he is being taken into custody. He should be told at the same time what he is accused of. It should be noted here that *apprehension,* in the Armed Services, has the same meaning as *arrest* has in civilian life. Just as a police officer informs a citizen that he is under *arrest* so does a naval officer tell a man that he is being apprehended or is being taken into *custody. Custody* is temporary control over the person apprehended until he is delivered to the proper authority (on board ship, the officer of the deck). In general, persons who have authority to apprehend may exercise only such force as is actually necessary. Petty officers should apprehend officers only under very unusual circumstances, such as to avoid disgrace to the service.

Restraint involves some deprivation of free movement of the person restrained. Restraint is never imposed as a punishment, and the degree of restraint used should be no more severe than that necessary to insure the presence of the offender at further proceedings in his case. Thus, even though a man has committed an offense or is suspected of such, he need not be restrained to any degree if his presence is assured at future proceedings.

Only the commanding officer may impose any degree of restraint on a commissioned officer or a warrant officer. If it is desired to restrain an officer, the commanding officer must be notified.

Only officers may ordinarily impose any degree of restrain on an enlisted man. However, the commanding officer may delegate this authority to warrant officers and enlisted men.

Confinement is an actual physical restraint imposed in serious offenses to insure the presence of the person.

Arrest is the moral restraint of a person, by an order, oral or written, to certain specified limits pending disposition of charges against him. It is not imposed as punishment. It is imposed only for probable cause, based on known or reported facts concerning an alleged offense. *Arrest* relieves a man of all military duties other than normal cleaning and policing. *Arrest* is imposed by telling a man (or officer) of the limits of his arrest.

One of the disadvantages of placing an accused in arrest is that he may no longer be required to perform his military duties, and if the authority ordering this type of restraint requires the accused to perform his military duties, the arrest is automatically terminated. Consequently, a lesser form of restraint is allowed. This is called, "Restriction in lieu of arrest."

Restriction is a restraint of the same nature as arrest, imposed under similar circumstances and by the same authorities, but it does not involve the suspension of military duties.

A prisoner at large (PAL) is a man under arrest or restriction and it is important that he be informed of which status is applicable in his case.

Persons apprehended aboard ship are delivered to the custody of the officer of the deck together with a misconduct report. The officer of the deck informs the executive officer (or command duty officer) and receives instructions regarding the nature of restraint to be imposed on the man. The restraint, of course, normally depends on the gravity of the offense. Assuming that formal restraint, such as arrest, is ordered, the officer of the deck notifies the offender, insuring that he, the offender, understands the nature of his restraint and the penalties for violation of restraint. The officer of the deck secures the offender's written acknowledgment of his notification by his signature upon the misconduct report slip, and then turns the offender over to the master-at-arms. The whole matter is logged, of course, with full details.

Restraint does not have to be imposed on an accused. The whole purpose of restraint is to insure the presence of the accused at a subsequent trial or disposition of his case. Thus, if the offense is relatively minor, and it can be assumed that the accused will not attempt to leave the area to avoid trial, no restraint is necessary. Confinement is used before trial only in such cases where there is a risk of the accused attempting to escape punishment. The lesser forms of restraint impose a burden on the accused because it is a punishable offense to violate the limits of the restraint. Restraint once imposed may not be removed except in the following circumstances: arrest and restriction in lieu of arrest may be lifted by the authority ordering the restraint, or a superior in his chain of command. Once a person is confined, he passes from the jurisdiction of the person ordering confinement, and can only be released by order of the commanding officer of the activity where the confinement takes place. On board ship, this situation poses no special problem because, generally, the authority ordering the confinement is also the commanding officer of the confining activity.

For further discussion of this subject, read Chapter II of *Military Law*. (See Bibliography.)

ASYLUM

Under international law, political or other refugees may be granted asylum on board a naval vessel. And in exceptional circumstances temporary refuge may be granted when life may be endangered by a mob. Any such action must be in complete accordance with the following:

Granting of asylum and temporary refuge.

1. If an official of the Department of the Navy is requested to provide asylum or temporary refuge, the following procedures shall apply:

A. On the high seas or in territories under exclusive United States jurisdiction (including territorial seas, territories and possessions):

(1) At his request, an applicant for asylum will be received on board any naval aircraft or water-borne craft or naval station.

(2) Under no circumstances shall the person seeking asylum be surrendered to foreign jurisdiction or control unless directed by the Chief of Naval Operations, Commandant of the Marine Corps or higher authority. Persons seeking asylum should be afforded every reasonable care and protection permitted by the circumstances.

B. In territories under foreign jurisdiction (including territorial seas, territories, and possessions):

(1) Temporary refuge shall be granted for humanitarian reasons on board a naval aircraft or water-borne craft or naval station only in extreme or exceptional circumstances wherein the life or safety of a person is put in danger, such as pursuit by a mob. When temporary refuge is granted, such protection shall be terminated only when directed by the Chief of Naval Operations, Commandant of the Marine Corps, or higher authority.

(2) While temporary refuge can be granted in the circumstances set forth above, permanent asylum will not be granted.

(3) Requests for asylum shall be referred to the U.S. Embassy, if any, in the foreign jurisdiction. Individuals requesting asylum shall be afforded temporary refuge only in the circumstances outlined in sub-paragraph (1).

C. The Chief of Naval Operations or Commandant of the Marine Corps, as appropriate, will be informed by the most expeditious means of all action taken pursuant to A and B above as well as the attendant circumstances. The appropriate U.S. Embassy or consular post will be similarly informed of actions taken pursuant to sub-paragraph 1.B(3) of this article. The Chief of Naval Operations or Commandant of the Marine Corps will cause the Secretary of the Navy and Department of State to be notified without delay.

2. Personnel of the Department of the Navy shall neither directly nor indirectly invite persons to seek asylum or temporary refuge.—Advance change to *Navy Regulations,* Article 0621.

REPORTING AND DETACHMENT OF PERSONNEL

An officer of the deck will appreciate that the first impression made on newly reporting officers and men is important. For this reason certain fixed procedures should be carried out. The officer of the deck should establish an officer's identity, should make appropriate arrangements for his baggage, and then see that he is escorted to the executive officer or the command duty officer. An enlisted man, after identification and assistance with baggage, should be turned over with his records to the chief (or duty) master-at-arms who will take him to the ship's personnel office. After the necessary paperwork is completed in the personnel office, the master-at-arms should assign the man a bunk and locker. This all sounds simple, but a large draft of new men received just before sailing will often present real problems. Whatever the means you employ, try to ensure that both men and officers are made to feel welcome and are processed on board as quickly and painlessly as possible.

CREW'S MESS

Each meal served in the general mess shall be sampled by an officer detailed by the commanding officer for that purpose. Should this officer find the quality or quantity of food unsatisfactory, or should any member of the mess object to the quality or quantity of the food, the commanding officer shall be immediately notified and he shall take appropriate action.— *Navy Regulations,* Article 1982.

It is normal procedure, when in port, for the command duty officer, or the officer of the deck, to eat at least one meal in the crew's mess during his watch. When underway, one of the watch officers should eat a meal with the crew daily. Officers eating with the crew should note not only the quantity and quality of the food, and that their portion is representative of that being served the men, but, equally important, the cleanliness and adequacy of mess gear, the manner in which food is being served, and the cleanliness of food handlers. It is not unusual for the commanding officer to unexpectedly eat with the crew in order to check on these important items himself.

Night Rations

It is a custom of long standing to serve a night ration to those having the midwatch. This helps people keep awake and sustains them through the night tasks which are often just as demanding as those of the day. In cold weather, a warm ration is especially welcome, either to those going on or coming off watch topside, as well as to those standing watch in the engineering spaces.

VISITORS AND OBSERVERS

Visitors aboard ship will require the attention of the officer of the deck. They may be distinguished officials or civilians, with VIP status, representatives of the press or communications media, officers and men from another ship coming aboard in the role of observers for a practice or exercise, or friends or dependents of crew members. According to their status, some will have papers to be checked: invitational travel orders, security clearances, or official orders, and such visitors must all be logged in.

Visitors should be properly met, and distinguished officials or officers should be accorded honors, if appropriate. Visitors who will remain on board over night should be escorted to their quarters. The Public Affairs Officer usually sees to this, and will also explain berthing and messing arrangements, as well as provide necessary wearing apparel, life jackets, and instructions on the ship's routine, and how to find their way about. Officers and men coming on board as observers will usually know their way around and need only to know where they are to eat. Observers will frequently need office space.

Prior arrangements for receiving all visitors will usually be made by the Executive Officer, and either that officer or the Commanding Officer will designate those whose status or rank rates special treatment. The Chief Master-at-Arms will normally handle enlisted visitors.

Chapter XI SAFETY

The officer of the deck shall ensure that necessary measures and precautions are taken to prevent accidents. Particular care shall be exercised in heavy weather, and when men are working aloft, over the side, or in confined spaces, and when inflammables and explosives, or any other dangerous materials are being handled. Means for recovery of persons falling overboard shall be available and ready for instant use.

Before turning over the main engines by power when not underway, the officer of the deck shall ascertain that it is safe to do so and that competent persons are stationed to give and execute the necessary signals; and he shall then obtain permission from the commanding officer.—*Navy Regulations,* Article 1014.

Safety must be practiced on a 24-hour day basis. Danger exists in every naval operation and aboard every naval vessel. Going to sea involves working with powerful machinery, high-speed equipment, intensely high temperature-pressure steam, volatile and exotic fuels and propellants, heavy lifts, high explosives, stepped-up electrical voltages, and the unpredictable, elemental forces of wind and wave. Young sailors are inexperienced and inclined to be careless if not downright reckless. It is an officer's responsibility to protect the lives of his men and the safety of his ship by observing all precautions.

There are innumerable safety regulations in various publications. Every piece of machinery and equipment must be operated in a safe manner, and specialized safety precautions have been provided for all such equipment to ensure safe operation. The *Naval Ships Technical Manual* contains safety precautions, as do various bureau manuals. The *Ship's Organization and Regulation Manual* for each type of vessel will contain safety regulations written for that particular type of ship. The following general instructions are merely an introduction to the whole subject of safety.

Ammunition (see also *"Underway Replenishment"*)

1. All personnel required to handle ammunition shall be carefully and frequently instructed in the safety regulations, methods of handling, storage, and uses of all kinds of ammunition and explosive ordnance with which the ship, aircraft unit, or station may be supplied.

2. No one shall be permitted to inspect, prepare, or adjust live ammunition and explosives until he thoroughly understands his duties, the precautions, and the hazards involved.

3. Only careful, reliable, mentally sound, and physically fit persons shall be permitted to work with or use explosives or ammunition.

4. All persons who supervise the inspection, care, preparation, handling, use, or disposal of ammunition or explosives shall:

a. Exercise the utmost care that all regulations and instructions are observed, and remain vigilant throughout the operation.

b. Carefully instruct and frequently warn those under them of the need for care and constant vigilance.

c. Prior to beginning the operation, ensure that all subordinates are familiar with the characteristics of the explosive materials involved; the equipment to be used; safety regulations to be observed; and the hazards of fire, explosion, and other catastrophies which the safety regulations are intended to prevent.

d. Be alert to detect any hazardous procedures or practices, or symptoms of a deteriorating mental attitude; and take immediate corrective action when such are detected.

5. Smoking is not permitted in magazines, nor in the

immediate vicinity of handling or loading operations involving explosives or ammunition. Matches, lighters, or spark- or flame-producing devices are not permitted in spaces in which ammunition or explosives are present.

6. Personnel engaged in working with explosives or ammunition shall be limited to the minimum number required to perform the operation properly. Unauthorized personnel shall not be permitted in magazines, nor in the immediate vicinity of handling or loading operations involving explosives or ammunition except for duly authorized inspections. Authorized visitors shall always be properly escorted.

7. When fuzed or assembled with firing mechanisms, mines, depth charges, rockets, projector charges, missiles, and aircraft bombs, shall at all times be handled and treated as if armed.

8. Live ammunition, rockets, or missiles shall be loaded into guns or on launchers only for firing purposes except where otherwise approved by the Naval Ordnance Systems Command, or as permitted below.

9. No ammunition other than inert ammunition shall be used for drill purposes, except that the following types of live ammunition may be used aboard aircraft carriers instead of inert ammunition for loading drills, when specifically authorized by the commanding officer and applicable radio frequency hazard restrictions and other appropriate safety regulations are adhered to:

a. Aircraft gun ammunition.

b. Bombs—conventional, or high explosive loaded.

c. Rockets and rocket launchers with installed rockets.

d. Guided missiles and torpedoes with exercise heads only.

10. Supervisors shall require the maintenance of good housekeeping in explosives spaces. Nothing shall be

stored in such spaces except explosives, containers, and authorized handling equipment.

11. No detonator shall be assembled in a warhead in or near a magazine containing explosives. Fuzing shall be done at a designated fuzing area.

Authorized Operators (see *"Hot Work"* and *"Special Equipment"*)

Boats

1. In motor launches, only the coxswain and the boat officer or the senior line officer may ride on the coxswain's flat. No more than two persons may be on the deck at one time.

2. Boat crews must keep their stations, especially when weather conditions are unpleasant, for it is usually during these times that vigilance is most needed.

3. Boats must always be properly loaded for the sea state. In heavy weather, the boat is loaded slightly down by the stern and the passengers and crew kept in lifejackets. Boat passengers will remain seated when a boat is underway and shall keep arms inboard of gunwales.

4. The coxswain, or boat officer when assigned, shall be responsible to the commanding officer for the enforcement of these regulations.

5. No boat shall be loaded beyond the capacities established by the commanding officer and published in the boat bill, without specific permission of the command duty officer, and then only in emergencies.

6. No person shall smoke in a boat under any circumstances.

7. No person other than those specifically designated by the engineer officer shall operate or attempt to operate a boat engine; test, remove, or charge a boat's battery, or

tamper in any way with the boat's electrical system; or fuel a ship's boat.

8. No person shall be assigned as a member of a boat crew unless he is a qualified swimmer; has demonstrated a practical knowledge of boat seamanship, Rules of the Road, and boat safety regulations; and has been duly qualified for his particular assignment by the first lieutenant.

9. All persons in boats being hoisted in or out, or hung in the davits, shall wear vest-type, inherently buoyant life preservers properly secured. Additionally, they shall wear safety helmets with chin straps unbuckled.

10. No person shall board a boat from a boat boom unless another is standing by on deck or in a boat at the same boom.

11. All members of a boat's crew shall wear rubber-soled canvas shoes when embarked in a ship's boat.

12. Fueling instructions must be posted in all power boats, and passengers must be kept clear of the boat while refueling.

13. Maximum operating speeds must be posted permanently upon the engine cover of all boats.

14. Standard equipment listed in the allowance list must be in boats at all times.

15. Prescribed lights must be displayed by all boats underway between sunset and daylight or in reduced visibility.

16. Life buoys must be carried forward and aft in each boat, secured in such a manner that they are easily broken out for use.

17. All boats leaving the ship shall have local charts with courses to and from their destination recorded thereon. Boat compasses and fog signaling equipment must be carried.

18. All boats will have sufficient life preservers on board to accommodate each person embarked, and they shall be readily available when rough seas, reduced visibility, or other hazards threaten.

19. No boat will be dispatched or permitted to proceed unless released by the OOD. Such release will not be given unless it has been determined that the boat crew and passengers are wearing life preservers, when advisable, and that weather and sea conditions are suitable for small boat operations.

20. Recall and lifeboat signals must be posted in the boats where they may be easily read by the coxswains.

21. A set of standing orders to boat coxswains must be prepared and kept in each boat.

Bolos (see *"Line Throwing Gun"*)

Cargo

Special precautions observed in handling cargo include:

1. Open hatches in use should be cleared of any adjacent loose equipment which might fall into them and injure personnel below.

2. Traffic about the hatch is restricted to the off side from where cargo is being worked. The area over which the loads are traveling is roped off to traffic.

3. Hatch beams or other structures in the way of hatches where cargo is being worked are secured by bolts or removed. Personnel engaged in moving hatch beams shall wear a safety line which shall be tended at all times.

4. Experienced personnel must always supervise the topping and lowering of booms. Before making any repairs or replacing any of the gear, booms should always be lowered on deck. When life lines are removed for any purpose, officers and petty officers concerned are required

to ensure that emergency lines are rigged and that every-one is cautioned to keep clear.

Closed Compartments

Danger of explosion, poisoning and suffocation exists in any closed compartment or poorly ventilated space, such as tanks, cofferdams, voids, and bilges. No person shall enter any such compartment or space until applicable safety regulations have been complied with and all danger has been eliminated or reduced to the lowest practicable minimum. The following precautions should be observed:

1. The seal around the manhole or other opening should be broken before all holddown bolts or other fastenings are completely removed, to allow dissipation of any possible pressure built up inside, and to make it possible to quickly secure the cover again if gas or water is present.

2. No person shall enter any such space without permission from the responsible division officer, who shall consult with his department head and the gas free engineer before granting permission.

3. No naked light or spark-producing electrical apparatus shall be carried into a closed space.

4. Safety lamps used in closed compartments must be in good operating condition. If the lamp fades or flares up, a dangerous condition exists and the space should not be entered.

5. No person shall work in such a compartment without a lifeline attached, and a responsible man stationed outside the compartment to tend the line and maintain communications with him.

Compressed Gases

Compressed gases used aboard ship include oxygen,

acetylene, carbon dioxide (CO_2) and plain compressed air. Helium, nitrogen, ammonia and certain insecticide fogs may also be used. All cylinders are identified in stencilled letters, and by color, as follows:

> *Yellow:* Flammable materials, such as acetylene, hydrogen, and petroleum gases.
> *Brown:* Poisonous materials, such as chlorine, carbon monoxide, sulphur dioxide.
> *Green:* Oxidizing material, particularly pure oxygen.
> *Blue:* Anesthetics and materials with similarly harmful fumes.
> *Gray:* Physically dangerous materials; gas under high pressure or asphyxiating if breathed in confined areas, such as CO_2, nitrogen, and helium.
> *Red:* Fire protection materials, especially carbon dioxide.
> *Black,* with *Green* striping: Compressed air, helium-oxygen, and oxygen-carbon dioxide mixtures.

All flammable gases, such as acetylene, become highly explosive when mixed in certain proportions with air. Even an inert gas like CO_2 can cause an explosion if the cylinder becomes too hot or cracks because of rough handling. The following rules should be obeyed without exception:

1. Gas cylinders and air cylinders must be kept away from high-temperature areas. Oil should never be allowed to come in contact with oxygen cylinder valves, since a violent explosion may result.

2. Gas cylinders must not be handled roughly, dropped, or clanked against each other. Gas cylinders should not be handled or transported without the cylinder valve caps in place.

3. Flames or sparks should not be permitted in any closed spaces where acetylene or oxygen tanks are stored, for seepage of gas from the tanks may have filled the com-

partment with a dangerous level of gas or pure oxygen.

4. Caution should be used around ammonia tanks and similar cylinders of poisonous gases. There is always the possibility that the gas is leaking from a loose valve or seeping through a defective connection.

5. In case of fire or other disaster, gas cylinders should quickly be moved from the danger area, and if necessary, thrown overboard.

Dangerous Materials (see *"Semisafe and Dangerous Materials"*)

Electrical and Electronic Equipment

This includes generators, electrically-powered machinery and mechanisms, power cables, controllers, transformers, and associated equipment, radars, radios, power amplifiers, antennas, electronic warfare equipment, computers, and associated controls.

1. No person shall operate, repair, adjust, or otherwise tamper with any electrical or electronic equipment (unless it is within his functional assignment in the department organization manual to perform a specific function on certain equipment) except in definite emergencies, and then only when no qualified operator is present. (Electric light and bulkhead electric fan switches are exempted.)

2. No person shall be assigned to operate, repair, or adjust electrical and electronic equipment unless he has demonstrated a practical knowledge of its operation and repair and of all applicable safety regulations, and then only when duly qualified by the head of department having cognizance over such equipment.

3. No person shall paint over or otherwise destroy or multilate any markings, name plates, cable tags, or other identification on any electrical or electronic equipment.

4. No person shall hang anything whatever on, or secure a line to, any power cable, antenna, wave guide, or other electrical or electronic equipment.

5. Only authorized portable electric equipment which has been tested by the electric shop shall be used.

6. Electric equipment shall be de-energized and checked with a voltage tester or voltmeter to ensure it is de-energized before servicing or repairing it, if possible. Circuit breakers and switches of de-energized circuits shall be locked or placed in the "off" position while work is in progress and a suitable warning tag shall be attached thereto.

7. If it is necessary to work on live circuits or equipment, every effort shall be made to insulate the person performing the work from the ground and to use all practical safety measures. If possible, rubber gloves shall be worn. Another man shall be standing by to de-energize the circuit and to render first aid.

8. No personal electrical or electronic equipment shall be used aboard ship until it is approved by the engineer officer and the executive officer.

9. Intentionally taking a shock from any voltage is always dangerous and shall not be done.

10. Bare lamps or fixtures with exposed lamps shall not be installed in machinery spaces. Only enclosed fixtures shall be installed in such spaces to minimize the hazard of fire caused by flammable fuels making contact with exposed lamps.

11. Personnel shall not be permitted to go aloft near energized antennas unless it is determined in advance that no danger exists. If any danger exists from rotating antennas, induced voltages in rigging and superstructure, or from high power radiation causing direct biological injury, the equipment concerned shall be secured and a suitable warning tag shall be attached to the main supply

switches. These precautions shall also be observed if any other antenna is in the vicinity, as on an adjacent ship.

12. Heads of departments shall ensure that electrical and electronic safety precautions are conspicuously posted in appropriate spaces, and that personnel concerned are frequently and thoroughly instructed and drilled in their observance.

13. Appropriate heads of departments shall ensure that all electrical and electronics personnel are qualified in the administration of first aid treatment for electrical shock and that emergency resuscitation procedures are posted in all spaces containing electronic equipment.

14. Appropriate heads of departments shall ensure that rubber matting is installed in operating areas in front and back of propulsion control cubicles, power and lighting switchboards, IC switchboards, test switchboards, fire control switchboards, ship announcing system amplifiers and control panels; areas in and around radio, radar, sonar, and countermeasures equipment spaces which may be entered by personnel in servicing or tuning energized equipment; and around work benches in electrical and electronic shops where equipment is tested or repaired.

Fire and Explosion Prevention

The reduction of fire and explosion hazards is the responsibility of every person on board, both individually and collectively. The gravity of these hazards is increased by the configuration of machinery spaces, the presence of fuel and heat, and the probable loss of systems which may contribute to the ship's fire-fighting capability. The following steps are essential:

1. Initiate action to ensure that all potential fire and explosion hazards are eliminated, including nonessential combustibles.

2. Replace, wherever possible, all combustible materials with less flammable ones.

3. Limit to a practicable minimum the amounts of essential combustibles carried.

4. Stow and protect all essential combustibles so as to reduce the probability of their causing or contributing to destructive fires.

5. Avoid accumulation of oil or other flammable materials in bilges and in inaccessible areas. Any such accumulations must be flushed out or removed at the first opportunity.

6. Stow oily rags in air-tight metal containers.

7. After use, stow paint, paint brushes, rags, paint thinners and solvents in authorized locations only.

8. Do not use compressed air to accelerate the flow from containers of oil, gasoline, or other combustible fluids.

9. Make regular and frequent (at least daily) inspections for fire hazards.

10. Train all personnel in fire prevention and fire fighting.

11. Enforce sound fire prevention policies and practices.

12. Maintain damage control equipment ready for any emergency.

Fire Watch (see *"Hot Work, 2"*)

Fuel Oil (see also *"Volatile Fuel"*)

1. While oil is being received on board, no naked light, lighted cigarettes, or electrical apparatus that is liable to spark should be permitted within 50 feet of an oil hose, tank, or compartment containing the tank or the vent from a tank. The carrying of any matches or cigarette lighters on the person while at work loading or unloading is prohibited. (see *"Underway Replenishment, 13"*)

2. No naked light, lighted cigarettes, or electrical fuses, switches (unless inclosed type), steel tools, or other apparatus that is liable to cause sparks should be permitted at any time in a compartment that contains a fuel-oil tank, fuel-oil pumps, or fuel-oil piping. However, smoking of cigarettes may be permitted in the engine rooms and on the fireroom floor in front of the furnaces of a boiler which is in operation. Electric lamps used in such compartments must have gas-tight globes. The term "naked light" includes oil lanterns as well as open lanterns, lighted candles, and lighted matches. Flashlights must not be turned on or off inside a fuel compartment lest a spark ignite vapors.

3. No person should be allowed to enter a fuel-oil tank until the tank has been freed of vapor, the person has obtained permission from the safety officer or CO, and the required precautions have been taken. Never enter a fuel-oil tank without wearing a lifeline attended by a person outside of the tank.

4. Fuel oil must not be heated to a temperature higher than 120° F.

5. Oil fires can be extinguished by smothering and cutting off all oxygen. Carbon dioxide extinguishers are preferred. Chemicals or water in the form of fog may be used. Sand and steam are also effective.

6. Compartments and tanks used for storage of fuel oil should not be painted on the inside.

7. Whenever a fuel-oil tank is to be entered, or any work is to be done in it, or any lights other than portable explosion-proof electric lights are used, and when work is to be done in the vicinity of an open tank or of pipes, all such tanks and pipes must be cleared of vapor after the fuel oil has been removed. No person should enter a fuel-oil tank for any purpose without obtaining permission from the safety officer or CO each time he wishes to enter.

Gasoline (see *"Volatile Fuel"*)

Heavy Weather

The safety of individuals require the following precautions:

1. Weather decks subject to the seas should be kept clear of all personnel except those who must be there for urgent duties. During heavy weather, word to this effect should be included in the plan of the day. Any location to which entry is forbidden should be publicized.

2. Extra life lines, protective nets, and snaking should be in place during heavy weather, particularly in areas where such evolutions as replenishment or recovery of a man overboard are being conducted.

Helicopters

During helicopter operations, only those personnel actually involved shall be allowed in the helicopter area. All other personnel shall remain clear or below decks. Personnel engaged in flight operations shall wear appropriate safety helmets. Passengers shall be led to and from a helicopter by a member of the handling crew or flight crew. All loose gear in the vicinity of the helicopter area shall be stowed elsewhere or secured to the deck. All personnel shall be instructed concerning the shrapnel effect caused when rotor blades strike a solid object.

Hot Work

Hot work is work involving welding, flame cutting, the use of open-flame equipment, or any heating of metal to or above a red heat. There are numerous ways in which hot work near flammable or explosive materials can create a dangerous situation. No person shall undertake a job involving hot work unless and until the gas-free engineer (or his authorized representative) has inspected the place where the job is to be done; indicated that the applicable safety regulations have been complied with; indicated that men can work in the area without danger of poisoning or suffocation; and indicated that the hot work can be undertaken without danger of fire or explosion.

1. No hot work shall be permitted without the permission of the commanding officer in each case underway or the duty officer in port.

2. When flammable or explosive materials will be exposed to welding or cutting operations, a fire watch shall be posted in the vicinity. If fire hazards exist on both sides of a deck or bulkhead being worked on, a watch shall be posted on each side. Fire watches shall remain on their stations for at least 30 minutes after a job is completed to ensure no smoldering fires have been started. Suitable fire extinguishing equipment shall be maintained near all welding and cutting operations.

3. No welding or burning shall be permitted in compartments of the ship where the explosives are stored.

4. Various synthetic materials yield toxic gases when burned or heated. Suitable warning signs shall be placed in areas where dangerous vapors may accumulate.

5. Only qualified men are permitted to operate welding equipment.

Life Jackets

Life jackets must be worn under conditions where the possibility exists that men will slip, fall, be thrown or carried into the water. The safest life jacket, when properly worn, is the standard Navy inherently buoyant vest type. Life jackets must be worn under the following conditions:

1. Working over the side in port and at sea, on stages, boatswain's chairs, or in boats or punts. "Over the side" means any part of the ship outside the life lines or bulwarks.

2. On weather decks during heavy weather, even when exposed only for the short time required to go from one station to another,

3. Handling lines or other deck equipment during such evolutions as transfers between ships, fueling underway, and towing.

4. In boats being raised or lowered, while entering boats from a boom or Jacob's ladder, in boats underway, and in rough water or low visibility. Ring buoys with a line and light attached must be available for use when a sea ladder or a Jacob's ladder is being used.

5. Transfer by highline or helicopter. Don life jackets prior to getting into the transfer seat or sling.

Lifelines

No person shall: lean on, sit on, stand on, or climb over any lifeline either in port or when underway. Men working over the side in port may climb over lifelines when necessary, but only if they are wearing life preservers;

No life line shall be dismantled or removed without specific permission of the first lieutenant, and then only if temporary lifelines are promptly rigged;

No person shall hang or secure any weight or line to any lifeline unless authorized by the commanding officer.

Lights

When in port at night, weather decks shall be well lighted. All accommodation ladders, gangways, and brows shall also be well lighted.

Lines and Rigging (see also *"Synthetic Lines"*)

When working with lines and rigging, the following precautions should be observed:

1. Lines or rigging under heavy strain should be eased

to prevent overstress or parting. Men must keep clear of heavily stressed line or wire, and under no circumstances, stand in the bight of a line or on a taut fall.

2. Hoisting heavy loads overhead shall be avoided. If it is essential to carry out such hoisting, the person responsible shall take steps to warn everyone away from the area directly beneath.

3. Boat falls, high lines, and mooring lines should be end-for-ended or changed at the first indication of wear or overstress. Failure to make such changes can result in serious casualty.

4. Lines not in use should be carefully made up and stowed clear of walkways and passages.

5. Lines must never be made fast to capstans or gypsy heads, but only to fittings provided for that purpose, such as cleats or bitts.

6. Steadying or frapping lines should be used on boat falls and large lifts to prevent uncontrolled swinging or twisting.

Line-Throwing Gun

A bolo or line-throwing gun is always used in the opening phase of replenishment operations, for which the following safety precautions must always be observed:

1. Bolo heavers and line-throwing gun-crew members must wear red helmets and highly visible red jackets to ensure easy identification.

2. The bolo heaver and line-throwing gunner must be thoroughly trained to place the line within easy reach of the receiving ship's crew, under existing conditions of range, wind, and relative motion.

3. Bolos and gun lines must be properly prepared for running. Even for the gun line, a loose coil in a bucket is preferable to a spindle.

4. When the receiving ship reaches the proper position,

both ships pass the word over the bull horn and topside loud speaker equipment: "Stand by for shot line—All hands take cover."

5. The officer in charge at each replenishment station in the firing ship sounds a 1-blast signal on a mouth whistle or passes the word "Stand by" on the electric megaphone. The officer in charge of the corresponding station in the receiving ship replies with a 2-blast signal on a mouth whistle or passes the word "Ready" on the electric megaphone when he is in all respects ready to receive the shot line and all of his crew have taken cover. After ascertaining that all hands in the vicinity of the target area are under cover, the officer in charge on the firing ship gives the order to fire. The bolo is not thrown nor the gun fired except by order of the officer in charge.

6. Only those members of each replenishment station designated by the officer in charge may leave cover to retrive the bolo or shot line. All other personnel in the receiving ship do not leave cover until all bolos or shot lines are on board and the word is passed on the topside loudspeaker equipment: "Shot (bolo) lines secure."

7. The receiving ship (except in the case of an aircraft carrier) does not fire her line-throwing guns unless ordered or requested to do so by the delivering ship.

8. Ships must ensure, by thorough indoctrination, that all hands take cover immediately on receipt of the word to do so.

Machinery

This includes all engines, motors, generators, hydraulic systems, or other apparatus supplying power or motive force.

1. Except in definite emergencies, and then only when no qualified operator is present, no person shall operate, repair, adjust, or otherwise tamper with any machinery

and associated controls unless assigned by his head of department to perform a specific function on such machinery.

2. No person shall be assigned to operate, repair, or adjust any machinery unless he has demonstrated a practical knowledge of its operation and repair, and of all applicable safety regulations, and then only when qualified by the head of the department having cognizance over such machinery.

3. Machinery undergoing repair shall have its power or activation sources tagged-out to prevent accidental application of power.

Painting

The poisonous effects of paint may be produded either by the vehicle or pigment. The vehicle is a volatile solvent. Excessive exposure to a vaporized solvent will produce irritation of the nose and throat, headache, dizziness, excitement, apparent drunkenness, loud or boisterous conversation, loss of memory and a staggering gait. A man showing such effects must be quickly removed from exposure to paint fumes; if not, he may become unconscious and fatality may result.

The pigment in paint may be poisonous because it usually contains lead. Pigment may be absorbed through the skin or inhaled as dust or atomized particles, particularly if a spray gun is used. The following precautions should be observed in painting:

1. Wash hands and clean under fingernails to protect from pigment poisoning.

2. Change soiled clothing as soon as possible.

3. Use respirators, and change filter frequently. (Respirators offer no protection against paint fumes.)

4. Men exposed regularly to spray-gun work should have fresh air supplied through a face mask.

Personnel Protection

1. When working or near rotating machinery, care shall be taken to avoid wearing clothing with loose ends or loops which might be caught by moving equipment.

2. Suitable leather or other heavy gloves shall be worn when working on steam valves or other hot units.

3. When working in the vicinity of steam equipment, the body shall be kept well covered to reduce the danger of steam burns (i.e., shirt buttoned, sleeves rolled down, etc.)

4. Protective goggles or helmet, and leather welding jacket shall be worn when brazing, welding, or cutting.

5. Men shall wear goggles whenever working with substances corrosive to eyes.

6. Men shall wear respirators when working where fumes or paint dust are excessive.

Power Tools (see "Tools")

Radiation

Radioactive material is present in a nuclear reactor core, in contaminants in the primary coolant, in nuclear warheads, in the sources used for calibration of radiation monitoring equipment, and in certain electronic tubes.

1. Nuclear warheads shall not be disassembled nor receive any maintenance on board ship.

2. Radiation sources shall remain installed in the radiation detection equipment or shall be stowed in their shipping containers in a locked storage.

3. Spare radioactive electronic tubes and fission chambers shall be stored in clearly marked containers and locked stowage.

4. All hands shall scrupulously obey radiation warning signs and shall remain clear of radiation barriers.

Safety Devices

1. Mechanical, electrical, and electronic safety devices shall be inspected at suitable regular intervals and additionally as unusual circumstances or conditions warrant. When practicable, such inspection shall include operation of the safety device while the equipment or unit is in actual operation. Machinery or equipment shall not be operated unless the safety devices are in proper working condition.

2. No person shall tamper with or render ineffective any safety device, interlock, ground strap, or similar device intended to protect the operators or the equipment.

Semisafe and Dangerous Materials

Semisafe materials are those materials which are considered safe so long as contained in unopened, nonleaking containers, it being understood that, in the event of leakage, any spilled material would be cleaned up with reasonable promptness and the leaking containers disposed of. Some of the more common semisafe materials are diesel oil, grease, lubricating oil, metal polish, paint, safety matches, and wax.

Dangerous materials are materials involving considerable fire hazards or having other dangerous characteristics whether or not in sealed containers. Some of the more common ones are acids, alcohol, anticorrosive paint, bleaching powder (chlorinated lime), calcium hypochlorite, compressed gases, gasoline, kerosene, lacquer, paint thinner, paint stripping compound, paint drier, rust preventive compound, storage battery electrolyte, turpentine, and varnish.

All semisafe and dangerous materials shall be stowed in the paint and flammable liquids storeroom unless another designated stowage area is provided. Naked lights and spark-emitting devices must not be used in compartments containing semisafe or dangerous materials.

Calcium hypochlorite and bleaching powder (chlorinated lime) must be stowed as follows: in a clean, cool, dry compartment or storeroom not adjacent to any magazine and safe from exposure to heat or moisture; isolated from flammable materials; and not in the same compartment with acids or other chemicals. Containers shall be inspected periodically to ensure they are tightly sealed and that exteriors or cans are free of rust. All defective containers must be removed from storage and consumed by immediate use or otherwise disposed of. Bleach in plastic containers must be stowed in a covered metal container.

Shoes

All persons shall wear shoes equipped with rubber heels except that boat crew members shall wear rubber-soled canvas shoes when embarked in ship's boats. Safety shoes must be worn in designated foot-hazardous areas. No person shall wear shoes with taps, cleats, or other metal device on the heels or soles on board ship or in ship's boats.

Sleeping Topside

Sleeping topside when the ship is underway shall be carefully supervised to ascertain that no cots are used and that there is no possibility of men rolling over the side.

Small Arms

Small arms are hand-held pistols, rifles, machine guns, line-throwing guns and flare guns, less than .50 caliber bore diameter.

1. No person shall be issued small arms unless he has

demonstrated to his department head or division officer that he is fully acquainted with the operation of and safety regulations pertaining to the weapon.

2. No person shall insert a clip or otherwise load any small arm unless he intends and is required to use the weapon in the performance of his duty.

3. Only designated personnel shall clean, disassemble, adjust, or repair small arms.

4. A small arm shall never be pointed at anyone unless it is intended to shoot him nor in any direction where accidental discharge may do harm.

Smoking

Safety demands strict control of smoking. No person shall smoke in any area or during any evolution described as follows:

1. In holds, storerooms, gasoline tank compartments, gasoline pump rooms, voids, or trunks; in any shop or space where flammable liquids are being used or handled; in the ship's boats; in bunks or berths; in magazines, handling rooms, ready service rooms, gun mounts, or turrets; in gasoline control stations, oil relay tank rooms, and battery and charging rooms; in the film projection room or in the vicinity of motion picture stowage; in the photographic laboratory; when bleeding oxygen; in any area where vinyl or saran paint is being applied.

2. In any area of the ship where ammunition is being handled.

3. When transferring ammunition, either loading or unloading.

4. In any part of the ship when receiving or transferring fuel oil, diesel oil, aviation gasoline, or other volatile fuel, except in spaces designated as smoking areas by the commanding officer.

5. During general quarters, general drills, or during emergencies, except as authorized by the commanding officer.

6. When the word "the smoking lamp is out" is passed.

Special Equipment

All personnel concerned with the operation of special equipment such as welin davits, winches, or booms must be thoroughly indoctrinated in the safety precautions peculiar to the use of such equipment. Applicable safety precautions must be posted in the immediate vicinity of the equipment. Only personnel who have been instructed in their duties and who have been authorized specifically by the first lieutenant are permitted to operate cranes, capstans, winches, and windlasses. Except in an emergency, operation of the machinery must be supervised by a responsible officer.

Synthetic Lines

Nylon, dacron, and other synthetic fiber lines, used for mooring and rigging applications, are characterized by high elasticity and a low coefficient of friction. The following precautions shall be observed when using synthetic fiber lines:

1. An extra turn is required when securing synthetic fiber line to bitts, cleats, capstans, and other holding devices.

2. When easing out synthetic fiber lines from bitts, cleats, or other holding devices, extreme care shall be exercised due to its high elasticity, rapid recovery, and low coefficient of friction.

3. Nylon line, on parting, is stretched one and one-half times its original length and snaps back. No one shall stand in the direct line of pull of nylon line when heavy loads are applied.

Tagout Procedures (see also *"Electrical and Electronic Equipment,"* and *"Working Aloft"*)

Proper use of tagout procedures for equipment and instruments can greatly improve personnel safety and help prevent costly accidents. Once a piece of equipment has been tagged, it cannot be untagged, operated, or used normally except by specified competent authority. General practice is as follows:

> *Red tag:* Used on valves or switches whose operation, due to test condition or derangement, would cause danger to personnel or damage to equipment.
>
> *Orange-yellow tag:* Used for precautionary purposes where temporary special instructions or unusual precautions apply.
>
> *Red and orange tags:* Used to indicate defective, disconnected, unreliable, or uncalibrated instruments, respectively.

Tools

Danger from electric shock and the risk of physical injury from flying particles accompany the use of portable pneumatic or electrically-powered tools. The rigorous use that electrically-powered tools receive, and the metal construction of the ship, increase the possibility of shorts and grounds and present a constant hazard to the safety of personnel using such tools.

1. No person shall be issued or in any way use a portable electric or pneumatic tool unless specifically authorized by his division officer, and then only after he has demonstrated a knowledge of the tool's operation and of the safety regulations incident to its use.

2. No portable electric tool shall be issued unless it has been carefully inspected and checked for proper insulation resistance.

3. No person shall use a portable electric or pneumatic tool for any purpose other than those specifically authorized by his department head.

4. No person shall use a portable electric tool unless the tool housing is grounded to the ship's metal structure, either through a grounded type receptacle and plug or by direct connection to the hull.

5. All persons using pneumatic or electrically-powered wire brushes, chippers, sanders, or grinders shall wear goggles or eye shields.

Toxic Materials

The issue and use of all materials that are potential health hazards shall be strictly controlled by the medical officer or other designated person.

Methyl alcohol, commonly used as duplicator fluid, paint thinner, cleaner, and antifreeze is hazardous if inhaled, absorbed through the skin, or swallowed. Swallowing even small amounts can cause permanent blindness or death. Methyl alcohol and products containing methyl alcohol shall only be released in the amount required and at the time needed to perform a specific job. It shall be used only in well-ventilated spaces and in such a manner that contact between alcohol and skin is avoided.

Halogenated hydrocarbons, normally used in gaseous or liquid form as solvents, refrigerants, fumigants, insecticides, paint removers, dry cleaning fluids, and as propellants for pressurized containers are also hazardous if inhaled, swallowed, or absorbed by the skin. They shall be used only with adequate ventilation, by authorized personnel under close supervision, and in such a way that contact with the eyes and skin is prevented.

Underway Replenishment

In this operation, speed is important, but safety must never be sacrificed for speed. All safety precautions must be reviewed prior to commencing the operation. It is impossible to anticipate all the hazardous situations that may arise, but the following list of general precautions provides an excellent start.

1. Only essential personnel shall be allowed in the vicinity of any transfer station.

2. Life lines shall not be lowered unless absolutely necessary; if lowered, temporary life lines shall be rigged.

3. When line-throwing guns or bolos are used, all hands on the receiving ship shall take cover. (see *"Line Throwing Guns"*)

4. Topside personnel engaged in handling stores and lines shall wear safety helmets and orange-colored, inherently buoyant, vest-type life preservers. If safety helmets are equipped with a quick-acting, break-away device, the chin strap shall be fastened and worn under the chin. If not so equipped, the chin strap shall be fastened behind the head or worn unbuckled. Between-ship phone talkers must not secure neckstraps around their necks, lest they be dragged over the side by their telephone lines.

5. Cargo handlers shall wear safety shoes. Those handling wire-bound or banded cases shall wear work gloves.

6. Personnel shall keep clear of bights, handle lines from the inboard side, and stay at least 6 feet from any block through which the lines pass. They shall also keep clear of suspended loads and rig attachment points until loads have been landed on deck.

7. Care shall betaken to prevent the shifting of cargo. Personnel shall not get between any load and the rail.

8. Deck space in the vicinity of transfer stations shall be covered with a slip-resistant deck covering.

9. A lifebuoy watch shall be stationed well aft on the engaged side. Provisions shall be made for rescuing anyone who falls overboard (i.e., if a lifeguard ship is not available, a boat shall be kept ready).

10. Suitable measures shall be taken to avoid the haz-

ards associated with radio frequencies. This is especially important when handling ammunition, gasoline, and other petroleum products.

11. Dangerous materials, such as acids, compressed gases, and hypochlorites shall be transferred separately from one another and from other cargo. The delivery ship shall notify the receiving ship of the type of dangerous material in each load prior to transfer. The receiving ship shall keep such dangerous materials separated, and shall stow them in designated storerooms as soon as possible.

12. When transferring personnel by highline, only a hand-tended, manila line shall be used. All personnel being transferred shall wear orange-colored, inherently buoyant life preservers (except patients in litters equipped with flotation gear). When water temperature is extremely low, immersion suits shall be worn, if possible.

13. When fuel oil is being received or transferred, the use of naked lights, or electrical or mechanical apparatus likely to spark, shall not be permitted within 50 feet of an oil hose in use, an open fuel tank, the vent terminal from a fuel tank, or an area where fuel oil or fuel oil vapors are or may be present. The term "naked light" includes all forms of oil or gas lanterns, lighted candles, matches, cigars, cigarettes, cigarette lighters, flame or arc welding and cutting apparatus, etc. Portable electric lights used during fueling shall have explosion-proof protected globes and shall be thoroughly inspected for proper insulation and tested prior to use. On ships being fueled, portholes in the ship's structure on the side from which fuel is being received shall be closed and secured.

14. When transferring gasoline, a ground wire shall be connected between the two ships before the hose is brought aboard, and shall be disconnected only after the hose is clear. Gasoline hoses shall be blown down by an inert gas upon the completion of any transfer.

Voids and Bilges (see *"Closed Compartments"*)

Volatile Fuels

Aviation gasoline, motor gasoline, JP-4, and JP-5 are highly volatile liquids giving off a vapor which, when combined with air in the proper proportion, forms an explosive mixture that can be set off by a slight spark or flame. Further, the vapor may travel along an air current for a considerable distance and then be ignited, the flash traveling back to the source of supply and causing an explosion or fire.

1. All spaces into which volatile fuel vapors issue shall be constantly and thoroughly ventilated.

2. No smoking and no naked lights (such as welding, cutting, etc.) shall be permitted in the vicinity of volatile fuel tanks or filling connections, drums, cans, stowage, piping, or spaces through which such piping passes.

3. Care shall be used to prevent the striking of sparks in locations where volatile fuel vapors may collect. Use only spark-proof tools.

4. When carried in cans for ship's own use, gasoline shall be stowed in the paint and flammable liquids storeroom. If no such storeroom is provided, gasoline shall be stowed on the weather-deck so that the containers may be readily thrown overboard.

5. Gasoline shall be issued only under the supervision of a reliable man who shall ensure all containers are securely closed and that all safety regulations are observed.

6. The metal nozzle at the end of a fuel hose shall be properly grounded to prevent sparks from static electricity. (see *"Underway Replenishment, 14"*)

7. Gasoline shall not be used for cleaning purposes under any circumstances.

8. Upon completion of loading or delivery, piping and hoses shall be carefully drained back into the ship's tanks or into containers which can be closed and sealed.

Welding (see *"Hot Work"*)

Working Aloft

Men wishing to go aloft shall first obtain specific permission from the officer of the deck, and then only to perform necessary work or duty. The officer of the deck is responsible for seeing that the following safety precautions are observed before granting permission:

1. Power is secured on all radio transmitting antennas and radar antennas in the vicinity and that power switches are tagged, "SECURED! MEN ALOFT."

2. The engineer officer has been instructed to lift no safety valves and, if men are to work in the vicinity, to secure steam to the whistle.

3. Men working in the vicinity of stack gases wear protective breathing masks and remain there for only a brief time.

4. All men use a short safety line secured around their waists and attached to the ship's structure at the same level.

5. All tools, buckets, paint pots, and brushes are secured by a lanyard when used in work on masts, stacks, upper catwalks, weather decks, or sponsons which overhang areas where other men may be present.

Working Over the Side

Men to be assigned to work over the side must be instructed in all safety precautions by their division officers before they will be permitted on scaffolding, stages, or in boatswain's chairs, and the following precautions must be observed:

1. Men working over the side must be supervised by a competent petty officer, and qualified men must be assigned to tend safety lines.

2. All men working over the side of the ship on stages, in boatswain's chairs, or in boats along the side of the ship shall wear inherently buoyant life preservers and, with the exception of men in boats, shall be equipped with safety lines tended from the deck above.

3. All tools, buckets, paint pots, and brushes used by men working over the side of the ship shall be secured by lanyards to prevent their loss overboard and injury to personnel below.

4. No person shall work over the side of the ship while underway without permission of the commanding officer.

Chapter XII BOATS AND VEHICLES

Boats shall be regarded in all matters concerning the rights, privileges, and comity of nations as part of the ship or aircraft to which they belong.

In ports where war or insurrection exists or threatens, the commanding officer shall:

(a) Require that boats away from the ship or aircraft have some appropriate and competent person in charge.

(b) See that steps are taken to make their national character evident at all times.—*Navy Regulations,* Article 0757.

In port he [the officer of the deck] shall require the coxswains of the lifeboats to inspect and report to him daily at sunset the condition of their boats as to readiness for service; and at sea he shall require a like inspection and report at the beginning of each watch.—*Navy Regulations,* Article 1013.

The officer of the deck shall insure that the ship's boats are properly manned and equipped and are not loaded beyond their safe capacity, consistent with weather conditions. He shall see that the required safety appliances are in place and in good order, and that the crews understand their use and observe all prescribed safety precautions.

He shall inform himself of all boats or other craft that come alongside or leave the ship, and shall permit them to lie at the gangway no longer than necessary. He shall promptly notify the officers concerned when stores or other materials or services arrive which require their knowledge or action.

He shall insure that the ship's boats and their crews present at all times a creditable appearance, that the boats are handled smartly, and that the crews observe the rules for preventing collisions and the regulations pertaining to honors and ceremonies.

He shall insure that boats are properly secured when not in use.

Boats and aircraft within sight of the ship shall be watched in order that aid may be sent promptly if needed.—*Navy Regulations,* Article 1016.

When embarked in a boat the senior line officer (including commissioned warrant and warrant officers) eligible for command at sea, has authority over all persons embarked therein, and is responsible under all circumstances for the safety and management of the boat.—*Navy Regulations,* Article 1331.

In the "Old Navy," boats were vital equipment of ships. Units of the fleet usually anchored in port instead of mooring to a wharf or pier as is the usual practice now. Ship's boats were the sole contact with the beach, and their appearance and the seamanship of their crews were a major factor in judging the service reputation of their parent ships. Officers took intense pride in the smartness of their boats and their interest was reflected in the attention of petty officers and nonrated men in caring for and operating their boats.

A ship's vehicles, passenger cars, station wagons, and trucks, are also a source of pride to a ship's company and a matter of concern to the officer of the deck. Like boats, vehicles must be inspected, dispatched, and safeguarded.

In the past many accidents have occurred and numerous lives have been lost because of improper preparation and poor handling of boats. While better berthing facilities have eliminated much boat traffic, the hazard still remains, particularly in foreign ports where ships anchor rather than moor to a pier. The requirement for careful supervision in the operation of boats is an important responsibility of the officer of the deck.

AT SEA

At sea the officer of the deck has relatively simple duties pertaining to ship's boats. Unless a boat is launched while the ship is underway, he is only concerned with the readiness of the lifeboats. This can best be assured by questioning the coxswains when they make their required report. Learn, if you do not already know it, the coxswain's own qualifications as well as those of his crew. Know where they are stationed and how long it takes to alert them. Know also who the men are who will lower the boat in an emergency and how long this process will take, as well as who is ordinarily in charge of the lowering. The boatswain's mate of the watch is your principal assistant for boats.

The readiness of the boat engine, the amount of fuel in the boat, and the special rescue equipment carried are other matters of interest to the officer of the deck. In cold weather, special precautions must be taken to keep the engine warm, either by frequent startings or by heaters. It should go without saying that boats at sea should be fueled to capacity. Special equipment will vary with different ships and their employment, but it is always a good idea for the officer of the deck to check the lifeboat's equipment once each watch. Have the coxswain make an inventory and report; he is always responsible for the condition as well as the appearance of his boat and crew.

All these matters are a part of the routine of a well-run ship, but the officer of the deck can never be complacent and assume that all is well, when, by asking a few questions, he can *make sure*. For if a lifeboat is ever needed and is not ready, or is launched with a green crew or short of fuel or gear, the officer of the deck is certain to be a responsible party.

IN PORT

In port, boats and vehicles present a major responsibility to the officer of the deck in their operation, appearance, and security.

Calling away, dispatching, fueling, and receiving boats and vehicles can be a complicated and most harassing business for the officer of the deck who has not organized his watch to handle it. Some sort of status board or sheet is almost mandatory to keep track of a number of boats and vehicles on a variety of missions. Assuming that you have an assistant maintaining a record of employment and conditions of readiness, there is still necessary an intelligent and personal supervision by the officer of the deck. Boats and vehicles should be inspected for appearance, their equipment should be checked, and the coxswain or driver instructed. If the instructions are complicated, send for the man and discuss the matter. If you have any misgivings about his memory, put your instructions in writing. Make your orders short, complete, and reasonable. Never send a boat or vehicle to wait for someone without putting a time limit on the trip. Otherwise, if the passenger or passengers fail to show up, you have lost the services of the vehicle or boat until you can get word to them, which might take hours. Boat crews and drivers are sometimes kept up long hours for no good reason because of some unforeseen change of plans ashore. The proper procedure for all boats and vehicles, except, of course, a gig, barge, or equivalent vehicle, is to direct them to wait for someone only for a certain time or until a specified hour.

Appearance

The subject of the appearance and smartness of a ship's boats has been mentioned before in this book. It is one that will always be prominent among officers who take pride in their ship and in their service. A smart boat reflects a smart ship and is often the means by which a ship and her crew are evaluated. Not only do fresh and neat paintwork and fancy knotwork make a good impression, but even more important is the manner in which the boat is handled. The officer of the deck is responsible for the good sea manners of coxswains, which includes the rendering of proper courtesies to passing boats and the avoidance of hot-rod landings and of excessive wake where damage might result.

The officer of the deck can be a major factor in maintaining high standards in the ship's boats. His critical appraisal of crew and boat as she comes alongside is the first step. If he then corrects any deficiencies possible he has done much to insure that his ship will be well represented by the boats that are employed during his watch. By the same token, an OOD should insure that ship's vehicles are clean and polished.

Capacity

The capacity of a Navy boat is indicated on the boat label plate secured in the boat when she was built. This is maximum capacity and should always be reduced in rough weather or when stores or other cargo are carried at the same time as passengers.

There is a technique in properly loading a large liberty boat that is worth learning. It is one of those small but significant marks of an efficient officer of the deck and a smartly run ship. After the chief petty officers have been embarked, the other men should be required to go forward in the boat and load from forward aft. It may take a little supervision to prevent men from filling up the center section first, but it will prevent people climbing over each other, or the dangerous practice of men walking along the gunwales.

Crews

The officer of the deck may have little to do with the training of boat crews, but he must make certain that those operating boats during his watch are qualified. Sometimes on a late boat trip a new man will appear as engineer, bow hook, or even as coxswain. Allow these men to go along for instruction if they wish to, but never as a substitute for a qualified crew member. It has even happened that after receiving his instructions from the officer of the deck the coxswain has delegated his job to an unqualified seaman. This sort of incident contributed to the swamping of a liberty boat a few years ago that caused the loss of eighteen lives. The point here is that the officer of the deck must know his boat crews and must be particularly alert to the qualifications of the coxswains.

Discipline

A familiar problem in handling liberty parties is the maintenance of good order and discipline, especially just before sailing on a lengthy cruise. High spirits and an uninhibited display of "smokestacking" and salty language are to be expected. When matters pass the bounds of decency or when they threaten the comfort and safety of the more reserved members of the liberty party, the boat officer or the senior officer aboard must maintain order. There is a correct and fairly easy way to do this, and also a wrong and sometimes disastrous method. The officer in charge should detail a number of petty officers, as many as circumstances require, to preserve order. The petty officers usually do so by separating the most exuberant of the troublesome men and persuading them to sit down and be quiet. The wrong method is for the officer in charge to attempt to deal with the noisy men directly, which can lead to disrespectful language or conduct and may even result in violence to the person of the officer who is trying to do the job singlehanded. It is important to note here the obligation that an officer has of avoiding, if possible, a situation involving a serious offense by an enlisted man. A hasty act by a man befuddled by drink could wreck his career.

It should be noted that in a boat the senior line officer eligible for command at sea is the responsible officer. It has happened that an officer did not realize that he was responsible until after an accident had occurred. In an emergency, of course, you have little time to stop and compare seniority with fellow officer passengers; the thing to do, if you believe the boat is in danger, is to act quickly and decide the matter of seniority later. With a boat officer on duty there is normally no reason for a senior passenger to interfere unless he believes a dangerous situation is developing which is beyond the capacity of the boat officer to handle. In this extremity, the senior line officer passenger (eligible for command at sea) should take charge. If he does take over he should do so decisively, informing the crew and the boat officer of his action. This action should only be taken in case of an emergency, since the boat officer has presumably been assigned his responsibility by competent authority.

Equipment

Boat compasses, life jackets, and other items of boat equipment must be checked by the officer of the deck as circumstances warrant. For long boat trips or when low visibility is likely, the boat compasses should be observed during the first trip in any port or anchorage, with headings and time on each course recorded in the boat's compass book. This practice will make boating much safer and more certain later on. Life jackets, foul weather clothing, harbor charts, and fire-fighting equipment are other items of boat equipment in which the officer of the deck should take a personal interest. Life jackets should be checked and their use directed when weather or sea conditions so indicate. The number of personnel allowed in a boat should not exceed the number of life jackets in that boat. Do not assume that boats belonging to other units, such as boat pools, are properly equipped; have them inspected if they are to be used by your ship.

Inspection

The engineer officer designates a junior officer or a particularly well qualified petty officer to inspect boat machinery daily. In addition, the first lieutenant makes periodic checks on the equipment carried in each boat and the condition of the boat itself. While these inspections can be assumed to be complete, they do not relieve the officer of the deck of exercising the prudence and foresight expected of a good seaman. The appearance and smartness of ships' boats always require additional attention on the part of the officer of the deck. When there is a question of safety or security, such as life jackets in a boat, there is, similarly, the need for personal supervision by the officer of the deck. He should not assume that routine inspections are enough to guarantee that certain equipment will be in a certain boat at a particular time.

Orders

When giving orders to the coxswain of a boat, do so in an explicit and seamanlike manner. Do not say, for example, "All right, coxswain, shove off and get the navigator at the Dock Street Landing." Instead, say: "Coxswain! When told to shove off, go to the Dock Street Landing and bring off the navigator, Lieutenant Commander Jones. If he does not show up by ——— o'clock return to the ship. Do you understand?" When he answers in the affirmative, say: "Shove off and carry out your orders." Remember that a boat "hauls out" to the boom, it does not "tie up" or "secure" to the boom. A ship "makes fast" to a pier, while a boat may "make fast" to the accommodation ladder (not the gangway). A boat may be "secured," but this means a more permanent fastening than to "make fast." The expression "tie up" is not a proper naval term and should be avoided.

Safety

A final aspect of boat operation is that of securing the boat when not in use. The safest procedure to follow, when practicable, is to hoist boats in at night or in bad weather. When this procedure is not practicable, the boats should be under surveillance when hauled out to the boom. Never permit boats to lie at the accommodation ladder unattended. Boats usually ride well at the boom; it is the practice of making fast astern that is risky in bad weather. Boat lines chafe through easily, and boatkeepers or boat sentries are normally employed in bad weather if there is any doubt about the safety of the ship's boats. (For detailed safety precaution governing boat operations, see Chapter XI, "Boats.")

Schedules

Boat schedules are normally prescribed by the executive officer and should be followed meticulously by the officer of the deck. Only the most unusual circumstances should cause a cancellation of a scheduled boat, particularly at night when there may be people ashore who are planning to return to the ship in that boat. If a scheduled boat trip must be canceled, get permission from the executive officer or duty head of department, and then pass the word.

It is quite common to have men and officers waiting to leave the ship who have the same destination as the gig or the barge. The officer of the deck should make every effort to learn the policy or practice of the senior officer concerned, and, if permissible, embark the people before the captain or admiral comes onto the quarter-deck. If doubt exists, it is quite appropriate to ask the senior officer if he desires to take any officers or men to his destination. If the answer is affirmative, as is invariably the case, make every effort to expedite loading the boat. Remember that juniors always enter boats (and vehicles) *first* and leave them *last.**

Security

One method to insure the safe and efficient operation of a boat is to provide a boat officer. This is only true, of course, when the officer assigned is qualified. An ensign fresh from Officer Candidate School, with no previous seagoing experience, would be of little value. A boat officer should be assigned:

1. In foul weather, fog, or high winds, existing or forecast.

2. For first boat trips in foreign or unfamiliar harbors.

3. For the return of large liberty parties, particularly late at night just before sailing.

A boat officer should wear a web belt and, except where prohibited by competent authority, a pistol as a badge of authority which distinguishes him from officer passengers. In cases where there are insufficient commissioned or warrant officers, it is customary to assign deck rating chief petty officers as boat officers.

* For an exception, see "Loading Liberty Boats," pages 214-215.

Chapter XIII HONORS AND CEREMONIES

The officer of the deck shall see that all regulations concerning salutes, honors, and ceremonies, except as modified by orders of competent authority, are carefully observed.—*Navy Regulations,* Article 1018.

The honors and ceremonies prescribed in these regulations may be dispensed with when directed by the Secretary of the Navy, or when requested by an individual to whom such honors and ceremonies are due.—*Navy Regulations,* Article 2101.

Honors and ceremonies are based on a long established code of customs, agreements, and regulations, which, in general, is common to all navies. With some important exceptions, these honors and ceremonies occur in port, and the manner in which they are rendered or carried out under your supervision as officer of the deck does much to make the reputation of your ship for smartness. Because of the frequent international character of honors and ceremonies, it is especially important that they be so rendered and conducted as to reflect credit on the Navy and on the United States.

Honors and ceremonies may vary from two side boys for an ensign to an official visit of the President or head of a foreign state. It is well, in your mind, to divide honors into two classes: those which you must know on the instant without looking them up, and those which you will normally have time to look up and which should not be trusted to memory. Most ships keep a "table of honors" posted on the quarter-deck.

The following pages contain enough pertinent extracts from Chapter 21, *Navy Regulations* to enable the officer of the deck, under normal conditions, to discharge his duties. On special occasions, such as the death of an important person, it will be necessary to refer to *Navy Regulations* itself.

With honors and ceremonies, as with nearly all your activities as officer of the deck, it is important to look ahead. Generally speaking, you should be able to estimate quite accurately the degree of readiness required under existing conditions. If anchored in bad weather at an advanced base, with air attack possible, you would not be likely to need side boys standing by. On another occasion it might be necessary to have the full guard ready at a moment's notice.

THE QUARTER-DECK

The commanding officer of a ship shall establish the limits of the quarter-deck and the restrictions as to its use. The quarter-deck shall embrace so much of the main or other appropriate deck as may be necessary for the proper conduct of official and ceremonial functions.—*Navy Regulations*, Article 2160.

The quarter-deck is that part of the ship so designated by the commanding officer. It is normally on the main deck near the gangways. It is marked off by appropriate lines, deck markings, decorative cartridge cases, or fancy work, and is always kept particularly clean and shipshape. *Men not on duty should not be allowed on or near the quarter-deck.* The dignity and appearance of the quarter-deck are symbols of the professional and seamanlike attitude of a ship and her crew. Be zealous in upholding both this dignity and appearance, together with the highest standards of smartness on the part of your personnel.

Tending the Side

The officer of the deck shall see that all persons coming aboard or alongside the ship are courteously treated.

Unless prevented by urgent duty, he shall be at the gangway to receive, and shall accompany to the side, all officers or distinguished visitors. When so prevented, he shall send a junior officer of the watch to represent him.

Except for those persons over whom he has no authority, he shall require all persons leaving or returning to the ship to report to him or his representative; on leaving the ship they shall report authority to do so.—*Navy Regulations*, Article 1017.

Gangways should always be tended smartly by the officer of the deck or one of his assistants. This should be done for reasons of both security and courtesy. Every person coming aboard should be greeted by a member of the watch immediately, his business ascertained and credentials examined, and appropriate steps taken to escort him below or else to send for the person he wishes to see. Officers' guests should be shown to the wardroom. It is considered a great mark of slackness and unseamanlike organization to let someone get on board without having been met properly.

When an officer comes aboard, his boat will normally lie alongside the accommodation ladder until it receives its orders. The officer of the deck should ask the visitor or his aide what orders are desired for his boat (gig, barge).

Side Boys

Side boys as the first members of the crew to come under the observation of an important personage or visitor, should always be particularly smart, with polished shoes, and immaculate uniforms. They should be kept together under the eye of a petty officer and not employed in any activity that will spoil their good appearance or take them away from the quarter-deck. See that they are properly instructed and are able to fall in properly without undue confusion. Similar care should be taken with the guard and band.

Piping the Side

The call "alongside" is sounded so as to finish just as the visitor's boat makes the accommodation ladder. During this call the side boys and the boatswain's mate stand at attention but do not salute.

The call "over the side" starts just as the visitor's head appears at quarter-deck level. When visitors approach over a brow, a corresponding point at the outboard end of the brow should be selected. Side boys and boatswain's mate salute on the first note, and drop their hands from salute on the late note. The boatswain's mate may salute with his left hand. Saluting and piping procedure is reversed when a visitor leaves.

OFFICIAL VISITS

Upon notification of an official visit, the officer of the deck should:

1. Check proper table of honors in *Navy Regulations*.

2. Notify admiral, chief of staff, commanding officer, executive officer, command duty officer, navigator, senior watch officer, flag lieutenant, commanding officer of the Marine detachment.

3. Have on deck a qualified bugler, a qualified boatswain's mate, and a quartermaster.

4. Inspect and rehearse side boys.

5. Inspect quarter-deck for appearance.

6. Station alert lookout, notify signal bridge to be alert and have personal flag ready.

7. Notify band.

8. Notify weapons officer if a salute is required.

Chapter 9, *Shipboard Procedures*, *NWP 50(A)*, contains detailed honors and ceremony procedures, with additional check-off lists for the officer of the deck.

HONORS AND SALUTES

Pertinent extracts from *Navy Regulations* are quoted here for ready reference by the officer of the deck.

Morning and Evening Colors.

1. The ceremonial hoisting and lowering of the national ensign at 0800 and sunset at a naval command ashore or aboard a ship of the Navy not underway shall be known as Morning Colors and Evening Colors, respectively, and shall be carried out as prescribed in this article.

2. The guard of the day and the band shall be paraded in the vicinity of the point of hoist of the ensign.

3. "Attention" shall be sounded, followed by the playing of the national anthem by the band.

4. At Morning Colors, the ensign shall be started up at the beginning of the music and hoisted smartly to the peak or truck. At Evening Colors, the ensign shall be started from the peak or truck at the beginning of the music and the lowering so regulated as to be completed at the last note.

5. At the completion of the music, "Carry On" shall be sounded.

6. In the absence of a band, "To the Colors" shall be played by the bugle at Morning Colors, and "Retreat" at Evening Colors, and the salute shall be rendered as prescribed for the national anthem.

7. In the absence of music, "Attention" and "Carry On" shall be the signals for rendering and terminating the salute.

8. During colors, a boat underway within sight or hearing of the ceremony shall lie to, or shall proceed at the slowest safe speed. The boat officer, or in his absence the coxswain, shall stand and salute except when dangerous to do so. Other persons in the boat shall remain seated or standing and shall not salute.

9. During colors, vehicles within sight or hearing of the ceremony shall be stopped. Persons riding in such vehicles shall remain seated at attention.

10. After Morning Colors, if foreign warships are present, the national anthem of each nation so represented shall be played in the order in which a gun salute would be fired to, or exchanged with, the senior official or officer present of each such nation; provided that, when in a foreign port, the national anthem of the port shall be played immediately after Morning Colors, followed by the national anthems of other foreign nations represented.—Article 2107.

Salutes to the National Ensign.

1. Each person in the naval service, upon coming on board a ship of the Navy, shall salute the national ensign if it is flying. He shall stop on reaching the upper platform of the accommodation ladder, or the shipboard end of the brow, face the national ensign, and render the salute, after which he shall salute the officer of the deck. On leaving the ship, he shall render the salutes in inverse order. The officer of the deck shall return both salutes in each case.

2. When passed by or passing the national ensign being carried, uncased, in a military formation, all persons in the naval service shall salute. Persons in vehicles or boats shall follow the procedure prescribed for such persons during colors.

3. The salutes prescribed in this article shall also be rendered to foreign national ensigns and aboard foreign men-of-war.—Article 2108.

Saluting Ships and Stations.

Saluting ships and stations of the naval service are those designated as such by the Secretary of the Navy or his duly authorized representative. The gun salutes prescribed in these regulations shall be fired by such ships and stations. Other ships and stations shall not fire gun salutes, unless directed to do so by the senior officer present on exceptional occasions when courtesy requires.—Article 2114.

"Passing Honors" and "Close Aboard" Defined.

"Passing honors" are those honors, other than gun salutes, rendered on occasions when ships or embarked officials or officers pass, or are passed, close aboard. "Close aboard" shall mean passing within six hundred yards for ships and four hundred yards for boats. These rules shall be interpreted liberally, to insure that appropriate honors are rendered.—Article 2130.

Passing Honors between Ships.

1. Passing honors, consisting of sounding "Attention" and rendering the hand salute by all persons in view on deck and not in ranks, shall be exchanged between ships of the Navy, and between ships of the Navy and the Coast Guard, passing close aboard.

2. In addition, the honors prescribed in the following table shall be rendered by a ship of the Navy passing close aboard a ship or naval station displaying the flag of the official indicated therein; and by naval stations, insofar as practicable, when a ship displaying such flag passes close aboard. These honors shall be acknowledged by rendering the same honors in return.—Article 2131.

Passing Honors to Officials and Officers Embarked in Boats.

1. The honors prescribed in this table shall be rendered by a ship of the Navy being passed close aboard by a boat displaying the flag or pennant of officials and officers.

2. Persons on the quarter-deck shall salute when a boat displaying a miniature of a flag or pennant passes close aboard.—Article 2132.

Passing Honors to Foreign Dignitaries and Warships.

1. The honors prescribed for the President of the United States shall be rendered by a ship of the Navy being passed close aboard by a ship or boat displaying the flag or standard of a foreign president, sovereign, or member of a reigning royal family, except that the foreign national anthem shall be played in lieu of the National Anthem of the United States.

Passing Honors to Officials Embarked in Ships.

Official	Uniform	Ruffles and flourishes	Music	Guard	Remarks
President	As prescribed by senior officer present.	4	National anthem	Full	Man rail, unless otherwise directed by senior officer present.
Secretary of State when special foreign representative of the President.	do	4	do	do	Crew at quarters.
Vice President	Of the day		do	do	Do.
Secretary of Defense, Deputy Secretary of Defense, or Secretary of the Navy.	do		do	do	Do.
An Assistant Secretary of Defense, Under Secretary or an Assistant Secretary of the Navy.	do		do	do	Do.

Passing Honors to Officials and Officers Embarked in Boats.

Official	Ruffles and flour-ishes	Music	Guard	Remarks
President	4	National anthem	Full	"Attention" sounded, and salute by all persons in view on deck. If directed by the senior officer present, man rail.[1]
Secretary of State when special foreign representative of President.	4	do	do	"Attention" sounded, and salute by all persons in view on deck.
Vice-President, Secretary of Defense, Deputy Secretary of Defense, Secretary of the Navy, an Assistant Secretary of Defense, Under Secretary or an Assistant Secretary of the Navy.	4	Admiral's march	do	Do.
Other city official entitled to honors on official visit.				Do.
Officer of an armed service.				Do.

[1] Those who man the rail will salute on signal.

Passing Honors Between Ships.

Officer of the Deck of Junior Ship	Officer of the Deck of Senior Ship	Bugle Call	Battery Whistle
1. Sounds "attention" starboard (port)			
	2. Sounds "attention" starboard (port)	"attention" starboard (port)	1 whistle starboard 2 whistles (port)
3. Sounds "hand salute" (guard presents arms and band sounds off if required)			
	4. Sounds "hand salute" (guard presents arms and band sounds off)	1 short note	1 short whistle
	5. Sounds "TWO" (in 3 seconds or after band sounds off)		
6. Sounds "TWO"		2 short notes	2 short whistles
	7. Sounds "carry on"	"carry on"	3 short whistles
8. Sounds "carry on"			

2. Passing honors shall be exchanged with foreign warships passed close aboard and shall consist of parading the guard of the day, sounding "Attention," rendering the salute by all persons in view on deck, and playing the foreign national anthem.—Article 2133.

Sequence in Rendering Passing Honors.

1. "Attention" shall be sounded by the junior when the bow of one ship passes the bow or stern of the other, or, if a senior be embarked in a boat, before the boat is abreast, or nearest to abreast, the quarter-deck.

2. The guard, if required, shall present arms, and all persons in view on deck shall salute.

3. The music, if required, shall sound off.

4. "Carry on" shall be sounded when the prescribed honors have been rendered and acknowledged.—Article 2134.

Dispensing with Passing Honors.

1. Passing honors shall not be rendered after sunset or before 0800 except when international courtesy requires.

2. Passing honors shall not be exchanged between ships of the Navy engaged in tactical evolutions outside port.

3. The senior officer present may direct that passing honors be dispensed with a whole or in part.—Article 2135.

Crew at Quarters on Entering or Leaving Port.

The crew shall normally be paraded at quarters on entering or leaving port during daylight, except when weather or other circumstances make it undesirable to do so. However, in lieu of parading the entire crew at quarters, an honor guard may be paraded in a conspicuous place on the weather decks on the following occasions:

1. Entering or leaving homeport, except when returning from or departing for extended deployments.

2. Entering or leaving U.S. ports other than homeport when the visit is operational in nature.—Article 2136.

Side Honors.

1. On the arrival and departure of civil officials and foreign

officers, and of United States officers when so directed by the senior officer present, the side shall be piped and the appropriate number of side boys paraded.

2. Officers appropriate to the occasion shall attend the side on the arrival and departure of officials and officers.—Article 2153.

Dispensing with Side Boys and Guard and Band.

1. Side boys shall not be paraded on Sunday, or on other days between sunset and 0800, or during meal hours of the crew, general drills and evolutions, and period of regular overhaul; except in honor of civil officials or foreign officers, when they may be paraded at any time during daylight.

2. Except for official visits and other formal occasions, side boys shall not be paraded in honor of officers of the armed services of the United States, unless otherwise directed by the senior officer present.

3. Side boys shall not be paraded in honor of an officer of the armed services in civilian clothes, unless such officer is at the time acting in an official civil capacity.

4. The side shall be piped when side boys are paraded, but not at other times.

5. The guard and band shall not be paraded in honor of the arrival or departure of an individual at times when side boys in his honor are dispensed with, except at naval shore installations.—Article 2154.

Honors at Official Inspection.

1. When a flag officer or unit commander boards a ship of the Navy to make an official inspection, honors shall be rendered as for an official visit, except that the uniform shall be as prescribed by the inspection officer. His flag or command pennant shall be broken upon his arrival, unless otherwise prescribed in these regulations, and shall be hauled down on his departure.

2. The provisions of this article shall apply, insofar as practicable and appropriate, when a flag or general officer, in command ashore, makes an official inspection of a unit of his command.—Article 2158.

Chapter XIV FLAGS, PENNANTS, AND BOAT HAILS

Each person in the naval service, upon coming on board a ship of the Navy, shall salute the national ensign if it is flying. He shall stop on reaching the upper platform of the accommodation ladder, or the shipboard end of the brow, face the national ensign, and render the salute, after which he shall salute the officer of the deck. On leaving the ship, he shall render the salutes in inverse order. The officer of the deck shall return both salutes in each case.

The salutes prescribed in this article shall also be rendered to foreign national ensigns and aboard foreign men-of-war.— *Navy Regulations,* Article 2108.

Closely related to and, in fact, overlapping the subject of honors and ceremonies is the subject of flags and pennants. This chapter will serve as a guide to the officer of the deck on the usage and customs related thereto. The material is largely based on *U.S. Naval Flags and Pennants and Customs DNC 27(A),* and *Navy Regulations.* The former publication is not well known; it should be studied by every officer on board ship who stands deck watches. Only the most basic and commonly used information will be presented here as a ready reference.

Many countries have variations to their national flag that are authorized for specific uses. The national flag used by men-of-war only is the *ensign;* that used by merchant ships is the *merchant flag.* The United States of America has only one flag, the *national colors,* which is used for all purposes. It may properly be called the *ensign* when used in the Navy.

Each landing party battalion that may be sent ashore from a ship has the national colors and an organization color, the U.S. Navy infantry battalion flag. Each company, when parading ashore and at other ceremonies, may display a *guidon*.

GENERAL RULES FOR DISPLAY

The distinctive mark of a ship or craft of the Navy in commission is a personal flag or command pennant of an officer of the Navy, or a commission pennant. The distinctive mark of a hospital ship of the Navy, in commission in time of war, is the Red Cross flag. Not more than one distinctive mark is displayed by a ship or craft at the same time, nor are the commission pennant and the personal flag of a civil official displayed simultaneously. Except as prescribed in *Navy Regulations* for certain occasions of ceremony and when civil officials are embarked, the distinctive mark mentioned above is displayed day and night at the after masthead, or, in a mastless ship, from the loftiest and most conspicuous hoist.

When the ship is not under way, the national ensign and the union jack are displayed from 0800 until sunset from the flagstaff and the jackstaff, respectively. A ship that enters port at night displays, when appropriate, the national ensign from the gaff at daylight for a time sufficient to establish her nationality; it is customary for other ships of war to display their national ensigns in return.

The national ensign is displayed during daylight from the gaff of a ship under way under the following circumstances, unless or as otherwise directed by the senior officer present:

1. Getting under way and coming to anchor.
2. Falling in with other ships.
3. Cruising near land.
4. During battle.

The union jack displayed from the jackstaff is the size

of the union of the national ensign displayed from the flagstaff.

SPECIAL RULES FOR THE U.S. ENSIGN
During Gun Salutes

A ship of the U.S. Navy displays the national ensign at a masthead while firing a salute in honor of a United States national anniversary or official, as follows, according to *Navy Regulations,* Article 2165:

1. At the main during the national salute prescribed for the 22d of February and the 4th of July.

2. At the main during a 21-gun salute to a United States civil official, except by a ship displaying the personal flag of the official being saluted.

3. At the fore during a salute to any other United States civil official, except by a ship which is displaying the personal flag of the official being saluted.

During a gun salute, the national ensign shall remain displayed from the gaff or the flagstaff, in addition to its display as prescribed above.

In Boats

Article 2166, *Navy Regulations,* states:

The national ensign is displayed from water-borne boats of the naval service:

1. When under way during daylight in a foreign port.

2. When ships are required to be dressed or full-dressed.

3. When going alongside a foreign vessel.

4. When an officer or official is embarked on an official occasion.

5. When a flag or general officer, a unit commander, a commanding officer, or a chief of staff, in uniform, is embarked in a boat of his command or in one assigned to his personal use.

6. At such other times as may be prescribed by the senior officer present.

Since small boats are a part of a vessel, they follow the

motions of the parent vessel as regards the half-masting of colors.

Dipping

When any vessel, under United States registry, or under the registry of a nation formally recognized by the government of the United States, salutes a ship of the U.S. Navy by dipping her ensign, it is answered dip for dip. If the national ensign is not already being displayed, it is hoisted especially for the purpose of answering the dip; the dip is returned, and, after a suitable interval, the ensign is hauled down. An ensign being displayed at half-mast is hoisted to the truck or peak before a dip is answered.

No ship of the U.S. Navy dips the national ensign unless in return for such compliment.

Of the colors carried by a naval force on shore, only the battalion or regimental colors are dipped in rendering or acknowledging a salute.

Half-Masting

In half-masting the national ensign it is, if not previously hoisted, first hoisted to the truck or peak and then lowered to half-mast. Before lowering from half-mast, the ensign is hoisted to the truck or peak and then lowered.

When the national ensign is half-masted, the union jack, if displayed from the jackstaff, is likewise half-masted.

At noon on Memorial Day, 30 May, each saluting ship fires a salute of twenty-one minute guns. All ships display the national ensign at half-mast from 0800 until the completion of the salute, or until 1220 if no salute is fired.

Colors are half-masted underway as well as when in port.

Following Motions of Senior Officer Present

On board ship upon all occasions of hoisting, lowering, of half-masting the national ensign, the motions of the senior officer present are followed, except as prescribed for answering a dip or firing a gun salute.

A ship displaying the flag of the President, Secretary of Defense, Deputy Secretary of Defense, Secretary of the Navy, an Assistant Secretary of Defense, Under Secretary of the Navy, or an Assistant Secretary of the Navy is regarded as the ship of the senior officer present.

Size of Colors to Be Prescribed

When two or more vessels are in company in port, the senior officer present makes a preparatory signal at 0745, giving the size of colors to be hoisted at 0800. If such a signal indicating size of colors is made at any other time during the day, colors shall be shifted when the signal is hauled down.

Display of Colors During Gun Salutes

While firing a salute to a foreign nation in one of its ports, while returning such a salute fired by a foreign warship, or while firing a salute on the occasion of a foreign national anniversary, celebration, or solemnity, a ship displays the ensign of the foreign nation at the main truck.

While firing a salute to a foreign dignitary or official entitled to twenty-one guns, a ship displays the national ensign of such dignitary or official at the main truck. While firing a salute to a foreign official entitled to less than twenty-one guns, or to a foreign officer, or when returning a salute fired by a foreign officer, the national ensign of the foreign official or officer is displayed at the fore truck.

DISPLAY OF THE UNITED NATIONS FLAG

The following policy concerning the display of the United Nations flag is quoted from Department of Defense Directive 1005.1:

1. The United Nations flag will be displayed at installations of the armed forces of the United States only upon occasion of visits of high dignitaries of the United Nations while in performance of their official duties with the United Nations, or on other special occasions in honor of the United Nations. When so displayed it will be displayed with the United States flag, both flags will be of the same approximate size and on the same level, the flag of the United States in the position of honor on the right (observer's left).

2. The United Nations flag will be carried by troops on occasions when the United Nations or high dignitaries thereof are to be honored. When so carried, the United Nations flag will be carried on the marching left of the United States flag and other United States colors or standards normally carried by such troops.

3. On occasions similar to those referred to in paragraph 2, above, U.S. Naval vessels will display the United Nations flag in the same manner as is prescribed for a foreign ensign during visits of a foreign President or Sovereign.

4. Except as indicated in paragraphs 1, 2, and 3, above, the United Nations flag will be displayed by United States Armed Forces only when so authorized by the President of the United States.

U.S. Naval vessels authorized to display the United Nations flag display it in the same manner as is prescribed for a foreign ensign during visits of a foreign president or sovereign.

PERSONAL FLAGS AND PENNANTS
Afloat

Except as otherwise prescribed in *Navy Regulations,* a flag officer or a unit commander afloat displays his personal flag or command pennant from his flagship. At no time does he display it from more than one ship.

When a flag officer eligible for command at sea is embarked for passage in a ship of the Navy, his personal flag is displayed from such ship, unless there is already displayed from such ship the flag of an officer his senior.

Flags or pennants of officers not eligible for command at sea are not displayed from ships of the U.S. Navy.

Broad and Burgee Command Pennants

The broad or burgee command pennant is the personal command pennant of an officer of the Navy, not a flag officer, commanding a unit of ships or aircraft.

The broad command pennant indicates command of:
1. A division of battleships, aircraft carriers, or cruisers.
2. A force, flotilla, or squadron of ships or craft of any type.
3. An aircraft wing.

The burgee command pennant indicates command of:
1. A division of ships or craft other than battleships, aircraft carriers, or cruisers.
2. A major subdivision of an aircraft wing.

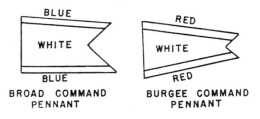

The broad and burgee command pennants are surcharged with numerals to indicate the organizational number within a type. Where two commanders within a type are entitled to display the same command pennant and when they have the same organizational number in different echelons of command, the commander in the higher echelon uses Roman numerals in the surcharge. In all other cases, Arabic numerals are used. Blue numerals are used on broad command pennants, and red numerals on burgee command pennants.

Bow and Flagstaff Insignia for Boats

A boat regularly assigned to an officer for his personal use shall carry insignia on each bow as follows:

1. For a flag or general officer, the stars as arranged in his flag.

2. For a unit commander not a flag officer, a replica of his command pennant.

3. For a commanding officer, or a chief of staff not a flag officer, an arrow.

Staffs for the ensign, and for the personal flag or pennant in a boat assigned to the personal use of a flag or general officer, unit commander, chief of staff, or commanding officer, or in which a civil official is embarked, shall be fitted at the peak with devices as follows:

SPREAD EAGLE:	For an official whose official salute is nineteen or more guns.
HALBERD:	For a flag or general officer whose official salute is less than nineteen guns.
	For a civil official whose official salute is eleven or more guns but less than nineteen guns.
BALL:	For an officer of the grade, or relative grade, of captain in the Navy.
	For a career minister, a counselor or first secretary of embassy or legation, or a consul.

STAR: For an officer of the grade, or relative grade of commander in the Navy.

FLAT TRUCK: For an officer below the grade or, relative grade of commander in the Navy.

                             For a civil official not listed above, and for whom honors are prescribed for an official visit.

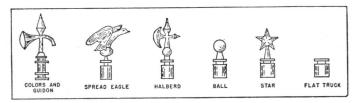

COLORS AND GUIDON   SPREAD EAGLE   HALBERD   BALL   STAR   FLAT TRUCK

When the National Ensign Is at the Masthead

The President's flag, if displayed at a masthead where a national ensign is required to be displayed during an official visit or during periods of dressing or full-dressing ship, shall remain at that masthead to port of the U.S. national ensign and to starboard of a foreign national ensign.

Except as provided above, a personal flag or command pennant is not displayed at the same masthead with a national ensign, but:

1. During a gun salute, it should be lowered clear of the ensign.

2. During an official visit, it should be shifted to the starboard yardarm in a single-masted ship and to the fore truck in a two-masted ship.

3. During periods of dressing or full-dressing ship:

a. If displayed from the fore truck or from the masthead of a single-masted ship, it should be shifted to the starboard yardarm.

b. If displayed from the main truck, it should be shifted to the fore truck in lieu of the national ensign at that mast.

c. If displayed from the after truck of a ship with more than two masts, it should remain at the after truck in lieu of the national ensign at that mast.

Flags or Pennants in Boats and Automobiles

When embarked in a boat of the naval service on official occasions, an officer in command, or a chief of staff when acting for him, displays from the bow his personal flag or command pennant, or if not entitled to either, a commission pennant.

An officer entitled to the display of a personal flag or command pennant may display a miniature of such flag or pennant in the vicinity of the coxswain's station when embarked on other than official occasions in a boat of the naval service.

An officer entitled to the display of a personal flag or command pennant may, when riding in an automobile on an official occasion, display such flag or pennant forward on such vehicle.

All flag officers are authorized to show stars of their rank on their assigned automobiles. The method of showing such stars is confined to six-inch by twelve-inch plates to be attached to license plates or located in the general vicinity of the license plates. Stars or replicas of personal flags are not painted on automobiles.

Half-Masting

Personal flags, command pennants, and commission pennants should not be displayed at half-mast for a deceased official or officer except as prescribed in *Navy Regulations*.

Civil Officials in Boats

A flag shall be displayed in the bow of a boat in the naval service whenever a United States civil official is embarked on an official occasion, as follows:

A union jack for:

1. A diplomatic representative of or above the rank of chargé d'affaires, within the waters of the country to which he is accredited.

2. A governor general or governor commissioned as such by the President, within the area under his jurisdiction.

The consular flag for a consular representative.

The prescribed personal flag for other civil officials when such officials are entitled to the display of a personal flag during an official visit.

For United Nations or North Atlantic Treaty Organization Officials

Personal flags of United Nations or North Atlantic Treaty Organization officials are not displayed when these officers are embarked in U.S. naval vessels, unless the officer holding such office qualifies for displaying his personal flag by being a U.S. Navy flag officer eligible for command at sea.

MISCELLANEOUS FLAGS AND PENNANTS

Absence Indicators

In ships, the absence of a flag officer, unit commander, chief of staff or a commanding officer is indicated from sunrise to sunset by the display of an absence indicator as prescribed in the table shown herewith. Substitute pennants as shown in the signal book are used.

In the case of the absence of a commanding officer who is acting as a temporary unit commander, both absentee pennants should be displayed.

Intention to Depart Officially

The display of the speed pennant, where best seen (in port), indicates that the official or officer whose personal flag or command pennant is displayed will leave the ship officially in about five minutes. When hauled down it means the official or officer is departing. An example of a flag officer shifting his flag would be:

1. Five minutes prior to departure, the flagship hoists the speed pennant at the main truck below the personal flag.

2. On departure, the flagship hauls down the speed pennant and hoists the flag officer's absentee pennant.

3. On arrival of the flag officer in the new flagship, that ship breaks his flag at the main truck.

4. Simultaneously (or as nearly as possible) with the breaking of the personal flag in the new flagship, the former flagship hoists a commission pennant and hauls down the personal flag and absentee pennant.

Church Pennant

Public Law 829 authorizes the use of the church pennant above the ensign "during church services conducted by naval chaplains at sea." The words "at sea" are interpreted for U.S. Navy purposes as meaning "on board a naval vessel." Shore stations, while not authorized to display the church pennant above the ensign, may display it separately if desired.

Ships are fitted with two halyards to the same point of hoist at the staff and gaff; this permits the display of the church pennant and the ensign simultaneously.

If divine services are being conducted at the time of morning colors, or if they begin at that time, the ensign is hoisted to the peak at the prescribed time. The church pennant is then hoisted and the ensign dipped just clear of the church pennant.

Use of Substitute Pennants

Sub.	Indication	Where normally displayed	Absentee
1st	Absence of an official from his ship for a period of 72 hours or less	Starboard main yardarm (outboard)	Absence of a flag officer or unit commander whose personal flag or command pennant is flying in this ship.
2nd	Same as 1st substitute	Port main yardarm (inboard)	Absence of chief of staff
3rd	Same as 1st substitute	Port main yardarm (outboard)	Absence of captain (executive officer it captain is absent for a period exceeding 72 hours)
4th	Same as 1st substitute	Starboard main yardarm (inboard)	Absence of civil or military official whose flag is flying in this ship

Should the ensign be displayed at half-mast, the church pennant should be hoisted just above the ensign.

Should divine services be conducted during time of evening colors, the church pennant is hauled down and the ensign hoisted to the peak just prior to the time for colors; the ensign is then hauled down at the prescribed time.

Union Jack for General Court-Martial

The union jack is displayed at a yardarm to denote that a general court-martial or court of inquiry is in session. It is hoisted when the court meets and hauled down when the court adjourns.

Meal Break

When the ship is at anchor, the meal break (crew's meal indicator) is displayed between sunrise and sunset on either yardarm during the crew's meal period. The meal break is the ECHO flag.

Battle Efficiency Pennant (Meat Ball)

The battle efficiency pennant is flown at the fore truck from sunrise to sunset, while at anchor, during the period provided in *Awards for Intra-Type Competition*.

When a guard flag, ready-duty flag, or Presidential Unit Citation pennant is displayed at the fore truck with the battle efficiency pennant, the latter should be flown below such other flag. The battle efficiency pennant is hauled down when BRAVO is displayed at the fore truck.

Homeward Bound Pennant

The use of the homeward bound pennant is traditional. Specifications for its design and rules for its use have never been firmly established. The usage set forth in *DNC 27(A)* is believed to conform with tradition.

PUC and NUC Pennant

At anchor, ships awarded the Presidential Unit Citation or the Navy unit commendation should fly the pennant, described in *DNC 27(A)*, at the fore truck from sunrise to sunset.

Special Flag Hoist Signals

The SOPA instructions may prescribe certain flag hoists for local use, such as request for garbage or trash lighter, or water barge.

DRESSING AND FULL-DRESSING SHIP

Ships not under way are dressed or full-dressed from 0800 until sunset when prescribed or when directed. Ships underway are not dressed or full-dressed.

When full-dressing is prescribed, the senior officer present may direct that dressing be substituted if, in his opinion, the state of the weather makes such action advisable. He may also, under such circumstances, direct that the ensigns be hauled down from the mastheads after being hoisted. (See *DNC 27(A)* for details of dressing and full-dressing, including the specified sequence of signal flags and pennants to be hoisted.)

BOAT HAILS

Night

All boats approaching a ship at night should be hailed as soon as they are within hearing distance. The watch aboard ship will call out, "Boat ahoy!" The coxswain will reply, as shown in the table below, to indicate the rank of the senior officer or official in the boat:

Officer or Official	Coxswain's reply
PRESIDENT OR VICE PRESIDENT OF THE UNITED STATES	"United States"
SECRETARY OF DEFENSE, DEPUTY OR ASSISTANT SECRETARY OF DEFENSE	"Defense"
SECRETARY, UNDER SECRETARY, OR ASSISTANT SECRETARY OF THE NAVY	"Navy"
CHIEF OF NAVAL OPERATIONS, VICE CHIEF OF NAVAL OPERATIONS	"Naval Operations"
FLEET OR FORCE COMMANDER	"Fleet" or abbreviation of administrative title
GENERAL OFFICER	"General Officer"
CHIEF OF STAFF	"Staff"
FLOTILLA COMMANDER	"_____ Flot _____"
SQUADRON COMMAND	"_____ Ron _____"
DIVISION COMMANDER	"_____ Div _____"

(The type and number abbreviation is used, i.e., Des-Flot-2, DesRon-6 DesDiv-22.)

MARINE OFFICER COMMANDING A BRIGADE	"Brigade Commander"
COMMANDING OFFICER OF A SHIP	"(Name of Ship)"
MARINE OFFICER COMMANDING A REGIMENT	"Regimental Commander"
OTHER COMMISSIONED OFFICER	"Aye, Aye"
OTHER OFFICERS (NOT COMMISSIONED)	"No, No"
ENLISTED MEN	"Hello"
BOAT NOT INTENDING TO GO ALONGSIDE, REGARDLESS OF RANK OF PASSENGER	"Passing"

Day

During hours when honors are rendered, the officer of the deck should challenge an approaching boat as soon as possible by raising his arm with closed fist in the direction of the boat and should train a long glass or binoculars on the coxswain. The coxswain should reply by holding up the number of fingers corresponding to the number, if any, of side boys which should be standing by to honor the senior officer in his boat. A wave-off from the coxswain would indicate no side boys are required.

Appendixes

Appendix A **SAMPLE NIGHT ORDERS**

The commanding officer's night orders are one of the most important documents in a ship. In many collision and grounding cases the commanding officer has been found at fault for various omissions in his night orders. Following is a sample set of night orders that fulfill minimum requirements for such orders.

STANDING NIGHT ORDERS

1. Standing night orders are generalized and permanent. Supplementary night orders will be issued daily as required, and will be initialled by each officer standing an underway operational watch, prior to relieving the watch.

2. You are required to understand and comply with applicable portions of *U.S. Navy Regulations, 1948; International* and *Inland Rules,* and pertinent type, force, and fleet regulations.

3. Rehearse in your mind action to be taken in the event of possible emergency such as vessel or light suddenly close aboard, dragging anchor, man overboard, main engine casualty, or steering casualty on this or any other ship. In addition, rehearse in your mind action to be taken in the event of a sudden tactical maneuver.

4. Officers reporting to relieve the watch should never relieve until they are thoroughly familiar with the circumstances. In any case where an oncoming watch officer feels that circumstances are such that he cannot relieve the watch, he shall immediately notify the captain.

5. Before relieving, observe formation, own position, and assure navigational safety. Call the captain and navigator if position will impair the safe navigation of the ship.

6. Do not relieve the watch until your eyes are properly adapted to the darkness. While on watch, subject your eyes to light as little as possible.

7. When at all possible consistent with normal duties, an officer should avail himself of sufficient rest before relieving a watch.

8. The officer of the deck shall require that all members of the watch furnish him with maximum help consistent with their ability and experience.

9. The use of standard phraseology is of the utmost importance to clear understanding. Use it and require that all members of the watch do likewise.

10. The officer of the deck is responsible for continual instruction of the members of his watch.

11. Notify the captain and the navigator of all changes in base course, speed, and disposition. When the navigator has a DR track laid down on the chart and visual or radar piloting leads you to believe that the ship is fifteen minutes or more ahead or behind the DR position, notify the navigator.

12. Verify the course frequently. Insure that your QM records compass comparisons every fifteen minutes and on every course change. Have recorded hourly compass and vital repeater comparisons. Notify me and the navigator at once of any discrepancies.

13. Be thoroughly familiar with all instruments and communications facilities on the bridge and in CIC. Be able to find them in the dark. Insure that navigation lights are operating or operable, as appropriate.

14. Apprise me promptly of sightings and radar contacts. Give me an estimate including bearing movement when possible. Notify me promptly when any contact outside the disposition of which we are a part gets within 10,000 yards or indicates from tracking a CPA of five miles

or less. Report and identify all navigational lights to the captain and the navigator. Take and record bearings on lights of all ships sighted. Advise me when any ships of this group or disposition are seriously off station.

15. Notify me immediately of changes in the weather including that of reduced visibility. In the event visibility is reduced to two miles or less, sound fog signals if the possibility of collision does exist. Stop engines if a fog signal is heard apparently forward of the beam and the position of the vessel whose fog signals you heard cannot be ascertained. Establish a fog-lookout watch in the eyes of the ship, with sound-powered phone communications to the bridge. Set proper material condition.

16. In the event heavy weather is expected, make all preparations to insure against damage or loss of equipment. In heavy weather take all precautions necessary to insure safety of personnel topside.

17. When necessary to change course to avoid a privileged vessel, do so early enough and with a clearly recognizable change of course. Do not cross ahead of such vessels.

18. CIC will plot all contacts and the OOD will insure compliance. Remember also that a continuous and accurate exchange of appropriate information between the bridge and CIC is essential to both the operations and safety of the ship. Insure that talkers relay information accurately, promptly, and completely. When exchange of such information is vital (such as an operational signal) check correct receipt, using direct communications if desired.

19. Keep required tactical publications handy and know how to use them.

20. Although "control" in the sense of positive recommendation may be passed to sonar or CIC under certain

circumstances, "conn" in the accepted sense, and the responsibility it entails, never leaves the bridge.

21. Completely and timely use of all aids and facilities such as radar, Fathometer, sonar, and lead line (when in difficult pilot waters) is axiomatic and expected. On the other hand, blind dependency upon such aids cannot be accepted.

22. When, in your opinion, use of running lights (despite darkened ship conditions) is essential to safety, *use them.* A ship at the bottom or badly damaged is of no value to anyone.

23. Take the following precautions to insure an efficient watch:

    a. Insure vigilance and attention to duty on the part of subordinates.

    b. Keep the bridge darkened at night.

    c. Permit no unnecessary noises.

    d. Require reports to be made in a clear, seamanlike, and concise manner.

    e. Require that each member of the watch realize that he is there for a specific purpose.

24. As captain, I am completely and inescapably responsible for this ship, its equipment, and the lives of all personnel on board. I depend upon and trust you to assist me in this function by informing me promptly and fully of any event or occurrence which bears on safety and operability of the ship.

25. Should a situation develop which in your opinion requires prompt action, you are authorized and directed to use your initiative to the best of your judgment, without awaiting my arrival on the bridge.

26. The captain is always on duty. Never hesitate to call me when in doubt. In the event I am awakened make sure that I understand the reports which are made to me.

Never hesitate to be forthright, positive, or even insis·
tent.

27. If you cannot reach me on normal circuits and cir·
cumstances demand, use any means available. If a loud·
speaker system is used, pass the positive word, "Captain
to the bridge."

CAPTAINS NIGHT ORDERS (Part I)

Ship .... Time Zone .... Date ....

Enroute from .... To ....

Operating with .... Area ....

OTC .... Flag Ship ....

Standard Tactical Data

Formation ....

Base Course ..... °T ..... °PSTGC Speed ..... KTS .....RPM

Axis .... °T. Guide .... Bear .... °T Dist .... Yds

Screen Data

Type screen .... Screen Axis .... Circle ....

No. Stations .... No. Ships .... Unassigned Sta's ....

Screen Cdr. .... Screen Cdr. Ship ....

Own Ship Station .... Patrolling Station Yes ( ) No ( )

Sta. Ship .... Sta. Ship .... Sta. Ship .... Sta. Ship

....

....

....

Own Ship Data

Engines on the Line .... Generators on the Line ....

Plant .... Ship Darkened Yes ( ) No ( )

Equipment Casualties .... ETR .... ETR........

....

....

....

CAPTAINS NIGHT ORDERS (Part II)

Weather Data

Sunrise .... Sunset .... Moonrise .... Moonset ....

Navigation and Weather Remarks ....
....
....
....
....

Night Intentions ....
....
....
....
....

1. Carry out standing night orders. Check them over to refresh your memory.

2. Eternal vigilance is the price of safety.

3. Call me when in doubt and in any event at ....

Signature (Commanding Officer) ....

Signature .... Signature ....
       (Navigator)   (Executive Officer)

Watch	OOD	JOOD
20-24		
00-04		
04-08*		

Watch Remarks ....
....
....
....
....

* Return to Captain by 0800

Appendix B **BEAUFORT SCALE**

Beau-fort no.	Sea miles per hour (knots)	Seaman's description	Effect at sea
0	Less than 1	Calm	Sea like a mirror.
1	1–3	Light air	Ripples with the appearance of a scale are formed but without foam crests.
2	4–6	Light breeze	Small wavelets, still short but more pronounced; crests have a glassy appearance and do not break.
3	7–10	Gentle breeze	Large wavelets. Crests begin to break. Foam of glassy appearance. Perhaps scattered white horses.
4	11–16	Moderate breeze	Small waves, becoming longer; fairly frequent white horses.
5	17–21	Fresh breeze	Moderate waves, taking a more pronounced long form; many white horses are formed. (Chance of some spray.)
6	22–27	Strong breeze	Large waves begin to form; the white foam crests are more extensive everywhere. (Probably some spray.)
7	28–33	Moderate gale (high wind)	Sea heaps up and white foam from breaking waves begins to be blown in streaks along the direction of the wind. Spindrift begins.
8	34–40	Fresh gale	Moderately high waves of greater length; edges of crests break into spindrift. The foam is blown in well-marked streaks along the direction of the wind.
9	41–47	Strong gale	High waves. Dense streaks of foam along the direction of the wind. Sea begins to roll. Spray may affect visibility.
10	48–55	Whole gale	Very high waves with long overhanging crests. The resulting foam in great patches is blown in dense white streaks along the direction of the wind. On the whole the surface of the sea takes a white appearance. The rolling of the sea becomes heavy and shocklike. Visibility is affected.

Beau-fort no.	Sea miles per hour (knots)	Seaman's description	Effect at sea
11	56–63	Storm	Exceptionally high waves. (Small and medium-sized ships might for a long time be lost to view behind the waves.) The sea is completely covered with long white patches of foam lying along the direction of the wind. Everywhere the edges of the wave crests are blown into froth. Visibility affected.
12 to 17	Above 64	Hurricane	The air is filled with foam and spray. Sea completely white with driving spray; visibility very seriously affected.

Appendix C. MATERIAL CONDITIONS OF READINESS

XRAY   Used only in well protected-protected harbors. All XRAY fittings closed at all times, except when actually in use, such as for issuing stores, repairs, or cleaning.

YOKE   Used in unprotected ports and for wartime cruising. All YOKE and XRAY fittings closed.

ZEBRA   Used for maximum battle protection. All XRAY, YOKE and ZEBRA fittings closed.

Classification of fittings

XRAY   Closed at all times except when actually in use.

YOKE   Fittings for which alternate ZEBRA accesses exist, and which are closed during condition YOKE, thus providing a higher degree of readiness and reducing number of fittings to be closed under condition ZEBRA.

ZEBRA   Normally open for operation of the ship, habitability, and access to battle stations. Closed during battle or emergencies.

WILLIAM Normally open during all conditions of readiness. Examples are sea suction valves and ventilation fittings in systems servicing heat generating spaces.

Black circle XRAY or YOKE May be opened without special authority while proceeding to or from battle stations. Other fittings so marked permit ammunition transfer and operation of vital systems. All such fittings opened only when actually in use.

Red circle ZEBRA May be opened on authority of the commanding officer to set modified condition ZEBRA to distribute food, open limited sanitary facilities, or ventilate battle stations and other vital areas such as magazines. When open, must be guarded for immediate closure if necessary.

Black "D" ZEBRA Closed for darkening ship.

Circle W Normally open during action, but may be closed, or stopped, as defense against NBC attack. Includes nonvital sea suction valves which, if secured, would not impair mobility or fire protection of the ship.

Based on ComCruDesLant Instructions

Appendix D. PROCEDURE FOR GETTING UNDERWAY—typical time schedule

Time	Event	Responsibility
6 hours	(1) Start gyros	Navigator, Duty IC man
3 hours	(1) Verify schedule for lighting off boilers	Engineer Officer
2 hours	(1) Ascertain from the Executive Officer:	OOD
	a. If any variation in standard time of setting Special Sea Detail;	
	b. Time of heaving in to short stay;	
	c. Disposition of boats;	
	d. Instructions concerning U.S. and Guard Mail;	
	e. Number of passengers, if any, and expected time of arrival.	
	(2) After obtaining permission from the Executive Officer, start hoisting in boats and vehicles when no longer required.	OOD
	(3) After obtaining permission from the Executive Officer, rig in booms and accommodation ladders not in use and secure them for sea.	OOD
	(4) Have word passed giving the time the ship will get underway.	OOD
	(5) Energize and check all CIC equipment.	CIC Officer
	(6) Conduct Radio Checks.	COMM Officer
1 hour	(1) Set material Condition YOKE (material Condition ZEBRA in reduced visibility).	Division Officers
	(2) Clear ship of visitors. Chief Master at Arms make inspection for stowaways.	
45 minutes	(1) Pass word "All hands shift into uniform of the day."	OOD
	(2) Muster crew on station.	Division Officers
	(3) "OC" and "R" Divisions man after steering and pilot house; test steering engine, controls, communications, and emergency steering alarm.	Navigator
	(4) Test engine order telegraph and revolution indicator.	Engineer Officer
	(5) Test anchor windlass.	Engineer Officer
	(6) Test running lights.	Engineer Officer
30 minutes	(1) Pass word "Station the Special Sea Detail."	OOD
	(2) Test Fathometer and sonar equipment.	Navigator/ASW Officer
	(3) Adjust Bridge PPI radar scope.	CIC Officer
	(4) Check navigation equipment on bridge. Check gyro repeaters against master gyro.	Navigator
	(5) Test sound-powered communication circuits.	OOD
	(6) Receive departmental reports of readiness to get underway, including material condition YOKE/ZEBRA set.	OOD

Appendix D. **PROCEDURE FOR GETTING UNDERWAY—typical time schedule** (*Continued*)

Time	Event	Responsibility
	(7) CMAA make report of inspection for stowaways.	CMAA
	(8) Record fore and aft draft of ship.	DCA
	(9) Direct engineering control to report when main engines are ready for testing. Upon receiving this report, obtain permission to test main engines from the commanding officer and direct engineering control accordingly. A qualified Officer of the Deck must be on the bridge when engines are tested.	OOD
	(10) Disconnect utility lines to pier and stow.	Engineer Officer
	(11) Pass the word "The Officer of the Deck is shifting his watch to the bridge."	OOD
15 minutes	(1) Report ready for getting underway to the Executive Officer who will report to the Commanding Officer.	OOD
	(2) If moored to a buoy, take in chain or wire, and ride to manila lines when ordered.	OOD
	(3) When directed, test the ship's whistle.	OOD
	(4) When directed, rig in brow.	First Lieutenant
	(5) As boats are hoisted or cleared away rig in booms and davits.	First Lieutenant
	(6) Check ship for smart appearance.	OOD
	(7) Obtain permission to get underway from SOPA or as designated.	
10 minutes	(1) Pass word "All hands not on watch, fall in at quarters for leaving port."	

Immediately prior to getting underway, warn engineering control to stand by to answer all bells.

Appendix E. **PROCEDURE FOR ENTERING PORT—typical time schedule**

Time	Event	Responsibility
Prior to entering restricted waters	(1) Deballast, as required.	Engineer Officer
	(2) Pump bilges when conditions permit (Oil Pollution Act 1954).	Engineer Officer
	(3) Dump trash and garbage when conditions permit.	First Lieutenant
	(4) Man Fathometer.	Navigator
1 hour	(1) Ascertain time of anchoring, (mooring) from the Navigator and notify Engineer Officer, Weapons Officer, First Lieutenant and engineering control.	OOD
	(2) Pass word "Make all preparations for entering port." Ship will anchor (moor _____ side to) at about _____.	OOD
	(3) Ascertain time for quarters for entering port from the Executive Officer.	
	(4) Check smartness of ship for entering port.	OOD
	(5) Obtain information concerning boating from Executive Officer and inform Weapons Officer.	OOD
	(6) Lay out mooring lines if required.	First Lieutenant
	(7) Prepare anchors for letting go.	First Lieutenant
	(8) Pass word "All hands shift into the uniform of the day."	OOD
30 minutes	(1) Blow tubes on all steaming boilers. Set material Condition YOKE. (Set material Condition ZEBRA in restricted visibility.)	OOD
	(2) Station the special sea and anchor detail.	OOD
	(3) Obtain from the Navigator information on depth of water at anchorage, and from Commanding Officer, anchor and scope of chain to be used and inform First Lieutenant. When mooring to a pier, inform Weapons Officer and First Lieutenant as to range of tide and time of high water.	OOD
	(4) Place propeller locks on torpedoes, and unload all hedge-hog projectors.	Weapons Officer
20 minutes	(1) Complete setting of all Special Sea Detail.	OOD
	(2) Ensure smart appearance of ship.	OOD
	(3) Direct Chief Master-at-Arms to inspect upper decks to see that crew is in proper uniform.	OOD
	(4) Swing lifeboat in or out as necessary.	First Lieutenant
	(5) Request permission to enter port from proper authority prior to anchoring or mooring.	OOD
	(6) Pass word "All hands to quarters for entering port."	OOD

Appendix E. **PROCEDURE FOR ENTERING PORT**—typical time
schedule (*Continued*)

Time	Event	Responsibility
15 minutes (Prior to mooring or anchoring)	(1) Station quarter-deck watch.	SWO
	(2) Assemble on the quarter-deck, the guard mail petty officer, mail clerk, movie operator, shore patrol or other details leaving the ship in the first boat.	On-coming OOD
	(3) If mooring to a buoy, lower boat with buoy detail as directed.	First Lieutenant
	(4) Stand by to receive tugs if previously requested and if required in going alongside.	First Lieutenant
Upon anchoring or mooring	(1) Rig out boat booms and lower accommodation ladders.	First Lieutenant
	(2) Lower boat as directed.	First Lieutenant
	(3) Record draft of ship fore and aft.	DCA
	(4) Secure main engines as directed by the Commanding Officer.	Engineer Officer
	(5) Secure the Special Sea Detail. Set inport watches.	OOD
	(6) Secure gyros only if permission is obtained from the Commanding Officer.	Executive Officer/ Navigator
	(7) Pass word: "The Officer of the Deck is shifting his watch to the Quarter-deck."	OOD

BIBLIOGRAPHY (and suggested reading)

Official Navy Department Publications

Bureau of Naval Personnel Manual
Manual of the Judge Advocate General
Naval Ships Technical Manual
Uniform Code of Military Justice
United States Navy Shore Patrol Manual
United States Navy Regulations
Allied Naval Maneuvering Instructions ATP1, Vol. I, II
Allied Naval Signal Book ATPIA, Vol. II
Cold Weather Operating Procedures NWP 35
Instructions for Keeping the Ship's Deck Log NavPers 15876
Ice Seamanship, HO 551
Manual of Synoptic Weather Observations for Ship's Deck Log
    OpNavInst 3140.27
Naval Arctic Operations ATP 17
National Search and Rescue Manual NWP 37A
Replenishment at Sea NWP 38D
Shipboard Procedures NWP 50A
U.S. Naval Flags and Pennants and Customs DNC 27A

Official Coast Guard Publications

Rules of the Road, International-Inland CG-169
Rules of the Road, Great Lakes CG-172
Rules of the Road, Western Rivers CG-184

Publications by the Naval Institute Press, Annapolis, Maryland

Command at Sea, RADM H. F. Cope, revised by Capt. H. Bucknell, USN, 3rd Edition, 1966.
Dutton's Navigation and Piloting, G. D. Dunlap and Capt. H. H. Shufeldt, USNR (Ret.), 12th Edition, 1969.
Farwell's Rules of the Nautical Road, revised by Cdr. Alfred Prunski, USCG (Ret.), 4th Edition, 1967.
Heavy Weather Guide, Capt. E. T. Harding, USN, and Capt. W. J. Kotsch, USN, 1965.
Military Law, LCDR Edward M. Byrne, USN, 1970.

Naval Shiphandling, Capt. R. S. Crenshaw, Jr., USN, 3rd Edition, 1965.

Sail and Power, Richard Henderson and Lt. Bartlett Dunbar, USN, 1967.

Simplified Rules of the Nautical Road, Cdr. O. W. Will, III, USN, 2nd Edition, 1968.

The Bluejacket's Manual, revised by Capt. J. V. Noel, Jr., USN and W. J. Miller, JOCM USN (Ret), 18th Edition, 1968.

Other Publications

Knight's Modern Seamanship, Capt. J. V. Noel, Jr., USN and W. J. Miller, JOCM USN (Ret.), 14th Edition, 1966, D. Van Nostrand Co., Inc., Princeton, New Jersey.

INDEX